KANT, DUTY ANI

'Philip Stratton-Lake has taken a fresh and subtle look at the foundations of Kant's moral philosophy, and throws a clear and powerful light both on Kant and on current issues in moral philosophy. His excellent book will be influential in teaching and in research.' – Graham Bird

Kant, Duty and Moral Worth is a fascinating and original examination of Kant's account of moral worth. The debate over whether or not Kant said moral actions have worth only if they are carried out from duty or whether actions carried out from mixed motives can be good is complex and lies at the heart of Kant's philosophy. Philip Stratton-Lake offers a unique account of acting from duty which utilises the distinction between primary and secondary motives. He maintains that the moral law should not be understood as a normative moral reason but as playing a transcendental role. Thus, a Kantian account of moral worth is one where the virtuous agent may be responsive to concrete particular considerations while preserving an essential role for universal moral principles.

Kant, Duty and Moral Worth is a lucid examination of Kant's moral thought which will appeal to Kant scholars and anyone interested in moral theory.

Philip Stratton-Lake is a lecturer in the Department of Philosophy at Reading University.

ROUTLEDGE STUDIES IN ETHICS AND MORAL THEORY

1 THE CONTRADICTIONS OF MODERN MORAL PHILOSOPHY
Ethics after Wittgenstein
Paul Johnston

2 KANT, DUTY AND MORAL WORTH
Philip Stratton-Lake

3 JUSTIFYING EMOTIONS
Pride and Jealousy
Kristján Kristjánsson

4 CLASSICAL UTILITARIANISM FROM HUME TO MILL
Frederick Rosen

KANT, DUTY AND MORAL WORTH

Philip Stratton-Lake

Routledge
Taylor & Francis Group
LONDON AND NEW YORK

First published 2000
by Routledge
11 New Fetter Lane, London EC4P 4EE

Simultaneously published in the USA and Canada
by Routledge
29 West 35th Street, New York, NY 10001

Reprinted in 2004

Routledge is an imprint of the Taylor & Francis Group

Typeset in Times by
Keystroke, Jacaranda Lodge, Wolverhampton
Printed in the United Kingdom by
TJ International Ltd, Padstow, Cornwall

British Library Cataloguing in Publication Data
A catalogue record for this book is available from the British Library

Library of Congress Cataloging in Publication Data
Stratton-Lake, Philip.
Kant, duty, and moral worth / Philip Stratton-Lake.
Includes bibliographical references and index.
1. Kant, Immanuel, 1724–1804—Ethics. 2. Ethics, Modern–18th century.
I. Title. II. Series.
B2799.F8 S77 2000
170′.92–dc 21 00-038246

ISBN 0–415–33557–4

FOR LINDA AND ALEC

CONTENTS

ACKNOWLEDGEMENTS

My thinking on the issues covered in this book has been greatly influenced by discussions with Jonathan Dancy. He has never quite succeeded in convincing me of the truth of particularism. Nonetheless, he has shaped my views in moral philosophy in more ways than I would like to admit.

I am grateful to the Departments of Philosophy at Keele and St Andrews for helpful discussions of earlier drafts of Chapters 1 and 2, respectively; and would like to thank the anonymous referees for Routledge for their constructive criticisms.

Philip Stratton-Lake

ABBREVIATIONS

I follow the practice of giving first the page reference in the relevant volume of Kant's *Gesammelte Schriften*, followed by the page reference in the English translation, except in relation to the first Critique where I follow the standard practice of referring solely to the pagination of the first (A) and second (B) edition.

Ak	*Gesammelte Schriften. Königlich Preußischen Akademie der Wissenschaften*, ed. de Greuter: Berlin, 1922.
CPR	*Critique of Pure Reason*, N. Kemp Smith, Basingstoke, Macmillan, 1985.
CPrR	*Critique of Practical Reason*, trans. L. W. Beck, New York, Macmillan, 1956.
Gr	*Groundwork of the Metaphysic of Morals*, trans H. J. Paton, New York, Harper and Row, 1964.
MM	*Metaphysics of Morals*, trans. M. Gregor, Cambridge, Cambridge University Press, 1991.
Rel	*Religion Within the Limits of Reason Alone*, trans. T. M. Greene and H. H. Hudson, New York, Harper, 1960.

INTRODUCTION

Context

From my very first reading of Kant's moral philosophy I was impressed by his claim that only actions done from duty have moral worth, and that no motive of inclination could confer moral value on any action done from it. This claim seemed to me then, and seems to me now, to be a deep truth about moral motivation, and the moral worth of actions. But this position did not sit easily with another view that has always struck me as correct, which is that the fact that I ought to do some action is no reason whatsoever for doing it. If an action ought to be done, then the reasons for doing it are the reasons why it ought to be done, and the fact that it ought to be done cannot be a reason why it ought to be done.[1]

Now these two views seem at first sight to conflict. How could Kant be right that only actions done from duty have moral worth if the fact that some act is our duty is not a reason to do it? I clearly did not want to commit myself to the absurd view that morally good actions are those that are done for no reason, but the conjunction of Kant's account of moral worth and the view that the fact that we ought to do some act gives us no reason to do it, made it difficult to avoid this conclusion. Of course I could abandon either Kant's account of moral worth, or my belief that thin deontic terms such as 'duty', 'ought', or 'should', do not give us reasons, but these both seemed to me to be true. The only recourse, then, was to look at Kant's theory of moral worth to see whether the notion of acting from duty could be understood in a way which did not generate this absurd conclusion. It is this that led me to write this book.

My aim was not only to resolve the above-mentioned dilemma, but also to present a rational reconstruction of Kant's views which would appeal to both Kantians as well as to those who are more sceptical about Kant's moral theory. This has meant discussing Kant's account of moral worth within a framework in which it is rarely discussed, a framework constituted by a concern for the concrete particular and by distinctions such as those between moral rightness and goodness, between normative and motivating reasons, and between what I call evidential and verdictive moral considerations.[2] Considering Kant's moral theory in this way may seem to some to be inappropriate. It may be thought that it is a mistake to bring alien concepts, distinctions and concerns to bear on Kant's thought. My view is that the converse is true. I think it is a mistake to defend Kant's moral theory with reference solely to concepts and distinctions of the framework within which he worked. This is philosophical provincialism. This is unsatisfactory because there are many questions we want, and ought to ask, but which Kant's terminology makes difficult to formulate clearly. These questions can, I believe, only be stated clearly if we utilise the abovementioned distinctions.

Furthermore, although Kant was not concerned with concrete particulars, this is, I believe an important concern in ethics. The fault certain Aristotelians make is not to focus on concrete particular considerations, but to tend to do this to the exclusion of the role strictly universal principles must play in moral thought. But a concern for abstract principles which ignores the important role of the concrete particular is an equally one-sided view. The trick is, I believe, to resolve what may be called the antinomy of particularism and universalism, between an exclusive concern for the concrete particular and an exclusive concern for abstract universal principles. There is I believe no such thing as Aristotelian and Kantian ethics, as if these different theories describe different phenomena. There is just ethics, and Kantian and Aristotelian ways of systematising this. My response, then, to those who maintain that my approach is illegitimate because it subjects Kant's theory to criteria it was not designed to work with, is simply to say that Kant's theory both can and should retain its plausibility when subjected to these criteria.

Summary of the argument

Because I want to appeal to moral philosophers in general rather than just to Kantian moral philosophers, I try, for the most part, to avoid getting embroiled in detailed exegesis of Kant's texts, and the particular scholarly worries these generate. I try, rather to focus on what I think Kant was getting at. The one exception to this is Chapter 2 where I spend considerable time trying to make sense of the many different things Kant says about the relation of moral feeling and moral motivation. I make this exception not because I get some sort of perverse delight from trying to resolve deeply puzzling exegetical issues in Kant (which I must admit, I do), but because I think addressing this particular exegetical issue raises important and interesting issues in moral motivation about the relation between our affective and cognitive sides. What is the connection between our recognition that we ought to do some action, and moral feeling? What is the nature of moral feeling? Is it only contingently connected to this recognition? If these mental states are necessarily connected, why is this? What is the connection between moral feeling and moral motivation? I think a careful study of the apparently contradictory things Kant says about moral feeling (reverence), consciousness of the moral law, and moral motivation raises all of these important questions and offers some interesting answers also.

The conclusions reached in Chapters 1 and 2 are negative. Here I reject different ways in which acting from duty might be understood. These critical chapters are necessary, however, since the two interpretations of acting from duty I reject are the two most common interpretations of Kant. Consequently, some time needs to be spent showing the ways in which these interpretations are inadequate.

In Chapter 1 I argue for the claim that the fact that I ought to Φ is no reason to Φ. I consider John McDowell's argument for this claim and ultimately reject it. In place of this I offer an argument based on what I call the 'symmetry thesis'. According to the symmetry thesis, the reason why a morally good person does what she should, and the reason why she should do that act are, under favourable conditions,[3] the same. Kant requires something like the symmetry thesis in order to maintain an internal connection between morality and rationality, for if there is such a connection between morality and rationality, then morally good people must at least be disposed to act on the basis of the reasons why they should act. Yet if we accept the symmetry thesis, then we must abandon the idea that a morally good person will do the right thing just because it is right. For this will imply what is clearly false, namely, that the (normative) reason why the act is right is that it is right. The best way to avoid this is, I maintain, not to abandon the symmetry thesis or the view that morally good actions are done from duty, but to abandon this standard interpretation of acting from duty.

If the fact that some act ought to be done is no reason to do it, then if we are to avoid ascribing to Kant an absurd view, we cannot understand acting from duty in the most natural way, which is as doing what (we think) is right just because (we think) it is right.[4] How, then, is acting from duty to be understood? The most natural alternative way of understanding acting from duty in Kant is as acting from respect for the moral law. But this makes it look as though morally good actions are motivated by a feeling caused by our consciousness of the moral law – the feeling of respect, or reverence – rather than by the moral law itself. In Chapter 2 I argue that respect is best understood as a complex mental state which includes both a cognitive and an affective aspect. The cognitive aspect is our consciousness of the moral law; the affective aspect is the feeling associated with this consciousness. I reserve the term 'reverence' for this feeling, and 'respect' for the complex state that includes both this feeling (reverence) as well as consciousness of the moral law. The question then is how these two aspects of respect are related. I argue that consciousness of the moral law is not causally related to the feeling of reverence, but that reverence is the way in which we are conscious of the moral law – that is, that respect is a reverential awareness of standing under an unconditional law. Now, if we think of respect in this way, then acting from respect for the moral law need not be understood as acting from a certain feeling (reverence), but from a certain cognitive state – our reverential awareness of the moral law.

But this is not the end of the story. For although this account of acting from duty means that we can avoid the idea that morally good actions are motivated by a certain feeling, it still looks as if such acts are motivated by a psychological state – our reverential awareness of the moral law. This is a problem because Kant often says that it is the moral law itself, not our respect for it, which is the one and only moral incentive.[5] Of course we have to be aware of it, for it to be our reason for acting, and this will be a reverential awareness. But it is not this awareness that is the sole moral motive for Kant, but its content – the moral law. How, then, are we to square this with his claim that *respect* for the moral law is the sole moral motive? I think this can be done if we note that he describes the moral law as the objective determinant, and respect as the subjective determinant of the will in moral action. I argue that this means that the moral law is the moral motive, and that respect is the state of being morally motivated. In this way we can, I think, capture everything Kant says about respect and moral motivation.

In Chapter 3 I move on to consider this interpretation of acting solely from duty, and argue that we should reject it. For to think of morally good actions in this way is to maintain that morally good people will, under favourable conditions, be motivated to do what they should solely by a thought about their maxim (whether or not it can be universalised, or whether its contradictory can be universalised), and this means that good people cannot be motivated to help others when they should by a thought about the other's need. I consider various ways in which this objection may be dealt with, and reject them. Since this conception of acting from duty means that morally good people cannot be motivated to help others by a thought about the other's need, I think we should reject this interpretation of acting from duty.

If, however, we reject this interpretation of acting from duty, we must also reject what I call the justificatory conception of the moral law. According to the justificatory conception, the moral law constitutes the normative reason why we ought to act in certain ways – that is, it constitutes the normative moral reason. This is because of the symmetry thesis. According to the symmetry thesis the (motivating) reason why a morally good person will do what she should, and the (normative) reason why she should do that act are the same, and vice versa. So if a good person ought to do a certain act just because of the lawlike nature of her maxim, then she will be motivated to do that act solely by this consideration. By a simple application of *modus tollens*, therefore, we can see that if we reject the idca that acting from duty is doing some act just because the maxim of the contradictory act cannot be universalised without contradiction, we must also reject the justificatory conception of the moral law.

But if the moral law does not act as the normative reason why we ought to act in certain ways, what role does it have? In Chapter 4 I argue that it has two roles. The first, and most important, is a transcendental role: the second, is a criterial role. To think of the moral law as playing a transcendental role is to think of it as the ultimate condition of the possibility of moral obligation. Kant held that the sort of practical necessity implicit in our experience of being morally obligated cannot be explained with reference to any object of the will, or law of nature, but must be explained with reference to an action's being subsumed under the form of law as such. It is only in this way that the distinctive sort of necessity involved in moral obligation is possible, for it is only by being subsumed under the pure concept of universality that some particular action can acquire the strict universality required to explain its unconditional necessity.

In its criterial role the moral law acts as a criterion by means of which we can check our verdictive moral judgements – that is, our judgements that we ought, or ought not to act in certain ways. If the maxim of the action we judge right can be willed as a universal law without contradiction, then this gives us reason to believe that our judgement is correct. If we judge that some act is wrong and its maxim cannot be willed as a universal law, then this will give us reason to believe that this verdictive judgement is correct.

The criterial role of the moral law is easily confused with the justificatory conception, but these should be kept distinct. According to the criterial conception, the moral law does not tell us why we ought to act in certain ways, but simply gives us a reason to *believe* that we ought to act in certain ways. In its criterial role, the moral law gives us epistemic reasons of a certain sort, whereas in its justificatory role its gives us practical reasons; and although the reason why we ought to act in certain ways should be able to act as a reason for us to believe that we ought to act in those ways, the converse is not true. We can, therefore, adopt the criterial conception of the moral law while rejecting the justificatory conception.

In Chapter 4 I also outline my preferred, alternative conception of acting from duty. I do this by utilising the distinction Barbara Herman and Marcia Baron make between primary and secondary motives. One's primary motive is the agent's reasons for doing a certain action. It has as its content the sort of consideration the agent would cite in support of her action. One's secondary motive expresses some general commitment of the agent – that is, the conditions under which she regards the considerations that figure in the content of her primary motives as providing reasons for action. To act from duty is to act from a certain motivational structure which involves a distinctive secondary and primary motive. One's secondary motive must be an unconditional commitment to morality. To be committed to morality in this way is not to have a certain desire, but is to regard oneself as having sufficient reason to act in a certain way in so far as one judges that one ought to act in that way. For morally obligatory actions one's primary motive will be the same as the normative reason why the act ought to be done. So if one ought to Φ because one promised that one would, then one's primary motive for Φ-ing will be 'because one promised to Φ', with an unconditional commitment to morality as one's secondary motive. To act from duty here is not only to regard the fact that one promised as a reason to Φ, but is to think of this fact in this way solely in so far as one judges that one ought to Φ.

The symmetry thesis means that Kant's account of moral worth requires a theory of normative moral reasons, but my rejection of the justificatory conception of the moral law means that he has no such theory. Consequently, such a theory has to be imported from outside. Given the criticism levelled against the justificatory conception of the moral law in Chapter 3, the theory of normative moral reasons must be such that it allows concrete considerations in the nature of the situation, such as the fact that someone needs help, or the fact that I have made a promise, to be basic normative reasons, and thus to enable morally good people to be motivated by such concrete facts. In Chapter 5 I argue that W. D. Ross's theory of *prima facie* duties satisfies this requirement. But given the way in which it is typically understood it will not seem like a theory of normative moral reasons at all. Ross's principles of *prima facie* duty are usually understood as specifying what, in general, we ought to do – that is, as expressing general, but overridable, moral verdicts. But a principle that states that we ought in general to Φ does not give us a reason to Φ, and if this principle is understood as specifying a *basic* moral consideration, then no justification can be offered for it. It does not, therefore, look as though Ross's principles of *prima facie* duty constitute a theory of normative moral reasons at all. It looks as though it cannot be used to fill the gap in Kant's account of moral worth left by the rejection of the justificatory conception of the moral law.

I think this objection is based on a deep misunderstanding of the very notion of a *prima facie* duty. Since this misunderstanding is so widespread I devote a chapter to clarifying Ross's theory. I consider the various accounts he offers of the notion and argue that he thought of these principles not as specifying a set of basic, but overridable, duties, but as specifying a set of basic normative moral reasons. But although the principles specify moral reasons, they are not themselves moral reasons. The principles themselves are best thought of as occupying the sort of transcendental role that the moral law has. The normative moral reasons are the concrete particular considerations that fall under these principles, and although these considerations could not be moral reasons if they did not fall under these principles, and ultimately, under the moral law, the principles are not themselves moral reasons for action.

If we accept that Ross's theory of *prima facie* duties gives us a theory of basic normative moral reasons, then we can utilise this theory to fill the gap in Kant's moral theory left by the rejection of the justificatory conception of the moral law. With this theory of normative moral reasons in place morally good agents will have as their primary motives only the concrete, particular consideration specified by the *prima facie* duty when they act solely from duty. Thus, if they ought to Φ, and the ground of this duty falls under the *prima facie* duty of fidelity, then the good-willed agent's primary motive for Φ-ing will be because she promised to Φ (governed of course by the secondary motive of an unconditional commitment to morality). If she ought to Φ and the ground of this duty falls under the *prima facie* duty of beneficence, then when she acts from duty her primary motive for Φ-ing will be that he needs help. This captures the idea that morally good people – that is, those who tend to do what they should from duty – will be motivated to help others when they should by thoughts about the state of the person to be helped, while fitting into the Kantian claim that only actions done from duty have moral worth.

In Chapter 6 I consider why we should agree with Kant that only actions done from duty can have moral worth, whether overdetermined actions have moral worth, and the moral worth of beneficent actions. I argue that duty is the only morally good motive because only this motive is non-accidentally related to the rightness of the actions done from it. It is non-accidentally related to rightness not in the sense that it guarantees that one does the right act. No motive can do that. It should, rather, be understood as non-accidentally related to rightness in the sense that *when* the act is right its being so expresses the agent's interest in doing what is right, rather than some non-moral interest.

But this motive's expressing the agent's interest in the morality of her action is not enough to support the view that no inclination can have moral worth, for if one acts from a non-derivative, *de dicto* desire to do the right thing, then when one's act is right its being so will also express the agent's concern for the rightness of her actions. The relation of the agent's motive to the rightness of her action must, therefore, not only be non-accidental, but must be non-accidental in the right way, and the right way is the way specified by the symmetry thesis. This rules out even the possibility that a non-derivative *de dicto* desire to do the right thing could have moral worth, for it is never the case that the fact that the agent has this desire is a normative reason why she morally ought to do certain acts.

I then consider over-determined actions. On my account of acting from duty an action is overdetermined if and only if:

1 one's secondary motive is an unconditional commitment to morality;
2 one would Φ (from inclination as a primary motive) in the absence of *any* moral judgement about the status of this act;
3 in the absence of cooperating inclinations the normative reasons why one ought to Φ would suffice (at the primary level) to motivate Φ-ing; and
4 the action is determined by both primary motives (the ground of duty, and inclination) operating separately, not by a happy marriage of the two.

Following Barbara Herman I argue that if the ground of duty is sufficient in the weak sense that one would Φ in the absence of a cooperating inclination, then one might not Φ if some opposing inclination were present; and this possibility is sufficient to show that the whole, overdetermined motivational structure is only accidentally related to the rightness of the action done from it. For whether or not someone with this motivational structure does the right thing will depend on the degree to which acting morally is demanding, or contrary to their interests.

This problem can be avoided if we think of the sufficiency of the ground of duty in a stronger sense. According to this strong sense the ground of duty is sufficient if the agent would Φ no matter what opposing inclinations she has. But this strong account of sufficiency is too strong. For whether or not one's action has moral worth in some set of circumstances depends on whether the ground of duty motivates one's action in *that* situation, not whether it would in some more demanding situation. One could hardly deny that someone's action has moral worth, because they would not do that action if, say, doing it would lead to their destruction, or ruin, or whatever. We must then work with the weaker account of sufficiency in overdetermined actions. But as we have seen, so understood, overdetermined actions lack moral worth.

The final issue I address in this chapter is whether beneficent actions can be morally good. Kant clearly thought that they could in the *Groundwork*, but is committed to maintaining that they cannot in the *Doctrine of Virtue*. This is because he there maintains that imperfect duties require, not the doing of some act, but the adoption of a maxim. Since beneficence is an imperfect duty, this means that we are not morally required to do beneficent actions, but only to adopt the maxim of beneficence. Yet if beneficent actions are not morally required we cannot knowingly do them from duty, and they cannot have moral worth.

This seems to me to be a deeply implausible implication. One of the reasons that seems to drive Kant to it is the attempt to introduce latitude in relation to imperfect duties. But latitude can be accommodated without having to abandon the view that beneficent actions can have moral worth. All we need do is think of imperfect duties as having disjunctive content, where the disjunctions are, in relation to the duty of beneficence, determinate beneficent actions. This allows latitude because the agent can choose between the various disjunctions of the particular obligation, and in so far as she does any one of these, she will have done what she should. Furthermore, the agent can act in accordance with this disjunctive obligation from duty, for she can be motivated at the primary level by the reasons why she ought to act in accordance with this disjunctive obligation. Since this way of accommodating latitude allows us to hold onto the view that beneficent actions can have moral worth, I maintain it is better than the way in which Kant attempts to accommodate latitude in the *Doctrine of Virtue*.

In the previous chapters I argued that this account of moral worth is not vulnerable to the criticisms levelled against the other two interpretations I consider. It may, however, be criticised on the ground that it is inconsistent with other key aspects of Kant's moral theory, namely, his constructivism, his view that morality and autonomy reciprocally imply each other (the reciprocity thesis), and his adherence to absolute side constraints. In Chapter 7 I address these issues. I argue that my account of moral worth is compatible with a certain form of constructivism. I concede that on my account Kant's constructivism is not central to his moral theory, but argue that this is how it should be. What is crucial to Kant's critical philosophy is not finding ways of getting others to believe certain judgements – be they about the existence of the external world, or about why we should act morally – but showing how it is possible that certain things obtain – objective knowledge and unconditionally necessary actions. The moral law in its transcendental role is what is central to Kant's moral philosophy. Its constructive, criterial role is a useful aid to moral judgement, but not central to his account of moral worth.

I argue that my account is consistent with his reciprocity thesis. This can be seen once we note the way in which Kant distinguishes spontaneity and autonomy. Roughly, an action is spontaneous if the consideration that motivates it does so only by being incorporated into the agent's maxim – that is, if it is done for the sake of reasons, rather than merely caused. This is what it means to act on the basis of self-given principles. An action is autonomous if it is both spontaneous and if the reason one acts from does not derive from some inclination or need the agent happens to have, but from the purely formal moral law. Only in this way is the will a law to itself. My account of moral worth is compatible with autonomy so understood, because the concrete considerations that act as the primary motive of good actions do not acquire their reason giving force by being instrumental to some inclination, but by being subsumed under the moral law in its transcendental role. The normativity of moral reasons is traced back to the moral law on my account. It is not, however, traced back along a justificatory route, but along a transcendental one.

Finally, I do not attempt to accommodate Kant's adherence to absolute side constraints, but argue, along with many other commentators that it is best to separate Kant's views about such constraints from his moral theory. The task is then to show that the application of the categorical imperative procedure does not generate absolute side constraints as Kant seemed to have thought.

Particularism and principles

I think that this revised account of moral worth in Kant is not only free of the difficulties to which the alternative accounts are subject, but also allows us to free ourselves from the opposition between various forms of particularism and principled ethics, on the one hand, and between Aristotelian and Kantian ethics, on the other. Particularists deny that there are any universally valid moral principles, and that moral judgement is and ought to be context sensitive. Some particularists, such as communitarians, are relativists, but not all are.[6] One could maintain that there are objective moral truths, but deny that these are determined by any set of exceptionless moral principles. Objectivist particularists typically maintain that certain actions ought to be done, not because they fall under some principle, but because they are called for by some concrete particular consideration in the nature of the situation. It is because our duty is determined by concrete particulars, rather than abstract principles that particularists tend to be Aristotelian, in the respect that they think that decisions as to what to do ultimately lie with perception, or judgement. Kantians, on the other hand, object that without moral principles moral judgement will be arbitrary.

Now in respect to the justificatory conception of the moral law I am on the side of the particularists. The view that the moral law is the normative reason why we ought morally to act in certain ways has always seemed me to be highly suspect, and I have recently become convinced that it is false. Whatever the reason is why we ought to keep our promises, tell the truth, help others, etc., it is not because the maxims of the contradictory actions cannot be willed as universal laws. My view is that the naïve, common-sense view on this issue is more or less correct and exhaustive, and doesn't need to be 'improved' or made respectable by any esoteric theory that nobody outside a philosophy seminar would dream of mentioning in support of their action. The reason why we ought to help others is because they need help, and for no other reason: the reason why we should do what we promised is because we promised, and that is all there is to it: the reason why we should show gratitude is because someone has helped us out in some way, and that is the end of the matter.

If it is certain concrete particular considerations in the nature of the situation that give rise to moral duties, then morally good people will be motivated by, and sensitive to, these considerations. The rejection of the justificatory conception of the moral law and moral principles enables Kantians to agree with particularists and Aristotelians about the ground of duty and about the sort of considerations that will motivate good people. This does not, however, mean that they must abandon the idea that moral principles have an essential role to play in morality, or that the moral law is the fundamental moral principle. For the idea that the moral law and particular moral laws have a transcendental role is quite compatible with the particularist's view about the ground of duty, and the Aristotelian picture of a morally good person. By distinguishing these different ways in which moral principles can function we can, therefore, transcend the opposition between particularism and Aristotelianism, on the one hand, and principled ethics and Kantianism, on the other. This in turn allows us to acknowledge the truth on each side of this opposition without watering down either view. This seems to me something to be welcomed.

1

DOING THE RIGHT THING JUST BECAUSE IT IS RIGHT

Introduction

For Kant, an action can have moral worth if and only if it is done from duty. Kant's notion of acting from duty is standardly understood as doing what is right just because it is right.[1] There is debate about whether Kant's view is that our action can have moral worth only if it done *solely* from duty, and about whether acting from duty is compatible with being inclined to do what one should.[2] Nonetheless, this debate tends to work within this standard understanding of acting from duty.

There are two standard criticisms of this account of moral worth. The first, the Humean one, maintains that one cannot act *solely* from duty, i.e., independently of any desire, because a desire for X is a necessary condition of being motivated to do X. This type of criticism does not apply to all conceptions of acting solely from duty, since some maintain that to act from duty is to act from a special sort of desire,[3] or from the relevant belief–desire pair.[4] Nonetheless, the notion of acting from duty in its Kantian, cognitivist, form is often criticised in this way. The second type of criticism comes from those who may be broadly categorised as Aristotelians, or virtue ethicists. They criticise acting solely from duty on the ground that it involves a kind of detachment from everyday relations which is alienating, or at least rules out acting from other desirable motives. I have little sympathy for the Humean theory of motivation,[5] but this is a topic which has received a great deal of attention and I do not wish to add to the literature here.[6] I shall say something later on in response to the latter criticism. For one of the main aims of this book is to show that the sort of things which worry Aristotelians can be accommodated within a Kantian framework if we interpret the notion of acting from duty as I suggest. I do not, however, want to get involved in this issue at this stage.

What I want to do in this chapter is argue that there is compelling reason to abandon the standard interpretation of Kant's notion of acting from duty. For if Kant is interpreted in this way, he will be unable to maintain that there is an essential and direct connection between morality and rationality. This is not a point about whether moral requirements are categorical or hypothetical imperatives.[7] Nor does it rest on a worry about possible conflicts between self-interest and morality, or about whether moral considerations really are self-standing reasons

– that is, whether they constitute reasons irrespective of whether treating them as such is in the agent's interest, or has survival value, or whatever. It is true that it is harder to show that moral considerations give agents reasons to act than it is to show that, say, desires or self-interest do. But I do not intend to address this issue. What I want to argue is that the particular moral consideration which Kant focuses on does not give us a reason to act. For the fact that I ought to Φ, or my belief that I ought to Φ, is not a normative reason to Φ. This is not to deny that there is an internal connection between my being obligated to Φ and my having reason, or even compelling reason, to Φ. For if one analysed 'I ought to Φ' as 'I have compelling reason to Φ', as W. D. Falk did,[8] then it would follow that whenever I ought to Φ I will have compelling reason to Φ. My claim is solely that this reason will never be the particular moral consideration which Kant maintains it is (under the interpretation of Kant we are considering), namely, the fact that I am morally required to Φ.

I begin by outlining John McDowell's argument for this conclusion and argue that it fails. In the next section I offer a different argument in support of his conclusion based on what I call the 'symmetry thesis'. Then I defend my argument from objections which might be raised against it. Finally, I conclude that if Kant's notion of acting from duty is understood as it commonly is, as doing what one should because one should, then he will be unable to hold onto the view that there is an essential and direct connection between morality and rationality.

McDowell's argument

John McDowell is, to my knowledge, the first to cast doubt on the view that the fact that one ought to do some act can be a reason to do it. He does not couch his criticism in terms of duty, or the thought of duty, but in terms of 'ought' or 'should' statements. But his criticism is aimed at Kant, so he clearly makes no special distinction between 'ought' and 'duty' statements. An 'ought' statement is one which has the simple form 'x ought to Φ'. Ought statements can relate either to particular acts, or to types of acts. They can thus express the fact, either that one ought, here and now, to Φ, or that one ought in general to do acts of type Φ. In either case, McDowell maintains, such statements do not express reasons for action. This is not the familiar Humean claim that mere thoughts, or beliefs are, by themselves inert. On the contrary, McDowell's criticism occurs in the context of a critique of this Humean thesis. Rather, his claim is based upon the view that a reason for acting 'must involve some appropriate specific consideration which could in principle be cited in support of the 'should' statement'.[9] If we think of moral requirements in this way, we will, he writes, be freed of

> the insane thesis that simply to say 'you should . . .' to someone is enough to give him a reason for acting; as if, when he protested 'But why should I?', it was sufficient to reply 'You just should, that's all'.[10]

The ought statement does not, McDowell maintains, support, or justify the obligatory action. But if it is not this moral consideration which justifies this action, what does? According to McDowell it is the reason (or reasons) why A is required to do this act. Whatever this is, it cannot be (or include) the fact that this act is morally required. Rather, it is the concrete specific considerations in the situation that call for this action, such as the fact that B is in need. A's failure to see that she ought to help B may stem from the fact that she failed to see that B needed help. If C pointed out *this* fact in response to A's enquiry, then he would have offered her a reason to help B, for he would have offered at least a *prima facie* justification for his claim that she ought to help B. He will not, however, have done so if he simply continues to insist that she ought to do this act.

McDowell's argument seems to run as follows:

(1) If F is a normative reason why I ought to Φ, then it must be possible to answer the question, 'why ought I to Φ?' with reference to F in an informative manner.
(2) If F were the fact that I ought to Φ, the answer to the question 'why ought I to Φ?' would be 'because I ought to Φ'.
(3) But this answer would be uninformative.

Therefore,

(4) The fact that I ought to Φ fails to meet the requirement stated in (1).

Therefore,

(5) The fact that I ought to Φ cannot be a normative reason why I ought to Φ.

This argument is plausible, but as it stands, it is not compelling. For one could capture the intuition expressed by the requirement stated in (1) in a way that enables the ought statement to function as a reason as follows:

> (1*) If F is a normative reason for me to Φ, then it must be possible to answer the question 'what reason is there for me to Φ?' with reference to F in an informative manner.

The fact that I ought to Φ could satisfy this requirement. For although it is uninformative to say that I ought to Φ because I ought to Φ, it is not uninformative to say that the normative reason I have for Φ-ing is that I ought to Φ.

One might respond to this objection as follows. One might claim that, in relation to reasons for belief, the following is true:

> (RB) any reason I have for believing that P must be able to function at the same time as a reason for me to believe that P is true.

If, for example, the results of the opinion polls over the last three weeks are reasons for me to believe that Labour will win the imminent election, then it must be possible for these results to be reasons for me to believe that it is true that Labour will win the imminent election. McDowell may try to link (1*) with (1) by an analogous principle in relation to normative reasons to act. This principle would run as follows:

> (RA) any reason I have for Φ-ing must be able to function at the same time as a reason why Φ-ing is right.

Granted this, McDowell could argue that if the fact that I ought to Φ can be a reason for me to Φ, it must not only be able to satisfy (1*), but would have to satisfy (1) also. But although it can satisfy (1*) it cannot satisfy (1). Consequently, it cannot be a reason for me to Φ, even though it satisfies (1*).

The degree to which this argument is successful will depend upon the degree to which we have reason to believe (RA). What reason do we have, then, to believe that (RA) is true? The only argument for this seems to be that it is the practical analogue of (RB). But this is not enough unless the reason why (RB) is true is applicable to (RA). If it is not, the mere fact that (RA) is structurally similar to (RB) will not give us reason to think that it is correct. What, then, is the reason for believing (RB)? There seems to be a very simple reason why (RB) is true, which is that to believe that P and to believe that P is true are equivalent. It is for this reason that anything which is a reason to believe that P will be a reason to believe that P is true. There is, however, no analogous equivalence in relation to (RA). My act of Φ-ing is not equivalent to my act's being right. I could not believe that P unless I believed that P is true, but I could Φ if Φ-ing were not the right thing to do. There is, therefore, no analog to the reason to believe (RB) in relation to (RA). But in the absence of such a reason, it is difficult to see how (RA) could be justified in a way that would not clearly beg the question at issue against those who believe that the fact that I ought to Φ can be a reason for me to Φ.

One could attempt to reformulate McDowell's argument by utilising a distinction Philippa Foot makes between verdictive and evidential moral considerations.[11] A verdictive moral consideration is the content of the conclusion of a piece of practical reasoning about the deontological status of some act. It is an overall verdict about whether some act is morally right, wrong or permissible, either in some specific situation or in general. Evidential considerations, on the other hand, are those which support, but do not constitute overall moral verdicts. These may be couched in overtly moral terms, such as considerations of rights, fairness, equality, or maximisation of good, but they need not be.[12] Someone's being in pain, or depressed, may be an evidential moral consideration, but is not expressed in overtly moral terms. Put in this language, McDowell can be understood as claiming that 'ought' statements are verdictive, but not evidential considerations. To hold that the ought statement is a reason to do the required act would be to treat this overall moral verdict as a piece of evidence which supports this very verdict. But no verdict constitutes evidence in support of itself, and, *a fortiori*, no verdict can be regarded as the *sole* piece of evidence for itself.

This is not to say that a verdictive moral consideration cannot at the same time function as an evidential moral consideration. The verdict that I ought to Φ may function as a piece of evidence in support of the verdict that I ought to Ψ, if, for example, Φ-ing is the only way in which I can Ψ. But this does not change anything. For although a moral verdict can function as evidence in support of a different moral verdict, it cannot function as evidence in support of itself. No verdict can do this.

One could attempt to support one's verdict that one ought, here and now, to Φ, with the statement that one ought always to Φ in situations of a certain type, along with the belief that this situation is of the relevant type. That is, a particular verdict could be supported by a generalised version of this very verdict. But this merely relocates the problem. For it is always meaningful to ask of any generalised version of an ought statement: 'Why ought I always to act in this way in this type of situation?'; and one does not answer this question simply by saying, 'because you ought always to act in this way in this type of situation'. Rather, to answer this question one would have to cite the general type of evidential moral consideration, or considerations, on the basis of which one judges the generalised ought statement to be true. But once this is done it will become apparent that it is not the generalised moral verdict that supports the particular verdict, but an instance of the type of evidential moral consideration which is cited in support of the generalised moral verdict. But then we are back where we started.

McDowell's line of argument can be further illuminated by considering the analogous case in relation to beliefs and reasons for believing, if we assume that such reasons are evidence which can be cited in support of a belief. The fact that I judge P to be true is not a reason for believing that P. For P's being true is a verdictive epistemic consideration, and as I have already noted, verdicts do not constitute evidence in support of themselves. Rather, the reasons for believing that P will be the reasons for judging that P is true – that is, they will be the evidence which can be cited in support of my belief that P. Whatever this evidence is, it will not include the fact that P is true. For I do not even explain why I believe that P simply by stating that P is true, let alone offer anyone else a reason to believe this.

It may, however, be conceded that the fact that I ought to do some act is not a sufficient reason to do it, but maintained that it is a necessary reason. So although we may have to reject the interpretation of Kant according to which an act can have moral worth only if it is done *solely* from duty, duty could, nonetheless, be *a* normative reason. Consequently, it may be objected that McDowell has gone too far in saying that duty is not a reason to do what morality enjoins, and that what he should have said is that it is not a sufficient reason. But if no verdict constitutes evidence for itself, then it will not only be the case that it cannot be the *sole* reason in support of itself; it cannot be *a* reason in support of itself either. So far then, this construal of McDowell's argument looks good.

Nevertheless, as it stands, his argument is not strong enough to support the strong conclusion that when one Φs solely because one ought to Φ, one acts from no reason at all. For although this verdictive moral consideration cannot be cited in support of itself, it may be argued that it can be cited in support of the action – that is, the act of Φ-ing. For the act of Φ-ing is not itself a moral verdict; and if the verdict is distinct from the action it favours, it may be held that the former may be used to justify the latter. The thought here would be that the evidential moral considerations will support the verdictive moral consideration, and this verdictive moral consideration will in turn support the doing of the action which is morally required. So understood, one's moral verdict will not be understood as evidence for itself, but for doing the required act.

It seems, therefore, that no formulation of McDowell's argument can be made to succeed. What I want to do now is offer an argument which supports McDowell's conclusion, but which is not vulnerable to the above objections.

The symmetry argument

My argument rests upon what I shall call the symmetry thesis. Christine Korsgaard proposes a strong version of the symmetry thesis and claims that Kant assumed this thesis in *Groundwork I*. She writes:

> Kant is analysing the good will, characterised as one that does what is right because it is right, in order to discover the principle of unconditionally good action. The assumption behind such an analysis is that *the reason why a good-willed person does an action, and the reason why the action is right, are the same*. The good-willed individual does the right thing because it is the right thing, so if we can discover why the good-willed person does it, we will have *ipso facto* discovered why it is the right thing.[13]

As it is formulated here, the symmetry thesis is the claim that:

> (S) The reason why a good-willed person does an action, and the reason why the action is right, are the same.

(S) is a thesis about the relation between motivating and normative reasons. It expresses the thought that the morally good person's motivating reason for Φ-ing will be the same as the normative reason for Φ-ing. The problem with (S), however, is that it is too strong. For, as Korsgaard describes it, the symmetry thesis is false. (S) would be true only if a morally good person never had false beliefs about the relevant facts, i.e., about the evidential moral considerations, and was never ignorant of them. But there is nothing about the concept of a morally virtuous agent that entails that her knowledge of the relevant facts is infallible, or that she will never be ignorant of the relevant facts. Someone might be perfectly virtuous, but nonetheless motivated to do what she thinks she should by the thought of something other than the reason, or reasons why she should do this act; and this might be because she is ignorant of some of the relevant facts. She might, for example, offer someone an aspirin because she thinks he has a headache, and because these are unpleasant. But it may be that his expressions of pain are caused not by a headache, but by an earache. In such a situation it cannot be maintained that the reasons why she should offer him an aspirin are that he has a headache and that these are unpleasant. For although it is true that headaches are unpleasant, he does not have one. This, then, cannot be a reason why she ought to give him an aspirin. Consequently, we should reject this strong version of the symmetry thesis.

We could, however, modify it to take into account the above criticism. According to this weaker version of the symmetry thesis,

> (S1) The reason why a good-willed person does an action, and the reason why the action is right, are the same, if she knows the relevant facts.[14]

This deals with the objection to (S). For this difficulty stemmed from ignorance of one of the relevant facts in the situation, namely, the fact that the other person has an earache. The relevant facts are the evidential moral considerations, such as the fact that someone is in distress or that an act of a certain sort will bring about a just distribution of some good. It is not, however, intended to include the fact that these facts constitute reasons why Φ-ing is morally right. To include this would run the risk of trivialising the symmetry thesis. By 'relevant facts' therefore, I mean the facts which are the reasons why one should Φ, but not the fact that these considerations are reasons to Φ.

But even though (S1) expresses a weaker version of the symmetry thesis than (S), it may, nonetheless, still be thought to be too strong. For, even if a virtuous person knew the relevant facts, she may sometimes act from reasons other than the ones in virtue of which her action is right. A morally good person might occasionally suffer from akrasia so that the reason why she should Φ, or the thought of this, was insufficient to motivate her to Φ. In such a situation she might be motivated to Φ by considerations other than the ones which give rise to the obligation to Φ, even though she knows the relevant facts. Furthermore, a good-willed person's judgement might not always be good. She might know the relevant facts, i.e., the evidential moral considerations, but believe that her action is made morally right by some other consideration. This would mean that she might Φ from reasons other than the reasons why she ought to Φ, even though she knows the relevant facts.

Although I think these are real possibilities for a morally good person, Kant needs something like (S1) if he is to hold onto the essential and direct connection between morality and rationality. For it is difficult to see how such a connection could be maintained if it were possible for a good-willed agent systematically to do what she should, but not from the reasons why she should do this.[15] To put this another way: it is difficult to see how such a connection could be maintained if the reason why an action is morally good, and the reason why it should be done, could come apart in a systematic way. One might be able to hold onto a *contingent* or *indirect* connection between morality and rationality if one rejected some version of the symmetry thesis. But this would fall short of what Kant desires. What is needed, therefore, is something which is weaker than (S) and (S1), but which still insists on some form of symmetry between the motivating reasons of a morally good person and normative reasons. This can be done with the following version of the symmetry thesis.

> (S2) A good-willed person is disposed to be motivated to do what she ought by the normative reasons why she ought so to act.

To say that a good-willed person is disposed to be motivated to do what she ought to by the normative reasons why she ought so to act is to say that if certain conditions are met, she will be so motivated. Alternatively, this can be expressed by saying that if she fails to be so motivated, it will be because one of these conditions has not been met. What, then, are these conditions? These will fall into three categories; conditions of knowledge, of practical rationality, and of ability. Two conditions fall under the first category. They are: (a) that she knows the relevant facts; and (b) that her judgement is good. The conditions of practical rationality are intended to rule out failures of practical rationality, such as weakness of will. If, therefore, a good-willed agent fails to Φ from the normative reasons why Φ-ing is right, this will be either because of some form of ignorance, or because of a breakdown in practical rationality.

These are fairly uncontroversial conditions. What is more controversial is what I have called the condition of ability. This condition is that she is *able* to do the right thing from the normative reasons why it is right. This condition needs to be added to cover the following possibility.[16] Consider a world in which there is an omnipotent, evil demon whose aim is to stop good people doing what they should in the light of the normative reasons why they should so act, even if the conditions of knowledge and rationality have been satisfied. He achieves this by making it the case that if a good person ever acts from the normative reasons why she should so act, he will make it such that this action is wrong, and he tells them this. Every good person knows, therefore, that she cannot do the right thing from the normative reasons why this is right. For they know that if they are motivated to act in this way, then their actions will be morally wrong. It is the mere possibility of such a situation which makes the condition of ability necessary.

It may be responded that this condition is unnecessary because it is covered by the conditions of knowledge. For if a good-willed agent Φ-ed from what she took to be the normative reasons why Φ-ing is right, the evil demon would make Φ-ing wrong. But then what she takes to be normative reasons why Φ-ing is right would not be such reasons. For something cannot be a reason why Φ-ing is right if Φ-ing is wrong. Her belief that these considerations are moral reasons will thus be false, and the knowledge condition will not be satisfied.

But the possibility under consideration does not make it impossible for the good person to know, or believe that Φ-ing is right, or even why it is right. For she can know that F is a reason why she ought to Φ, if she is not motivated by F, and she can know that Φ-ing is right if she is not motivated to Φ by F. It does not therefore, make it impossible for such a person to know the relevant facts, or judge correctly that some evidential moral consideration is a normative reason why she should Φ. All it makes impossible is for the good person to do the right act from the reasons why it is right. For if she acts from these reasons, the evil demon will ensure that what she does is in fact wrong.

Could an omnipotent being make an act wrong which would otherwise be right? This depends upon the extent to which one thinks that the rightness or wrongness of an act is context dependent. Suppose I have promised A that I would Φ. Then Φ-ing will be the right thing to do. Whether or not the evil demon could make this act wrong will depend upon whether its being right is subject to a *ceteris paribus* clause. One need not be a consequentialist to think that if my keeping my promise would cause terrible suffering to innocent people, then this act might be wrong. But this is all that is needed for the omnipotent, evil demon to make this act wrong, if he chooses. For he might bring it about that these terrible consequences will occur only if the good person does this act from the normative reason why it is right. If she does it for some other reason, these consequences will not follow, and the act of keeping her promise will be the right thing to do.

It is not clear that Kant, or Kantians would accept this *ceteris paribus* clause. For keeping one's promise, like truth-telling, is for Kant a perfect duty, and these allow of no exceptions.[17] If keeping one's promise is right in all circumstances, then the *ceteris paribus* clause would not apply, and the evil demon would not be able to make this act wrong, even if he were omnipotent.[18] But many Kantians try to argue that Kant is not committed to this extreme view, and that it can sometimes be right to lie, or break one's promise – for example, it may be right to lie to a murderer to save his potential victim's life.[19] But even those who do adhere to an absolute prohibition on this class of acts, do not believe that all acts are absolutely prohibited. Acts which fall under imperfect duties are subject to a *ceteris paribus* clause. And this class of acts may be all that is needed to make the ability condition necessary.

But whether or not one thinks that an ability condition needs to be built into the disposition, the introduction of the notion of a disposition to do the right thing from the reasons why it is right accommodates the difficulty raised against (S1), without abandoning the thought behind the symmetry thesis. For if there is an essential and direct link between morality and rationality, and if one is a moral person, then one must at least be disposed to be motivated to Φ by the normative reasons why one ought to Φ. If one were not even disposed so to act, we would have to say that such a person was not morally good.

The trouble is that if one accepts any version of the symmetry thesis, which one must if one is to insist upon an essential and direct connection between morality and rationality, and if one interprets Kant's account of acting from duty as

Korsgaard and many others do, one will fail to hold onto *any* connection between morality and rationality. For if the good-willed agent is disposed to do the right thing from the normative reasons why it is right, and such an agent does, or is disposed to do, the right thing because it is right, it follows that these acts are right because they are right – that is, that the normative reason why they are right is because they are right. But this cannot be correct. Whatever it is that makes an act obligatory it cannot be the fact that it is obligatory. Just as someone is not made happy by the fact that they *are* happy, but by some other fact, such as the fact that they are reading a good book, or watching a good football match, or whatever, so acts cannot be made obligatory by the fact that they are obligatory.[20] Whatever it is one thinks makes some act obligatory will depend upon one's moral theory: consequentialists (who are not Analytical Consequentialists) maintain that it is the good consequences of the act, whereas deontologists such as Ross maintain that there is not a single evidential moral consideration in virtue of which acts are morally right. But whatever one's view is about the type of considerations that can give rise to obligations, no one can seriously maintain that acts are morally right because they are morally right; and given any version of the symmetry thesis, Kant seems to be committed to this odd view. Some version of the symmetry thesis is, therefore, required if Kant is to hold onto an essential and direct link between morality and rationality, while at the same time this thesis falsifies the view that a morally good person will be motivated to do what she should by the thought of duty.

The claim that neither the fact that we should Φ nor the belief that we should – is a normative reason for Φ-ing does not commit us to the view that moral considerations are not reasons. This implication only seems to follow if one fails to distinguish evidential from verdictive moral considerations. All I have denied is that *verdictive* moral considerations are ever reasons to act in accordance with these verdicts. I have not denied that evidential moral considerations, i.e., considerations of rights, fairness, good consequences, promises, etc., are reasons to act in accordance with the moral verdicts they support. Nothing I have said casts doubt on the view that *evidential* moral considerations are reasons. I have not even denied that verdictive moral considerations can support *different* verdicts. The fact that I ought to Φ can be a reason for Ψ-ing, but not for Φ-ing.

The distinction between normative and motivating reasons

Since it is the symmetry thesis that is the cause of the difficulty, one might attempt to defend the Kantian account of moral motivation we are considering by attacking this thesis. One might argue that no version of the symmetry thesis can be correct, because the reasons why some act is morally required cannot literally be identical with the reason from which a morally good person would do this act.[21] For one might think that one ought to do certain acts, such as help the needy, simply because of the fact that they need help, but argue that this fact cannot be the reason from which anyone acts, because motivating reasons are essentially a different type of thing from justifying reasons. Motivating reasons are psychological states such as beliefs or desires. But it is not these psychological states which give rise to obligations, but certain facts about the world, such as the fact that I have made a promise, or that someone I can help is in distress. It is not your *belief* that you have made a promise, but the fact that you have made one, that gives rise to the moral requirement for you to do what you have promised. Since normative reasons cannot be motivating reasons, no version of the symmetry thesis can be correct.

To begin to respond to this objection we should distinguish two claims: (1) that the way in which a consideration functions as a motivating reason is different from the way in which it functions as a normative reason – that is, that these are different functions, even if one and the same consideration has them; and (2) that one and the same consideration, or type of consideration, cannot function in these very different ways – that is, one and the same thing cannot be both a normative reason for me to Φ and a motivating reason for me to Φ. The truth of the first claim is in no way incompatible with the truth of any version of the symmetry thesis. For the symmetry thesis does not imply that the way in which a consideration can function as a normative reason is identical with the way in which it functions as a motivating reason, or vice versa. All that is claimed is that in the case of obligatory actions, one and the same consideration will function in these two very different ways for a good-willed agent (assuming, of course that the relevant conditions are met). One may hold the view that the notion of practical normative reasons can be reductively analysed in terms of occurrent or dispositional motives, as Falk and Williams do.[22] But one is not committed to this view simply in virtue of adhering to the symmetry thesis. All one is committed to is the view that one and the same consideration will be disposed to function both as a normative and as a motivating reason for a good-willed agent. The truth of (1), therefore, is quite consistent with the truth of the symmetry thesis. Does (2) pose a threat?

(2) expresses the claim that the consideration which functions as a motivating reason is essentially distinct from the consideration which functions as a normative reason – that is, the consideration which is the good-willed individual's (motivating) reason for doing what she should, *cannot* be one and the same consideration that is the normative reason and which gives rise to the obligation. This is because motivating reasons are essentially a different type of thing from normative reasons, i.e., because essentially different types of things function as motivating reasons than function as normative reasons. It may be held that only psychological states can function as motivating reasons, but that it is not psychological states, but certain facts (where the notion of a fact is used simply to refer to the content of these psychological states) which function as normative reasons. On this view, if, for example, I am morally required to Φ because I promised my friend that I would Φ, then, this fact cannot be the reason why I Φ-ed. It cannot function as my motivating reason because my motivating reason must be a psychological state, such as my belief that I made a promise, or this belief plus a desire to keep my promises. According to (2) therefore, the symmetry thesis cannot be correct,

because it assumes something that is false, namely that one and the same consideration can function both as a normative and as a motivating reason.

But even if it were true that the reasons from which we act cannot be identical with the reasons that give rise to moral requirements (because the former are psychological states, and the latter are not), this would not require the abandonment of the symmetry thesis, but would require only that we modify it. We would not be able to maintain that the reason from which a morally good person would be disposed to do the right thing will be identical with the reasons why it is right. For her motivating reason will be, e.g., the *belief* that she has promised to Φ, or the *belief* that someone needs help, whereas the reason why it is right for her to keep her promise, or help the other person is the *fact* that she has promised to Φ, or the *fact* that he needs help. But we could maintain, quite plausibly, that

> (S3) A morally good individual is disposed to be motivated to do the right thing by psychological states which *have as their content* the normative reason why this act is right, and vice versa.

This modified version of the symmetry thesis will mean that I will have to modify very slightly the argument I use in support of the claim that the mere fact that one ought to Φ is not a reason for Φ-ing. But since there still remains a necessary connection between the normative reasons why we should do certain acts, and the motivating reasons from which a good-willed individual would be disposed to do those acts, the substantive point of the argument would remain.

Supporting counterfactuals

It may be objected that we will be unable to accommodate the relevant counterfactuals if we abandon the thought that a good-willed individual is disposed to do the right thing because it is right. What are the relevant counterfactuals? Here are three:

1 A good-willed individual would not Φ if she thought that Φ-ing were wrong.
2 A good-willed individual would not Φ unless she judged that Φ-ing is either permissible, or obligatory.[23]
3 In situations in which there are conflicts of duty, a good-willed individual would not Φ unless she judged that Φ-ing is morally required.[24]

These counterfactuals seem to be true of a good-willed individual. The question is, therefore, whether we can accommodate these counterfactuals if we deny that a good person will be motivated to do the right thing because it is right. I think we can if we draw a distinction in the theory of motivation analogous to one which is often made in a theory of causality.

Some want to distinguish something's being a cause from its being causally relevant on the ground that something may be causally relevant, but not a cause. One may, for example, think that only events are causally efficacious, but think that properties of things which are not events can be causally relevant. One might think that what causes a sensation of red in me is not the surface properties of the red thing, but the event of light reflecting off the object. But if one holds this view, it is plausible to think that, at least some of the surface properties of the red object are causally relevant in the sense that this event would not cause a sensation of red in me if they had been different.

A similar distinction can be made in the theory of motivation. Certain counterfactuals, such as the ones listed above, may be true of someone, but not imply that the belief that Φ-ing is right is a motive for her Φ-ing. For the counterfactual may be true not because the belief, or its content, are motives, but because they are motivationally relevant. If one is a good-willed agent, the reason why this belief cannot be one's motive is because of the symmetry thesis. The reason for thinking that these counterfactuals are motivationally relevant is just that they are true. Absent weakness of will, and the like, a good-willed agent would not Φ if she thought that Φ-ing were wrong, or unless she judged that it was either right or merely permissible, or if, in a situation in which there is a conflict of duty, she judged that Φ-ing is morally required.[25] We can, therefore, accommodate these counterfactuals even though we reject the idea that a good-willed agent would do the right thing because it is right.

The possibility of practical reason

It might be objected that reason can only be practical if we can do what we believe we should just because we believe we should do this act. John Broome, for example, argues that it is not enough for reason to be practical that we can, through a process of theoretical reasoning, reach a belief about what we should do. It is also necessary that we be able to do this act just because we believe we should do it. His argument runs as follows:

> Imagine people who have normative beliefs – they believe they ought to do one thing or another – but who never do what they believe they ought to do because they believe they ought to do it. If one of them happens to do what she believes she ought to do, the explanation is always something other than her belief. We could not say these people are guided by reason in their acts, nor that reason is truly practical for them.[26]

If Broome is correct, and it must be possible for us to do what we believe we should just because we believe we should, then this would cast doubt on the claim that this belief, or its content, constitutes no reason at all. For it would be very odd indeed if the practicality of reason depended upon our ability to act from considerations which are not reasons. One might bite the bullet here, and simply accept that this odd implication follows. But I do not see why we should accept this. For I do not see why we should think that the practicality of reason depends upon the possibility of acting solely from this verdictive moral consideration.

The thought at work in Broome's argument is that if we cannot do what we believe we should, just because we believe we should, then even if this belief were arrived at by means of reason, reason would not be practical, because this reasoning would not have carried through to the relevant action. It would have come to a dead end with the belief, and something else would have motivated the action. But why should we think that the explanation of the action must work through the belief about what we should do if reason is to be practical?

Broome seems to work with the idea that we reach an overall moral verdict because we believe that the reasons support this verdict, and that this reasoning will only be *practical* if we act because of this verdict. But there is no reason to suppose that this verdict need figure in the explanation of the action in order for our reasoning to be practical. We needn't do the act we believe we should solely, or even partially, because we believe we should do it, but solely because of the reasons why we believe we should do it. Our beliefs about these reasons would then support both our belief about what we should do and the corresponding action. But if these reasons can explain our action (as well as our belief that we ought to do this act), then surely this is all that is needed for reason to be practical. Beliefs about what we should do are not the only type of normative beliefs. Beliefs about what we have reason to do are also normative, and will be practical if *they* can explain action. Surely if we can do what we believe we should solely because of the reasons why we think we should do this, then reason can be practical. But if this is correct, then Broome's claim that if reason is to be practical we must be able to do this act just because we believe we should do it, must be mistaken.

The value of acting from duty

It might be argued that when duty functions as a motivating reason, it has a distinctive moral value; and that it is *this value* which constitutes the reason why the relevant act should be done. Thus, it might be said, Kant is not committed to the claim that the reason why certain acts ought to be done is because they ought to be done (which is, of course, no reason at all), but only to something like the view put forward by H. W. B. Joseph. Joseph held that the goodness of a good motive can be what makes certain actions right.[27] Certain acts ought to be done, he maintains, because of the value of the motive from which, if done, they will be done. This view has, more recently, been put forward by J. L. A. Garcia, who argues that concepts such as 'morally right', and 'ought', are what he calls 'input concepts'.[28] By this he means that the moral rightness of an act is not determined by the value of the consequences that follow from it, but by the moral value of the motives and intentions from which it is done.

But this response is inadequate. First, the view under consideration is that the reason why certain acts are morally required is because of the value of the motive from which, if done, they will be done. If this is correct, it follows from the symmetry thesis that the good-willed agent's reason for doing what she should will be the value of the motive from which she would do this act. But this does not make sense. One cannot maintain that what motivates the morally good person is nothing other than the value of their motive. For this implies that such agents are motivated by something other than the value of their motives. They will also be motivated by whatever motive *has* this value. Assuming this motive is the motive of duty, one would be forced to claim that what motivates morally good people is both the thought of duty, and the value this thought has when it functions as a motive.

But this would give rise to a different difficulty. For it would rule out the view that a good willed agent acts *solely* from duty. She could not act solely from duty, but because she should do this *and* because it is good to be motivated by this verdictive moral consideration. But perhaps those who interpret Kant in this way would be happy to modify their interpretation in this way.

But then Kant will be subject to a third problem. For if this modified Kantian account is accepted, it follows from (S2) that certain actions are morally required because of the value of the motive from which, if done, they will be done, and because they are morally required. But this still implies that *one* of the reasons why we should Φ is because we should Φ – which is, of course, no reason at all. We could only free Kant from this difficulty by maintaining that a morally good person will be disposed to act *solely* from the value of her motive. But, as we have already seen, this does not make sense. This modified account of Kant's view does not, therefore, free him from the specific difficulty at issue.

The analysis of 'ought'

But surely, it will be maintained, if someone points out to me that a certain act ought to be done, they will, at the same time, have pointed out to me a reason why I should do this act? No matter how tempting it is to think this is correct, the previous arguments have shown that it cannot be the case that when someone points out that some act is morally required that they have, at the same time, pointed out a, let alone *the*, reason to do the act. But if this is right, we need to give some account of why it is so tempting to think otherwise.

One way in which this might be explained would be if we could analyse 'ought' statements in terms of reasons for action. Two such analyses are offered by W. D. Falk and, more recently, Michael Smith. These analyses can not only explain why it is so tempting to think that if someone points out to me that a certain act ought to be done, they will, at the same time, have pointed out to me a reason why I should do this act, but can also make clear why this temptation should be resisted. My view is that Falk's analysis is the correct one, and that what Smith takes to be an analysis is (non-analytically) true because Falk's analysis is true. I do not, however, intend to defend this view here. My aim is simply to argue that if either of these analyses is true, it will be able both to explain why it is so tempting to treat ought statements as reasons, and why we should not treat them in this way.

Falk notes that the statement 'I ought to Φ' is often understood externally, as expressing the fact that I am from outside myself demanded (either by God, society or simply by the situation I am in) to Φ.[29] He argues, however, that it can be understood internally, as expressing the fact that I have overriding, or compelling reason to Φ.[30] Since Falk identifies practical reasons with motives, the internalist sense of 'I ought to Φ' is, for him, equivalent to the claim that 'I have an overriding motive, or compulsion to Φ'.[31] For this reason he calls (what I have referred to as) the internalist sense of 'ought' the motivational sense, and thinks that this is the sense of 'ought' we have in mind when we think that there is an internal connection between 'ought' statements and either occurrent or dispositional motives. One could, however, accept Falk's analysis of 'ought' statements in terms of compelling reasons, but reject his identification of practical reasons with motives. One might, as for example, Parfit does,[32] maintain that one can have a reason to Φ even if one is not motivated by this consideration and would not be motivated by it if one deliberated from one's existing motivational set. So whether this internalist analysis of 'ought' statements implies Falk's motivational analysis will depend upon one's view about whether there is a substantive distinction between normative and motivating reasons, or between normative reasons and motives.[33]

My point is simply that if this internalist analysis of 'ought' is correct, and whether or not it entails the motivational analysis, then this would explain why it is so tempting to think that if someone points out to me that a certain act ought to be done, they will, at the same time, have pointed out a reason why I should do this act. For on this analysis, in so far as you convince me that I ought to Φ, you will in effect have convinced me that I have compelling reason to Φ; and this gets a close enough connection between beliefs about what we should do, and what we have compelling reason to do, to explain the temptation to identify moral reasons with ought statements. It is true that this explanation will work only if the analysis of 'ought' is transparent. If it is opaque, then even if the analysis is correct, it will not follow that if I believe I ought to Φ I will believe I have compelling reason to Φ. But this analysis is, I think, close enough to common sense to warrant the assumption that if one believes one ought to Φ one will have, at least an implicit, belief that one has compelling reason to Φ, and this is all that is needed here.

But although this analysis of 'ought', if accepted, can explain why it is so tempting to think of 'ought' statements as reasons to do the required act, it also shows why it is mistaken. For it is one thing to think that I have compelling reason to Φ in so far as I believe that I ought to Φ, and quite another to think that the content of the latter belief is the, or even one of the compelling reasons I take myself to have. To put this another way; the fact that I take myself to have compelling reason to Φ, is not itself one of the compelling reasons I take myself to have (to Φ), just as the fact that there is a compelling argument for P is not itself a compelling argument for P. The reasons will be the evidential moral considerations that can be cited in support of this verdictive belief.

Another analysis of 'ought' which might explain why it is so tempting to think of 'ought' statements as reasons to do the required act, is that offered by Michael Smith.[34] According to Smith, 'ought' statements are analysed in terms of statements about what our ideal rational self would want us to do. If this analysis is correct and more or less transparent – a big if! – it could explain why it is so tempting to think of obligations as reasons. Indeed, Smith himself holds that categorical ought statements are normative reasons.[35] But although this analysis, like Falk's, might explain this, this temptation should be resisted, even if Smith's analysis is correct. The argument for this rests on a modified, but equally plausible, version of the symmetry thesis.

> (S4) a fully rational agent is disposed to be motivated to Φ by the normative reasons why she should Φ.

What we need to ask is: 'Is the fact that I would be motivated to Φ if I were fully rational a normative reason for me to Φ?' If (S4) is granted, the answer to this question will be 'no'. For given (S4), the normative reason, or reasons why I should Φ will be identical with my motivating reason, or reasons for Φ-ing (if the knowledge, practical reasons, and ability conditions are satisfied). But surely if I were fully rational I would not be disposed to be motivated to Φ by the belief, or fact, that I would be motivated to Φ if I were fully rational. If I were fully rational, and were asked why I did what I ought morally to have done, the sort of answer I would be disposed to give would be, 'because I promised to', or 'because so and so needed help' , or 'because she did me a favour in the past', or 'because Φ-ing maximised good', or something of this sort. I would not answer, 'because I promised to and because I would be motivated to do this if I were fully rational'; and I certainly would not answer with reference *solely* to the second conjunct.

Perhaps I would not refer to this verdictive moral consideration under this description if I were fully rational. Perhaps I would reply, 'because this was what I morally should have done', or 'because I promised, and this was what I morally should have done'. But then I would be subject to the earlier criticism. For given (S4) it will turn out that the reason why I ought to Φ will either be because I ought to Φ, or because I promised to Φ and because I ought to Φ. But the fact that I ought to Φ is not a reason why I should Φ at all. So even if Smith's analysis of 'ought' is correct, it will not follow that the 'ought' statement expresses a reason to act in accordance with it. Indeed, given the assumption we have been working on, this will turn out to be false.

Conclusion

The above considerations mean that we must abandon the idea that a morally good person would be disposed to be motivated to do what she should by the thought of duty, and *a fortiori* the idea that she would be disposed to be motivated solely by this thought. For if we insist that a morally good person would act solely from this motive we will be unable to hold onto the connection between morality and rationality which is so central to Kant's thought. This is because we will be forced to concede that morally good people are disposed to be motivated by considerations which are not (normative) reasons at all.

If, therefore, we are to hold onto the view that a morally good person will act solely from duty and that there is an essential and direct connection between morality and rationality, we must interpret Kant's notion of acting from duty in some other way. In the next two chapters I consider an alternative interpretation according to which acting from duty is understood as acting from respect for the moral law. I shall argue (in Chapter 3) that although this gets around the difficulty we have been considering here, it is vulnerable to another, equally devastating objection. There is, however, a third way in which Kant's notion of acting from duty can be understood, which I offer in Chapter 4, which avoids both of these difficulties.

2

RESPECT AND MORAL MOTIVATION

Introduction

In the last chapter I argued that Kant cannot hold onto the view that there is an essential and direct connection between morality and rationality if his claim that a morally good person would tend to do what she should solely from duty is understood as a claim that she would do what she should just because she should so act. This is because the fact that I ought to Φ is not a normative reason to Φ. If, therefore, a morally good person were one who tends to Φ solely because she ought to Φ, she would tend to be motivated to act by a consideration which is not a reason why she should act in this way. The reason why we should do the required acts is not the fact that they are morally required, but the reason why these acts are morally required. If there is an essential and direct connection between morality and rationality, then a morally good person will tend to act from these reasons. But whatever these reasons are, they cannot be or include the fact that the relevant act is morally required. For the fact that some act should be done, or is right, cannot be cited in support of the claim that this act should be done, or is right. It cannot, therefore, be a normative reason in support of this action.

There are two ways in which one might respond to this argument. One could claim either that a good-willed person is not one who tends to act from duty, or that acting from duty should not be understood as doing what one should just because one should. The first type of response is too drastic, and should be adopted only if the second response proves hopeless. For the notion of acting from duty is so central to Kant's ethical thought that if it were abandoned it is difficult to see that anything distinctively Kantian would be left. If we are to defend Kant from this criticism, therefore, we must respond in the second way. This is the line I wish to pursue in Chapters 4 and 5. There I shall offer an alternative interpretation of acting from duty which builds on Barbara Herman's and Marcia Baron's distinction between primary and secondary motives. Before I do that, however, I want to consider an alternative way in which this line of argument might be pursued.

Kant claims not only that duty is the sole moral motive, but that respect for the moral law is. According to the standard interpretation, to act from respect for the moral law is just to do the right thing because it is right. But we have seen that this interpretation is unsatisfactory. A different way of understanding Kant's theory of moral worth would be to start from an account of what it is to act from respect for the moral law, and interpret acting from duty in the light of this. In this, and the following chapter I clarify, and assess, this understanding of acting from duty.

In this chapter I focus on the notion of respect and its relation to moral motivation. Despite the importance of respect (*Achtung*) in Kant's ethics, it is by no means clear what he means by it or what its role in moral motivation is. Some maintain that respect is a certain feeling, others, that it is consciousness of the moral law, while yet a third group argue that it is both of these. The debate about the role of respect in Kant's account of moral motivation is about whether the feeling of respect or consciousness of the moral law is the moral incentive. These are clearly interconnected issues, the resolution of which is crucial if we are to understand Kant's account of moral worth. In this chapter I shall argue for the view that respect is a complex mental state involving a cognitive aspect, consciousness of the moral law, and an affective aspect, what Kant calls moral feeling. This is not a new interpretation of respect. What is novel about my version of this interpretation is the way in which I understand the two aspects of respect to be related.

Other commentators maintain that the cognitive and affective aspects of respect are causally related. But, I argue, this interpretation is inconsistent with Kant's view that moral feeling can be known *a priori* – that is, that it necessarily accompanies consciousness of the moral law for finite rational beings. If, however, we think of moral feeling as the way in which we are conscious of the moral law, we can explain why Kant held that the affective aspect of respect always accompanies the cognitive aspect (for finite rational wills). For this description of our consciousness of the moral law expresses in other words the distinctive way in which the moral law appears to us; and since the moral law can appear to us *only* in this way, moral feeling is the only way in which we can be conscious of it. I finish by considering a further ambiguity which is neglected in the literature, namely, that Kant seems to oscillate between the view that it is respect for the moral law, on the one hand, and the moral law itself, on the other, which is the sole moral incentive. I first argue, contra Beck, that this ambiguity should be taken seriously, and second, that Kant's considered view is that respect is not the moral motive at all, but the state of being morally motivated.

Kant's different claims about respect

For the most part Kant describes respect as a certain feeling caused by the moral law. For example, in the *Critique of Practical Reason* he states that 'respect for the moral law . . . is a feeling produced by an intellectual cause',[1] and in the *Groundwork* he says that, 'respect is a feeling . . . *self-produced* by a rational concept, and therefore specifically distinct from feelings of the first kind, all of which can be reduced to inclination or fear.'[2] He also consistently refers to respect as a feeling throughout his discussion of it in Chapter 3 of the Analytic of the *Critique of Practical Reason*. The 'rational concept' referred to in the above passages is the moral law. The feeling of respect is thus understood as caused by the moral law. It is for this reason that Kant describes it as the one and only moral feeling in the *Groundwork* and in the *Critique of Practical Reason*.[3] It is usually assumed that since the moral law can only cause a feeling in us if we are conscious of it, it is not the moral law itself, but our consciousness of this law which is the immediate cause of moral feeling. According to this view, therefore, the moral law causes our consciousness of it, and this consciousness in turn causes moral feeling. We will see later on that there is reason to question the accuracy of this interpretation. For now, however, I simply note it without comment.

This feeling is described in the *Groundwork* in analogy to fear and inclination, and in the second *Critique* in terms of pleasure and elevation, on the one hand, and pain and humiliation on the other.[4] In so far as the moral law is recognised as having an authority over us which takes no account of our inclinations, the feeling it causes can be understood in analogy to fear. As such, it is thought of as a feeling of humiliation and pain. But in so far as the moral law is considered as *self*-imposed, the feeling it causes may be regarded in analogy to inclination. For in this respect it is conceived of as a feeling of elevation which is similar to pleasure. There is a tendency to overplay the analogy with fear, or pain, and to ignore, or downplay the analogy respect has with inclination and pleasure. But it should be emphasised that the feeling of respect caused by the moral law is not merely one of humiliation and pain, but of elevation also.[5]

I have noted the passage in which Kant states that respect is a feeling produced by the moral law. Elsewhere in the *Groundwork* he states that the moral law is the *only* object of respect.

> For an object as the effect of my proposed action I can have *inclination*, but *never respect*, precisely because it is merely the effect, and not the activity of a will. Similarly for inclination as such, whether my own or that of another, I cannot have respect: I can at most in the first case approve, and in the second case sometimes even love – that is, regard it as favourable to my own advantage. Only something which is conjoined with my will solely as a ground and never as an effect . . . and therefore only bare law for its own sake, can be an object of respect.[6]

His view on this matter is complicated, however, by the fact that he also states that law-giving (*Gesetzgebung*),[7] the ideal will (*Wille in der Idee*),[8] and persons (but not things),[9] are the sole, or appropriate objects of respect. But although Kant's various statements about the object of respect are confusing, there is a close enough conceptual link between the moral law, law-giving, the ideal will, and persons to see them as expressing a coherent view.[10] For they can all be reduced to his initial claim that it is the moral law alone which is the object of respect.

We can first eliminate the ideal will as a contender for being the sole object of respect once we note that the distinctive characteristic of the ideal will is that it is one which gives itself its own law.[11] Thus, when Kant states that it is this ideal will which is the sole object of respect, he can be taken as referring to the characteristic such a will has of law-giving. What, then, is the connection between law-giving, the moral law and personality? In the long footnote on respect in the *Groundwork* Kant writes that 'all respect for a person is properly only respect for the law'.[12] So his claim that only persons can be respected is simply a different way of stating that only the moral law is respected. For what we respect in persons, he maintains, is the moral law in them. This reduces Kant's claims about the sole object of respect to two – the moral law and law-giving. But it is a simple matter to reconcile these two statements. For Kant may be understood as stating that it is not so much the giving of the law which is respected, but the law which is given, and this is just what he states at *Ak* IV, 400. Once all this is noted, therefore, Kant's various descriptions can be taken as different expressions of the same point, namely, that the moral law is the one and only object of respect.

So far, then, we have seen that respect is described by Kant as a distinctive sort of feeling, namely, one whose sole object is the moral law. In the *Critique of Practical Reason* Kant picks out another distinctive characteristic of respect – that is, that it can be known *a priori.*[13] By this he does not mean that the feeling of respect can be known independently of any experience, but that it is a necessary and universal element of moral experience.[14] Thus, just as space is something which is necessarily presupposed in all sensible experience, so moral feeling is a necessary and universal ingredient of moral experience.[15] This means that this affective state *necessarily* accompanies our consciousness of the moral law.

This is, however, only true of finite rational beings. A perfectly rational being, or holy will, not only would not feel respect for the moral law, but *cannot* be conscious of the moral law with respect. For, he writes, respect

> presupposes the sensuousness and hence the finitude of such beings on whom respect for the moral law is imposed; thus respect for the law cannot be attributed to a supreme being or even to one free from all sensibility, since to such a being there could be no obstacle to practical reason.[16]

Thus, we have seen that Kant describes respect (1) as a feeling which can be understood in analogy to, but not defined in terms of, pain and pleasure, or humiliation and elevation; (2) that it is the one and only moral feeling; (3) that the sole object of this feeling is the moral law; and (4) that this feeling necessarily accompanies consciousness of the moral law for finite rational beings. We have resolved a difficulty pertaining to the third characteristic of respect. There are, however, two problems relating to the first characteristic of respect, with which we must now deal. The first is that in the *Metaphysics of Morals* Kant states that by 'moral feeling' he means a receptivity, or susceptibility (*Empfänglichkeit*) to have certain feelings. But if moral feeling is understood in this way, then it will turn out not to be a feeling at all, for a susceptibility to have a certain feeling is not itself a feeling. Second, Kant sometimes identifies respect with our consciousness of the moral law itself and of its supreme authority; and this has led some commentators to maintain that respect is not a feeling, but that moral feeling is simply the effect of respect.

The first of these difficulties can be dealt with fairly easily. For although in the *Metaphysics of Morals* moral feeling is desribed as a susceptibility to have certain feelings,[17] rather than as a certain feeling itself, this does not mean that he no longer thought of respect as a feeling. For in the *Metaphysics of Morals* Kant no longer identifies respect with moral feeling. Rather, moral feeling is described as one 'moral endowment' and respect another (along with conscience and *love* of one's neighbour).[18] And when he describes respect, he is quite clear that it is 'a feeling of a special kind'.[19] So although the modification in Kant's terminology in the *Metaphysics of Morals* is unhelpful, it does not introduce any serious difficulties for the view that respect is a feeling.

The passages in which Kant describes respect as consciousness of the moral law and of its authority raises a more serious difficulty with any account which interprets it simply as moral feeling. In the *Groundwork* Kant states that respect 'means merely consciousness of the *subordination* of my will to a law without the mediation of external influences on my senses',[20] and that 'immediate determination of the will by the law and consciousness of this determination is called "*respect*"';[21] while in the *Metaphysics of Morals* he states that 'respect for the law . . . is identical [*einerlei*] with consciousness of one's duty'.[22] Ralph Walker has recently argued that these passages express Kant's considered view about what respect is, and thus maintains that he thought of it as a cognitive rather than as an affective state.[23] He brushes aside Kant's description of respect as moral feeling as merely manifesting confusion.[24]

But the sheer number of times Kant refers to respect as a feeling, and the sparsity of his descriptions of it as consciousness of the moral law undermine the plausibility of this approach. Even where Kant does describe respect as consciousness of the moral law, he never does so unambiguously. In the same footnote in the *Groundwork* where he describes respect as consciousness of the moral law, Kant also describes it as a certain feeling, and in the *Metaphysics of Morals* his claim that respect is consciousness of the moral law is not unequivocal. The full passage runs, 'Respect for the law, *which in its subjective aspect is called moral feeling*, is identical with consciousness of one's duty.'[25] It is not clear what Kant means by the 'subjective aspect' of respect in this passage. (I shall return to this later.) Nonetheless, the presence of this clause means that even here Kant does not describe respect unambiguously as a cognitive state.

What motivates Walker to give these passages such disproportionate weight is not the sheer weight of textual evidence – for it does not have this weightiness – but a different consideration altogether. This interpretation is motivated by a desire to accommodate Kant's claim that respect is the only moral incentive with his statement that, in relation to moral motivation, the will should not be determined by any feeling whatsoever.[26] But although it is difficult to see how his view that the moral law itself should be the sole moral incentive fits with his conception of respect as a certain feeling caused by the moral law, and his view that this feeling is the sole moral incentive, it is illegitimate to try to resolve this difficulty by simply ignoring the overwhelming number of references to respect as a moral feeling. The passages where Kant states that respect is consciousness of the moral law need to be accommodated. They should not, however, be accommodated at the expense of the numerous passages where he describes it as moral feeling.

Respect as a complex state

Richard McCarty has recently tried to achieve this goal by interpreting respect as a single complex mental state consisting in a cognitive and an affective state causally related to each other.[27] This interpretation of respect simply absorbs Kant's different descriptions of it into a single account, so that it is not thought of merely as the effect of our consciousness of the moral law, but as including this very consciousness. So although respect is understood as including moral feeling, it is not conceived of as being nothing but this. Rather, respect is here interpreted as being both consciousness of the moral law and the moral feeling caused by this consciousness.

This interpretation is suggested by the passage in the *Metaphysics of Morals* Walker cites in support of his interpretation of respect. For as I noted earlier, the full passage runs: 'Respect for the law, which in its subjective aspect is called moral feeling, is identical with consciousness of one's duty.' Kant does not actually use the word 'aspect' (*Absicht*). But nonetheless this passage strongly suggests that he thinks of respect as having two aspects, and thus supports the view that he did not think of moral feeling merely as the effect of respect (conceived of as a mere consciousness of the moral law), but as an aspect of this.

This interpretation has the further virtue of leaving it an open question which aspect of respect constitutes the moral motive. This is a virtue because it enables us to reconcile Kant's statement that respect is a certain feeling with his view that respect is the sole moral motive, on the one hand, and that moral motivation is not mediated by any feeling whatsoever, on the other. For it enables us to maintain that it is not the affective aspect of respect which motivates in morally worthy acts, but the cognitive aspect. But, surprisingly, McCarty does not exploit the full potential of his interpretation of respect in this way, and argues that it is the affective aspect which motivates in morally worthy acts.[28] Yet this view about which aspect of respect constitutes the moral motive undercuts what I take to be one of the main reasons one might find the two-aspect interpretation attractive. For what generates a reluctance to accept Kant's descriptions of respect simply as a feeling is the view that this does not fit with his motivational cognitivism, his view that the moral law itself should be the sole, and immediate incentive in morally worthy acts. It is this difficulty which leads Walker to give such disproportionate weight to the passages where Kant describes respect as consciousness of the moral law. What makes McCarty adopt the view that it is the affective aspect of respect which constitutes the moral motive is that he ascribes to Kant the Humean view that thoughts, by themselves, are inert.[29] But the ascription of such a view to Kant is deeply implausible. For one of Kant's main aims in his ethics is to show that pure reason can be practical, and to do this is just to show the falsity of the Humean thesis.

If, therefore, one were to adopt this interpretation of respect one would be better off maintaining that it is the cognitive aspect of respect which constitutes the moral incentive.[30] This account would then appear to be able to accommodate everything Kant says about respect and moral motivation. There are, however, two problems with this interpretation of respect as it has been described so far. The first stems from the way in which the constituent components of it are regarded as related to each other.[31] The second is that it ignores those passages where Kant describes the moral law itself, not the respect we have for it, as the sole moral incentive.

I shall attempt to resolve these difficulties in the following two sections. What, then, is the first difficulty? The first difficulty is that the view that moral feeling is merely causally related to consciousness of the moral law does not fit with Kant's belief that respect can be known *a priori*. By this he means that the affective aspect of respect, i.e., moral feeling, can be known *a priori*. But if moral feeling is merely the effect of our consciousness of the moral law it is by no means clear how such knowledge would be possible. For the effect will be governed by causal laws of nature; and although it will be true that, given these laws, the effect will necessarily occur, since these laws are not themselves necessary, moral feeling will not be a necessary ingredient of moral experience for finite rational beings in the strong sense that Kant requires.

One might try to get around this difficulty by maintaining that consciousness of the moral law has the property of being disposed to cause moral feeling. For one could then argue that this property is an essential one. But even if one could argue that this dispositional property is essential to our consciousness of the moral law, one would still not have shown that the affective aspect of respect can be known *a priori*. For dispositions are standardly understood as embodying subjunctive conditional claims to the effect that if certain conditions obtain, a certain effect will obtain. So understood, a disposition to cause moral feeling would only accommodate Kant's view that moral feeling necessarily accompanies consciousness of the moral law if the conditions that figure in the disposition necessarily obtained; and whatever those conditions might be it is highly improbable that this would be the case.

The view that respect is a complex mental state consisting of consciousness of the moral law and the moral feeling this effects needs, therefore, to be modified in a way which enables us to explain why Kant held that moral feeling can be known *a priori*. In what follows I offer such an account which is, I maintain, suggested by Kant's view about the way in which the moral law appears to finite rational beings.

Moral feeling as the way in which we are conscious of the moral law

McCarty's account of respect as a single complex state offered the possibility of accommodating Kant's description of it both as consciousness of the moral law and as moral feeling, but could not explain why he thought that moral feeling could be known *a priori*. This deficiency stemmed from the fact that, according to this interpretation, the two aspects of respect are conceived of as causally related. If, therefore, we are to make good this deficiency, we will have to conceive of the two aspects of respect as more intimately related. I suggest that the best way to do this is to think of moral feeling not as the effect of our consciousness of the moral law, but as the way in which we are so conscious. But what does it mean to say that moral feeling is the way in which we are conscious of the moral law?

This can be clarified if we distinguish between 'respect' and 'reverence'. Mary Gregor and Ralph Walker use these terms to distinguish *Achtung* conceived of as consciousness of the moral law (respect) and as moral feeling (reverence).[32] Like Gregor and Walker, I think the concept of reverence picks out well the moral feeling Kant maintains is involved in our consciousness of the moral law. I do not, however, want to use 'respect' simply to denote the cognitive aspect of *Achtung*, but to refer to the whole complex state. Thus, in the way in which I will use these terms, respect will be regarded as a complex mental state which involves both consciousness of the moral law and the feeling of reverence.

This distinction between respect and reverence enables me to clarify what it is I mean when I say that moral feeling is the way in which we are conscious of the moral law. What I mean when I say that moral feeling – that is, reverence – is the way in which we are conscious of the moral law is that we are aware of the moral law reverentially. Respect is, therefore, a *reverential awareness of the moral law*. The negative aspects of the feeling of reverence (pain and humiliation) stem from the fact that the moral law appears to us as constraining our inclinations, i.e., as limiting their authority. The positive aspect of reverence (pleasure and elevation) stem from the fact that we recognise the moral law as a self-legislated principle of our will, and hence regard the way in which the moral law appears to us, not as an external constraint, but as a self-constraint.

Kant nowhere describes respect explicitly in this way, but it receives support from the passage in the *Metaphysics of Morals* where Kant states that duty 'could be presented to us only through [*durch*] the respect we have for it'.[33] Assuming this passage is expressing something more than the trivial truth that we can only be conscious of the moral law through our consciousness of it, it must be taken as saying that we can only be conscious of the moral law through the affective aspect of respect. If we think of moral feeling simply as the effect of our consciousness of the moral law, this passage does not make sense. For how could our consciousness of the moral law be enabled by something which is the effect of this very consciousness? If, however, we think of moral feeling as the way in which we are conscious of the moral law, this passage makes perfect sense. We are conscious of the moral law through, or by means of, moral feeling, because this is the only way in which this consciousness can exist.

Why did Kant think that we could be aware of the moral law only in this way? Why did he not allow that we could be conscious of it indifferently, or even with contempt? This amounts to the question of why he thought that moral feeling could be known *a priori*. The answer to this question may be found by considering the way in which the moral law must appear to us, and why it must appear in this way.

According to Kant, the moral law can appear to finite rational beings only as a command.[34] By 'command' Kant means the necessitation (*Nötigung*) of the will. If the will is determined solely by reason, and no other incentives are present, i.e.:

> if reason infallibly determines the will, then in a being of this kind the actions which are recognized to be objectively necessary are also subjectively necessary – that is to say, the will is then a power to choose *only that* which reason independently of inclination recognizes to be practically necessary, that is, good.[35]

To say that what is recognised as objectively necessary is subjectively also, for a perfectly rational will, is to say that such a will necessarily wills what it ought. Consequently, the moral law does not appear as a command, constraint, imperative, or duty for such a will. '"*I ought*" is here out of place, because "*I will*" is already of itself necessarily in harmony with the law'.[36] For a finite rational being, however, i.e., one which is 'exposed also to subjective conditions (certain incentives) which do not always harmonize with the objective ones',[37] actions which are recognised as objectively necessary are subjectively contingent. Consequently, 'the determination of such a will in accordance with objective laws is *necessitation*'.[38] To say, therefore, that the moral law appears to finite rational beings as a command, is to say that it appears to them as necessitating certain actions – that is, it appears as an imperative.[39] Since actions required by the moral law are recognised as necessary not merely as a means to some contingent end, but as necessary in and of themselves, the moral law appears to finite rational wills as a *categorical* imperative.

The moral law appears to us as an imperative because we do not necessarily will in accordance with it. It appears, therefore, as a *constraint* for a finite rational will.[40] It is easy to take the notion of a constraint as implying that our natural inclinations are in some way essentially opposed to the requirements of the moral law.[41] But Kant thinks that the moral law appears to us as necessitating, or constraining, not because our natural inclinations are intrinsically immoral, but because of the *contingency* of the connection between what we are inclined to do and what we ought to will. The notion of a constraint should not, therefore, be understood as presupposing a conception of inclination as essentially opposed to morality (a view that Hegel and Hegelians are fond of ascribing to Kant), but as expressing the fact that the moral law places a rational *limit* on the practical possibilities open to us in certain circumstances, and is recognised as such.[42] The moral law does not appear to a perfectly rational being as a rational *constraint* because it does not limit the possibilities open to such a will. This is because such a being does not have possibilities open to it which can conflict with, and hence can be limited by, the moral law.

This understanding of constraint as a rational limitation brings to light a crucial aspect of the way in which the moral law appears to us. In so far as it appears to us as a *rational* limitation it will not appear to us as a mere constraint, but as a *self*-constraint. In so far as the moral law appears to us as a rational constraint, it will appear to us, at least in so far as we regard ourselves as rational, or noumenal agents, as a self-constraint. Because the moral law appears to finite rational beings as a self-constraint in the sense of a rational limitation, its being recognised as constraining will not depend upon a contingent opposing inclination. All it presupposes is the contingency of the co-operating inclination, if one is present. The moral law will appear to a finite rational being as a self-constraint, therefore, irrespective of the degree of virtue present in the agent, or of the degree to which she wants to do what she ought. Given that the conformity of our inclinations to the moral law is *always* only contingent, the moral law can *only* appear to us as a (categorical) imperative.

How does this explain why Kant thought that we can only be aware of the moral law reverentially? This can be explained if we reject the view that the distinctive way in which the moral law appears to us is something distinct from, and causally related to, the distinctive way in which we are conscious of the moral law. To do this is to regard the way in which we must be conscious of the moral law as a different description of the way in which the moral law must appear to us. Thus understood, the claim that we can only be aware of the moral law reverentially is just another way of saying that the moral law can appear to us only as a self-constraint. If there is such an identity, then the arguments Kant brings to bear in support of his claim that the moral law necessarily appears to us as a self-constraint will, at the same time, constitute arguments for his claim that we can only be aware of the moral law reverentially, and the puzzle will be solved.

Is this identity claim plausible? I think that it is. It is not clear what more Kant could mean when he says that the moral law necessarily appears to us as a rational self-constraint over and above the claim that we are aware of it as subordinating our will to a law without the mediation of external influences; and since this is just what it is to be conscious of the moral law reverentially,[43] it is difficult to see that Kant could mean anything more than that we are aware of the moral law reverentially when he says that the moral law necessarily appears to us as a rational self-constraint. If this is accepted, then we will have explained why Kant thought that we can only be aware of the moral law reverentially.

Kant's claim may seem implausible to many. It may be objected that criminals and amoralists are aware of the moral law with indifference, or contempt, rather than with reverence, and that to insist otherwise is to fly in the face of the empirical evidence. I shall, later in this chapter, give reasons for thinking that Kant's strong claim is not as implausible as it may at first appear. In order to do this, however, I will need to address the second of the two difficulties with McCarty's account mentioned previously. It is to this that I now turn.

The role of the moral law

So far I have argued that respect is a complex mental state consisting of consciousness of the moral law and its authority, as well as moral feeling. But although the constituent elements of respect are distinct, they are not independent of each other for a finite rational will in the sense that one could exist without the other. Moral feeling cannot exist without a consciousness of the moral law, because the moral law is the only object of this feeling; and consciousness of the moral law cannot exist without moral feeling because this feeling is the only way in which we can be conscious of the moral law. It is only if we think of respect in this way that we can explain why Kant thought that the affective aspect necessarily accompanied the cognitive aspect for finite rational beings. This modification of McCarty's account of respect can, therefore, deal with the first of the two difficulties mentioned previously.

We now need to address the second of these difficulties. McCarty maintained that it is the affective aspect of respect which is the sole moral incentive. I argued that his interpretation would be better if he claimed that it is the cognitive aspect, as this would fit better with Kant's motivational cognitivism. Given my modification to McCarty's account, we do not have to choose which aspect of respect constitutes the sole moral incentive. The moral incentive is respect for the moral law – that is, the sole moral incentive is our reverential awareness of the moral law and of its authority. The problem with this is that Kant often says that it is the moral law itself, not our respect for it, which is the one and only moral incentive. In the *Groundwork* he states that in relation to moral motivation the will must be determined 'solely by the law, without any further incentive',[44] and this is repeated in the *Critique of Practical Reason*. Here he states: 'What is essential in the moral worth of actions is that the moral law should directly determine the will',[45] and further on he writes: 'The [moral incentive] of the human will (and that of every created rational being) can never be anything other than the moral law.'[46] L. W. Beck claims that these passages cannot be interpreted literally on the ground that the moral law itself 'is just not the sort of thing that can be an incentive'.[47] I think this view is mistaken. What may make Beck think that the moral law is not the sort of thing that can be an incentive is that we sometimes think of incentives, or motives as a kind of force which pushes us in a certain direction. We conceive of motives in this way when, for example, we talk of someone committing some act out of rage, or jealousy. If the moral law were conceived of as a motive in this sense, then it would not be a practical law at all, but would be something like a law of nature, or rather something governed by a natural law. But we also think of motives not as forces pushing us along, but simply as reasons we have for doing certain acts (where these reasons are not understood causally). When, for example, Poirot is looking for a suspect's motive, what he is looking for is not some psychological force which caused the action, but for the agent's reason for doing this.

Now although the notion of an incentive may suggest the first sense, Kant's considered view is that incentives are reasons for action which can be recognised as a good reasons by the agent.[48] Incentives should not, therefore, be thought of as something like Humean passions which move us to act. For Kant, such a conception is incompatible with our freedom.[49] We are not moved to act by some impulse, but move ourselves on the basis of reasons we take to be valid, and these are, in Kant's terminology, the incentives from which we act. But if we think of incentives as practical reasons which can be recognised as such and incorporated into the agents maxim, then there is no reason to suppose, as Beck does, that the moral law itself is the wrong sort of thing to be an incentive. For to say that it is an incentive for finite rational beings is just to say that it is a principle, the authority of which each of us recognises, and which each of us can, if we choose, make the ground of our action.

But Beck has a further reason for denying that the moral law itself can be interpreted as the moral incentive. He argues that, since we have to be conscious of the moral law in order to be motivated by it, it must be this consciousness, not its object, which is our incentive. But this conclusion is too strong. For the fact that we have to be conscious of the moral law in order for it to be a reason from which we act does not stop its being the, or a reason from which we do that action when we are conscious of its commands and make it the ground of our act. Humeans would insist that motivating reasons have to be psychological states, since they must always include a desire, and this is a psychological state. But since Kant rejects the Humean thesis that motivating reasons must be or include desires, there is no reason why he should think that motivating reasons should be psychological states rather than their contents, and there is reason to reject this interpretation of Kant.

Since Beck gives us no good reason for ignoring the various passages in which he states that it is the moral law itself which is the moral incentive, we cannot side-step the difficulty these passages introduce simply by ruling them out as a possibility. It seems, then, that there is a genuine ambiguity in Kant about what the moral incentive is: he seems to have thought either that it is *respect* for the moral law, or that it is the object of respect – *the moral law itself.*

In the *Groundwork*, however, Kant offers a third alternative. Here he writes that the moral law is the *objective* determinant, and respect the *subjective* determinant of the will.[50] By 'determinant' here he seems to mean 'incentive'. Thus understood, this passage states that the moral law is the objective moral incentive of the will and our respect for it is the subjective moral incentive. But how should this contrast be understood? Kant might have in mind the distinction between an objective and a subjective principle that he makes in *Groundwork II*.[51] Here he states that an objective principle is one on which one ought to act, and a subjective principle is one on which the subject *in fact* acts. If we understand the contrast between subjective and objective incentives in this way, then the moral law will be understood as an incentive from which one ought to act, and respect for the moral law the incentive from which the agent acts (when she acts morally). Since an incentive can only determine the will in so far as it is incorporated in to the agent's maxim, this will have to be understood as stating that the moral law is the incentive which ought to be incorporated into the agent's maxim, and respect is the incentive which is, or has been, incorporated into the agent's maxim when she acts in accordance with this imperative.

This may be what Kant is trying to say here, but if it is, it is very odd. For one would expect him to say that the moral law, not our reverential awareness of it, should also be our subjective principle. Why should Kant think that the fact that we ought to incorporate the moral law into our maxim implies that we must incorporate a psychological state (respect) into our maxim? What does this psychological state add to the content of one's maxim when it figures in it? Since it is the content of this psychological state which is action guiding, not the psychological state itself, I think we should reject this interpretation of the contrast between a subjective and objective determinant of the will.

A different view is suggested in Chapter 3 of the Analytic of the *Critique of Practical Reason*.[52] Here Kant seems to be suggesting that we first recognise the objective validity of the moral law; that this recognition involves the feeling of reverence (as the way in which we are conscious of the moral law and its authority); and that this feeling in turn induces us to accept the law as our subjective principle or maxim.[53] Here respect does not seem to figure in the content of the moral maxim, but is what motivates our incorporating the moral law into our maxim, thus making this objective principle our subjective principle.

The problem with this, however, is that it does not fit with Kant's claim in the second *Critique* that 'the objective determining ground must at the same time be the exclusive and subjectively sufficient determining ground of [morally worthy] action'[54] and in the *Groundwork* that 'the will is determined here solely by the law without any further motive'.[55] Consequently, whatever Kant means by his distinction between a subjective and an objective determinant, or incentive, it cannot be one between two different incentives which are individually necessary and jointly sufficient for moral motivation.

The passages cited above strongly suggest that his view is that the objective determinant, i.e., the moral law, is or must be the sufficient incentive of the will if our willing is to be good. But if respect is not, after all, the, or a, moral incentive, we need to know what Kant means when he describes it as the subjective determinant of the will. I think a coherent account of the role of respect in moral motivation is suggested by what Kant says about moral interest in the *Groundwork*, and I will finish this section by sketching out what I take this view to be. We will then be in a position to answer the objection raised previously.

Kant identifies the concept of a moral interest with respect for law. 'All moral *interest*, so-called, consists solely in *respect for* the law.'[56] In the *Groundwork* Kant defines interest as 'that in virtue of which [*wodurch*] reason becomes practical – that is, becomes a cause determining the will'.[57]

A subjective determining cause, or ground of a finite will is an *incentive*.[58] Thus, according to this definition, a *moral* interest is that in virtue of which the moral law constitutes an incentive, or motive to do what one ought. Since moral interest is equated with respect, it follows that respect is that in virtue of which the moral law constitutes an immediate incentive for us. Kant is not here expressing the view that respect is the moral incentive, but that, in finite rational beings, moral motivation *presupposes* respect. For all motivation, including moral motivation, presupposes an interest, and in relation to morality, this interest is respect. It is, however, one thing to say that respect is necessary for a finite rational being to be morally motivated, and quite another to say that this psychological state constitutes the moral motive for such a being. I propose, therefore, that when Kant says that respect for the moral law is the subjective determinant of the will, he does not mean that it is, in some sense, a subjective *incentive*, but that it is a subjective condition of the moral law's being an immediate incentive of the will for beings like us.

But why, it might be asked, should he think that respect is a necessary condition for the possibility of the moral law being an immediate incentive of the will of finite rational agents if he does not think that it is an incentive which prompts us to incorporate the moral law into our maxim? There are, I believe, three reasons for this. The first, is simply the trivial point that some consideration cannot motivate us unless we are conscious of it. So if the moral law is to motivate us, we must be conscious of it, and respect is Kant's term for this (reverential) consciousness. The second is that I can only be motivated immediately by the moral law if I am conscious of its unconditional authority – that is, if I am conscious of 'the *subordination* of my will to a law without the mediation of external influences on my senses' and of 'a value which demolishes my self love'.[59] But the only way in which we can be aware of something's unconditional authority is reverentially. Consequently, it is not only our awareness of the moral law which is presupposed in order for it to be an immediate incentive of the will, but a *reverential* awareness of it; and this is just what respect is.

Finally, respect is a necessary condition for the possibility of the moral law itself being an immediate incentive of the will because this psychological state is *what it is to be motivated* in the distinctive way in which we are when we are morally motivated. Our reverential awareness of the moral law is not the moral motive, but the state of being morally motivated. This claim is supported by the fact that Kant does not describe respect as ground of determination (*Bestimmungsgrund*), but as the state of being determined itself (an *unmittelbare Bestimmung des Willens*[60]). The incentive is not the state of being determined, but that which gets one's will into this state (the *ground* of determination), and what gets the will into this state is not our consciousness of the law, but the law itself.[61] So although it will be true that one will have an incentive to do what the law enjoins in so far as one is conscious of the moral law, it will not be true that one's consciousness is this incentive. The incentive is, as Kant clearly states in his more careful moments, the law itself.

Moral motivation and internalism

Previously I said I would respond to the objection that Kant's claim that we can only be conscious of the moral law reverentially is falsified by the empirical evidence. Criminals and vicious individuals might be aware of the moral law, but why should we assume that they must be aware of it reverentially? Isn't it more plausible, the objection runs, to assume that they are aware of it with indifference, or even contempt? One might try to respond to this objection by utilising the argument Kant puts forward for the claim that the moral law can appear to us only as a rational self-constraint. For since the way in which we are conscious of the moral law is just another way of describing the way in which the moral law must appear to us, if these arguments support the latter, then they will support the former also. This would not, however, meet the objection. For according to this objection any argument which claimed to show that we can only be conscious of the moral law reverentially must either be invalid or unsound, because the conclusion is contradicted by the empirical facts. But given my interpretation, the moral feeling of reverence is not only the way in which we are conscious of the moral law, but also the state of being motivated to do what the moral law enjoins. Once this latter point is noted, Kant's claim that we can only be conscious of the moral law reverentially will not seem as blind to the empirical facts as it may at first appear. For it amounts to the claim that we cannot be aware of the moral law without being motivated to do what it enjoins.

In order to see this, we need to note that the moral law can never appear to us in complete abstraction from some content. The moral law itself is just the pure form of universal necessity. But we can only become aware of this in so far as we recognise that some act is practically necessary, or necessitated. We are, then, only ever aware of the moral law in so far as we are aware of being, or believe that we are, obligated to do some action. But we can only recognise that we are morally obligated to Φ if we recognise that the normative concept 'obligatoriness' is applicable to this act. On Kant's account, the normativity of this concept is ultimately traceable to the pure form of universality, i.e., the moral law itself. Nonetheless, I can become conscious of the moral law only in so far as I recognise that some act falls under some morally normative concept, such as 'ought', 'duty', 'obligation'. If the feeling of reverence is understood, not as the moral motive, but as the state of being morally motivated, Kant's claim that we cannot be aware of the moral law without reverence will amount to internalism – that is, the view (not to be confused with Williams' view that practical reasons must be internal) that if an agent judges that it is right for her to Φ in circumstances C, then she is motivated to Φ in C or she is practically irrational.[62] I do not intend to defend internalism here, but it is a very plausible view. As Smith puts it:

> Having convinced me that I should give to famine relief you seem to have done everything you need to do to convince me that I have reason to do so. And having convinced me that I have reason to give to famine relief

> – absent weakness of will or some other psychological failure – you seem to have done everything you need to do to motivate me to do so.[63]

Whether or not internalism is true, it is certainly plausible to believe that there is a conceptual connection between believing that I should Φ and being motivated to Φ. Thus, if the feeling of reverence is the state of being morally motivated, and we can only become conscious of the moral law in so far as we are conscious of being morally obligated, then it is equally plausible to think that there is a conceptual connection between consciousness of the moral law and the feeling of reverence. If all of this is correct, then Kant's claim will not only appear plausible, but his arguments for this claim can be seen as arguments for internalism. Unlike many, Kant does not merely assume the truth of internalism, but tries to show why it is true. If, therefore, we interpret Kant in the way I suggest we can not only reconcile the various things he says about respect and moral motivation, but can also make plausible his claim that moral feeling can be known *a priori*.

3

ACTING FROM RESPECT FOR THE MORAL LAW

Introduction

We are considering an interpretation of acting from duty which starts with an account of what it is to act from respect for the moral law, and interprets acting from duty in accordance with this account. To act from respect for the moral law is best understood as acting from the moral law;[1] and to act from the moral law is to act from the mere universality of one's maxim. But if the moral law, or mere universality, is to be something one can act from, it must be able to guide action. To this end Kant offered three formulations of the moral law: the formula of universal law, the formula of the end in itself, and the formula of the kingdom of ends.[2] The first is a purely formal expression of the moral law – that is, it is a formulation which makes no reference to an end. The second is the material formulation, and specifies the unconditional end of moral action. The third is the synthesis of the first two. But although these are distinct formulations, they are intimately related as form, matter and complete determination.[3]

In this chapter I shall offer an account of acting from duty understood in accordance with the idea of acting from respect for the moral law. I shall then argue that, although there is textual evidence in support of this interpretation, we should not understand Kant in this way. For in so far as he understands morally worthy acts as ones which are done *solely* from duty, this interpretation will have the deeply implausible implication that a morally good person cannot be motivated by the needs of others. I then locate the source of the problem with the idea that we ought to do certain acts just *because* they are commanded by the categorical imperative – that is, in the idea that the categorical imperative is the normative reason why we ought to do certain acts, or, to put this another way, is the ground of duty. Abandoning this interpretation of acting from duty, therefore, will entail abandoning the idea Kant occasionally puts forward that the reason why we ought to do certain acts is because of the lawlike nature of our maxims. This will mean that we will have to offer a different account of (a) acting from duty, (b) the role of the moral law, and (c) the ground of duty. I shall carry out these tasks in Chapters 4 and 5.

Acting from respect for the moral law as acting from the categorical imperative

Since we have three distinct formulations of the moral law which are capable of guiding action, the question is: From which formulation would a good-willed agent act? It may turn out that a good-willed agent would be one who acts solely from *any* one of these formulations, or that she would have to act from one particular formulation in order to be morally good. This interpretation of acting from duty would appear quite appealing if it at least allowed, if not required, a good-willed person to be one who acted solely from a concern for treating others, as well as herself, as ends in themselves – that is, one who acted solely from the formula of the end in itself. But although this would make the interpretation of Kant under consideration attractive, I do not think it is one we can adopt. It is true that for Kant a good-willed person will be one who has made rational nature, or humanity, her ultimate end, as the formula of the end in itself, *qua* material formulation of the moral law, sets the unconditional *end* of action.[4] But what we are considering is not what *ends* a good-willed person would have, or have internalised, but what it is that would *motivate* her to adopt, and pursue these ends; and Kant is clear that the moral worth of actions can stem solely from a merely *formal* motive, i.e., one which abstracts from all ends.

> That the purposes we may have in our actions, and also their effects considered as ends and motives of the will, can give to actions no unconditioned and moral worth is clear from what has gone before. Where then can this worth be found if we are not to find it in the will's relation to the effect hoped for from the action? It can be found nowhere but *in the principle of the will*, irrespective of the ends which can be brought about by such action; for between its *a priori* principle, which is formal, and its *a posteriori* motive, which is material, the will stands, so to speak, at a parting of the ways; and since it must be determined by some principle, it will have to be determined by the formal principle of volition when an action is done from duty, where, as we have seen, every material principle is taken away from it.[5]

It is tempting to read this passage as claiming simply that a motive lacks moral worth if it expresses an end we just happen to desire.[6] But Kant's point here is that a motive has moral worth only if it is purely formal, and hence abstracts from any *end* whatsoever, including the unconditional end in itself. Thus, since an action 'must be determined by some principle, it will have to be determined by the formal principle of volition when an action is done from duty, where . . . every material principle is taken away from it.'[7] If one's action cannot be determined by any material principle when it is done from duty, and the formula of the end in itself is a material principle – the formulation of the moral law which expresses the matter of morality – then this formulation cannot be the one from which a good-willed agent would act. The formula of the kingdom of ends would be ruled out for the same reason. For as the complete determination of the moral law, this formula includes both the form and matter of the supreme moral principle, and is hence not purely formal. These passages suggest, therefore, that Kant not only thought that the formula of universal law is the most reliable guide[8] to action, but also that it is the sole determinant, or motive of moral action.

This is not to say that when we act morally we have no end in view.[9] For Kant, all willing involves the willing of some end.[10] Consequently, moral willing does. The point is that no end, not even the end in itself, will function as a motive when one's willing is morally good. One's motive will be the purely formal one of universality as such, as it is expressed in the formula of universal law. The morally good person will be one who wills those ends which support, or respect, the autonomy of others – that is, their rational nature as ends in themselves – because the maxim of her action is lawlike. According to the interpretation we are considering, therefore, the good-willed individual is one who is motivated solely by the universal validity of her maxim as this is expressed in the formula of universal law – that is, she would be one who acts solely from this formulation of the categorical imperative. From now on, therefore, I shall refer to the formula of universal law whenever I mention the categorical imperative, unless I state otherwise.

This interpretation of acting from respect for the moral law is supported by the fact that Kant sometimes describes the categorical imperative as the ground of duty. For example, towards the end of *Groundwork I* he states that if a maxim cannot be willed as a universal law, 'it is to be rejected, and that not because of a prospective loss to you or even to others, but *because* it cannot fit as a principle into a possible enactment of universal law.'[11] This passage suggests that Kant conceived of the categorical imperative as constituting the normative reason *why* we ought to forbear certain actions. This conception of the categorical imperative is also suggested by the following passage from *Groundwork II*.

> Now all imperatives of duty can be derived [*abgeleitet*] from this one imperative as their principle, even although we leave it unsettled whether what we call duty may not be an empty concept, we shall still be able to show at least what we understand by it and what the concept means.[12]

In the second half of this passage Kant talks of the categorical imperative as telling us *what the concept of duty means*. However, his opening claim that specific duties can be derived from the categorical imperative lends further support to the view that he believes that the categorical imperative is the ground of these duties. Let us call this the *justificatory* conception of the categorical imperative. The idea here seems to be that we ought (have a duty) to do certain acts, e.g., to keep our promises, to be truthful or to help the needy, because the maxim of opposite actions – that is, the maxims of acts of promise breaking, lying, or failure to help the needy – cannot be conceived, or willed as universal laws. If Kant thinks of the categorical imperative in this way, i.e., as the reason why we ought to do certain acts, then it will be the reason why a morally good person will tend to do these acts. This is because the symmetry thesis identifies the normative reasons why one ought to Φ with the motivating reasons why a good person will Φ, and vice versa (under favourable conditions).

It may, however, seem deeply counter-intuitive to ascribe to Kant the view that the categorical imperative is the sole justification for the various moral obligations we have. It would seem far more plausible to hold that the categorical imperative is the ultimate, or most basic justification for moral requirements, but that other evidential moral considerations are also reasons why we should do certain acts. But despite the fact that this would be a far more plausible view, it is difficult to see how we could ascribe it to Kant. For the view that the moral law, as it is formulated in the categorical imperative, is only one of the reasons, albeit the most basic one, why we ought to do certain actions is incompatible with his view that a good-willed person would tend to act solely from respect for the moral law.[13] For if the moral law is only one of the reasons why we ought to act in certain ways, and the good-willed person is one who tends to act from the reasons why she should so act, then she will be one who tends to do what she should, not merely from respect for the moral law, but from these other considerations also. But if these other considerations, whatever they are, are motives which are necessary conditions of morally good acts, then the motive of respect for the moral law as such cannot be sufficient. It is clear, however, that Kant thought that respect for the law is not only necessary, but also sufficient for the moral worth of the actions done from it.[14]

This is further supported in the *Metaphysics of Morals* where Kant states that:

> For any one duty only *one* ground of obligation can be found; and if someone produces two or more proofs for a duty, this is a sure sign either that he has not yet found a valid proof or that he has mistaken two or more different duties for one.[15]

If for any duty there can be only one ground, and if the moral law is the ground of duty, then it must be regarded as the sole reason why we ought to do certain acts. It is true that this passage strongly implies that different obligations have different grounds; and this militates against the view that there is one ground for all duties, and that this is the moral law. But part of what I am trying to show in this work is that there is not a single account of acting from duty in Kant, or of the ground of duty. Sometimes he talks as if the moral law is the sole determinant of right actions, while at others, especially in the *Metaphysics of Moral*, he puts forward the more intuitive view that different obligations are generated by different considerations.[16] The interpretation of acting from duty I shall propose in Chapters 4 and 5 will work with the latter view. The one I am considering at present, however, is working with the former. But whether or not Kant thought that one consideration generates all obligations, it is clear that he thinks that for any one duty, there can be only one ground. So if the justificatory conception of the categorical imperative is accepted, the categorical imperative will have to be regarded as the sole normative reason why we ought to act in certain ways.

We could, of course, abandon the view that for any obligation there can be only one ground, and thus hold onto the more plausible view that the categorical imperative is *a* but not *the* reason why we ought to do certain acts. But then the first difficulty will re-emerge. For if the moral law is not the sole normative reason why we ought to do certain acts, then it will not be a motive which is sufficient to make an action morally good. Given the symmetry thesis, the other normative reasons would be necessary for the moral worth of the actions they motivate. We could abandon the symmetry thesis and the view that there can only be one ground of duty for any obligation. But although Kant would then be able to hold onto his central thesis that the moral law is a motive sufficient to make actions morally good without being committed to the view that the moral law is the sole reason why such actions should be done, he would be unable to hold onto the view that there is an essential and direct link between morality and rationality. For it would then be possible for the moral worth of actions to come apart from any normative reason why those actions should be done. If we are going to take seriously the justificatory conception of the categorical imperative, therefore, we will have to think of it as the sole ground of duty.

Nonetheless, this may not seem a very promising interpretation of acting from duty for other reasons. For the categorical imperative is usually regarded merely as a criterion for assessing one's motivating reasons and principles, not as the sole consideration which will motivate a morally good person.[17] To regard the categorical imperative as a criterion is to regard it as a means by which we can come to know that some principle, or reason, which informs our deliberation is either permissible or impermissible. To treat it as one's sole motivating reason, on the other hand, is to regard it as actually *giving us reason* to act in certain ways. There is, furthermore, good reason to think of the categorical imperative in this way. The worry is that if we think of the categorical imperative as having more than a criterial role it will generate deeply implausible conclusions.[18] For not all actions whose maxims can be willed as a universal law, and hence pass the categorical imperative test, are morally required. Some are merely permissible. Consequently, if we think of the categorical imperative as in some way generating obligations, these apparently permissible acts will turn out to be morally obligatory.[19]

I do not wish to deny that there is plenty of evidence in Kant to support the view that he regarded it solely as a criterion of moral action, rather than as its sole ground – on the contrary, I shall later argue that this is how we should understand Kant. Kant conceived of the categorical imperative in a number of different ways, and did not clearly distinguish these.[20] All I wish to claim here is that if Kant is interpreted as claiming that a morally good person would act solely from the categorical imperative, he would be committed to these absurd consequences.

Whether or not he is will depend upon how we understand acting from respect for the moral law. If this is interpreted as stating that a morally good person would tend to do what she should solely because her maxim can be willed as a universal law without contradiction, then he would be stuck with this difficulty. For if the reason why a morally good person does what she should tends to be identical with the normative reason why she should so act, it will turn out that the sole consideration which makes actions obligatory is that their maxims can be universalised without contradiction. But as we have already noted, the maxims of merely permissible actions can be universalised without contradiction. Thus, if mere universalisability makes acts morally obligatory, it will follow that (apparently) merely permissible acts will be regarded as morally obligatory.

But this problem can be avoided simply by understanding acting solely from respect for the moral law in a different way. In relation to prohibited acts, we can understand this as forbearing some act just because its maxim cannot be universalised without contradiction, and in relation to obligatory acts, we can understand it as doing what one should just because the maxim of the contradictory act cannot be universalised. For the sake of simplicity, let us call maxims of obligatory actions, i.e., those acts whose contradictory expresses a maxim which cannot be willed as a universal law without contradiction, '*lawlike*' maxims. The term 'universally valid maxim' will be reserved solely for the maxim of merely permissible actions, i.e., those whose maxim is universalisable, and where the maxim of the contradictory act is also universalisable. So understood, a good-willed person would tend to keep her promise, for example, solely because the maxim of this act is lawlike, i.e., because the maxim of failing to keep one's promise cannot be willed as a universal law, and she would be truthful just because the maxim of failing to be truthful cannot be universalised. This interpretation will not make merely permissible acts morally obligatory. For although these have universally valid maxims, they are not lawlike in the sense in which I am using this term. If I fail to do some merely permissible act, such as reading the paper in the morning, having lunch at 1.00 p.m., or drinking tea after dinner, my maxim will still be universalisable.

Now if Kant thought that we ought to do, or forbear certain acts simply *because* their maxims are lawlike, and if the reason why a relevantly informed agent Φs will tend to be identical with the reason why she ought to Φ, then a good-willed agent will be one who tends to be motivated solely by the lawlike nature of her maxims.

I don't want to claim that this is the only way in which the notion of acting from duty can be understood in Kant, and certainly not that it *should* be understood in this way. As we noted in Chapter 1, the notion of acting from duty can be understood in a more common-sensical way as doing what one should, just because one should, and in Chapters 4 and 5 I shall propose a third interpretation that I believe is the most plausible account in Kant. All I claim here is that Kant's notion of acting from duty can be understood in this way, and that one can avoid the criticisms raised in Chapter 1 if one does.

The problem raised in Chapter 1 was that if we think of acting from duty as doing what we should just because we should, then we will be committed to the absurd view that the only reason why we ought to do certain acts is because we ought to do them, which is, of course, no (normative) reason at all. Thus, if a morally good person is one who tends to act solely from duty, she will be one who tends to act from a moral consideration which is neither a, or the, reason why she should do those acts; and the connection between morality and rationality will be lost. If we interpret acting from duty in Kant as acting from the categorical imperative, however, it seems as though this connection can be maintained. For there is no reason to think that the categorical imperative *could* not be the reason why we ought to perform certain actions.

But, despite the fact that there is textual evidence for this interpretation, and though it is not vulnerable to the difficulties discussed so far, it is nonetheless one we ought to reject. For if we interpret Kant's notion of acting from duty in this way, he will be committed to the deeply implausible view that a morally good person cannot be motivated by the needs of others. She might make the needs of others her end, and may do so for no selfish, or ulterior motive. Nonetheless, she will not be able to adopt this end *because* some other person, or persons are in need. Thus, this interpretation makes Kant vulnerable to the type of criticism that has been levelled against him by some of his Neo-Aristotelian critics.[21] If the categorical imperative is the sole reason why certain acts ought to be done, and is hence the sole reason why a good-willed person will tend to do those acts, then in a case where she helps someone in need, and is morally required to do so, she cannot act *because* this person is in need, but simply because the maxim of her action is lawlike. It is not a fact about the needy person, but a fact about herself, about her maxim, which will motivate the Kantian good-willed person. So although this interpretation of acting from duty would save the connection between morality and practical reason, it does so only on the deeply implausible assumption that a morally good person could not be motivated, or at least could not tend to be motivated solely by the needs of others.

Moral motivation and the needs of others

I have claimed that if we interpret acting from duty as acting from respect for the moral law, then we will be committed to the view that a morally good person will not be able to be motivated to help others by a thought about the other person, but solely by a thought about herself, about the lawlike nature of her maxim. If correct, this would clearly be a deficiency in Kant's account of moral worth. But this criticism assumes that for Kant an action has moral worth only if it is done *solely* from duty, i.e., solely from respect for the moral law. But this assumption has so far received no support. One would be acting from duty if one acts from duty *and* inclination, or from duty *and* from sympathy.[22] Since acting from duty is sufficient for an action to have moral worth, then, it may be said an action has moral worth if it is done from duty and from inclination, or from duty and sympathy. But if this is correct, then a morally good person could be motivated to help someone when they should by a thought about the other person even if acting from duty is understood as acting from respect for the moral law. For, in so far as one is motivated by the lawlike nature of one's maxim, and by the need of the other person, one will be acting from respect for the moral law (and from concern for the other person). One's action would, therefore, have moral worth. The issue that has to be addressed, therefore, is whether motivationally overdetermined actions can have moral worth. If they cannot, then the above criticism of the account of morally worthy actions will not work.

Kant never explicitly considered the issue of whether overdetermined actions have moral worth. It is, therefore, difficult to present a decisive view one way or the other simply on the basis of textual evidence. There are passages which support the view that he did not think that such actions could have moral worth. For example, in the second *Critique* he writes that, 'the objective determining ground must at the same time be the exclusive and subjectively sufficient determining ground of action if the latter is to fulfil not merely the letter of the law but also its spirit'.[23] Here he claims that for an action to have moral worth, duty must not only be a sufficient motive, but must be the exclusive motive also. If duty must exclude all other motives for an action to have moral worth, then overdetermined actions cannot have moral worth. But passages such as this one cannot decide the issue of whether overdetermined actions have moral worth in the absence of an account of why Kant thought duty is the only morally good motive. For, the only way this issue can be decided is by first giving an account of why Kant thought that only actions done from duty have moral worth, and then seeing whether overdetermined actions satisfy the requirements of this account. I do not, however, intend to consider the issue of why Kant thought only actions done from duty have moral worth until Chapter 6 (where I shall argue that they cannot). The issue of whether overdetermined actions have moral worth cannot, therefore, be decided here. I shall, nonetheless, work on the assumption that the above passage reflects Kant's view, and that an action can have moral worth only if it is done solely from duty. I shall justify this assumption later.

Granted this assumption, if acting from duty is understood as acting from respect for the moral law, then morally worthy actions will be those, and only those, done solely from respect for the moral law. If this is right, then, on this interpretation of acting from duty, Kant seems to be committed to the view that a morally good person will be motivated to help others when she should solely by a thought about the lawlike nature of her maxim. This would be odd, because it will mean that she will not be able to be motivated to help others when she should by a thought about the other person.[24]

Two responses may be offered to this criticism. First, it may be objected that, on Kant's account, a good-willed individual, acting solely from duty, does not act simply in order to fulfil her duty, but in order to provide help. Second, it may be objected that I have failed to take into account the distinction many commentators make between duty as a primary and as a secondary motive,[25] and that it is this failure which makes Kant's account look so implausible. I shall deal with each of these in turn, and argue that both responses fail to deal adequately with the worry I have.

The first response is to maintain that it does not follow from the fact that someone is acting solely from respect for the moral law, that she is acting solely in order to fulfil its commands; and that it is consistent for someone to help another *out of* duty, but *in order to* provide help. Thus, it may be argued, thoughts about the other person's condition can be present in someone who acts solely from duty even if this is understood as acting solely from respect for the moral law.

In order to see whether this objection deals adequately with my worry, we need to be clear precisely what it is that is being stated when one claims that one can act from duty not *in order to* fulfil one's duty, but to provide help. As I understand this it is a claim to the effect that the good-willed agent would do the act which is the best way of providing help, and that she could do this solely from duty. Perhaps A helps B because she judges that she should help B in these circumstances. She decides that the act of Φ-ing is the best way to help B in the circumstances, and thus Φs in order to help B (as a way of helping B) from duty. Understood in terms of the categorical imperative, A would Φ in order to help B because the maxim of this action is lawlike, i.e., it can be willed as a universal law while the maxim of the contradictory act cannot be so willed. It is not at all clear, however, that this deals with the problem at issue. For once A has decided that Φ-ing is the best way of helping B, she will Φ solely from duty – that is, solely because her maxim is lawlike – not because B needs help. A may Φ in order to provide help solely from duty. But her motivating thought will have as its content the lawlike nature of her maxim not B's need.

The same point holds if we understand Φ-ing in order to provide help (from duty) as capturing the thought that the good-willed agent does not *aim* to do her duty (to have lawlike maxims), but to help the needy person. What is distinctive about the good-willed person is not what she aims at, but what motivates her to aim at this end.[26] In a situation in which she is required to help someone she will thus aim at this end (the end of helping the other person) *from the motive* of duty. But my worry is not that the good-willed individual aims at the dutiful act only in so far as it is thought of under the description 'morally required', but that she will aim at this end not because the other person needs help, but solely because the maxim of her act is lawlike. This is not a worry about the description under which the agent aims at this end, but about the reasons why she aims at it; and given the justificatory conception of the categorical imperative her reason for aiming to help the other person will not be because he needs help, but because her maxim is lawlike. Thus, the worry I have is not dealt with by pointing out that the good-willed agent can act in order to provide help.

It may, however, be argued that I have failed to distinguish between duty as a primary and secondary motive; and that when we do distinguish the different ways in which duty can motivate, it will turn out that a Kantian good-willed individual can be motivated to do a morally required act by considerations about the other person's condition, even if acting from duty is understood as acting from respect for the moral law.

Barbara Herman distinguishes between duty as a primary and as a secondary motive. A primary motive is the agent's motivating reason, i.e., it is what motivates the agent to do some particular act, and may be the thought of duty, or a reason of inclination, love or friendship. A secondary motive is a regulative notion governing the type of acts the agent will do (from some primary motive). In cases where an act is not obligatory, one cannot act from the primary motive of duty. For one cannot do a merely permissible act solely because it is one's duty.[27] In such cases one's primary motive must be a non-moral one, such as friendship or love. Nonetheless, a good-willed agent's action will still be governed by duty as a secondary motive. What this means is that the permissible act will be performed only on the condition that it is permissible.[28] It will thus be done from a non-moral primary motive, but governed by duty as a secondary motive.[29]

It may be that Herman's distinction between duty as a primary and secondary motive offers a response to my worry that a Kantian good-willed individual will be motivated to do what she should solely by thoughts about the lawlike nature of her maxim, and hence cannot be motivated by thoughts about the condition of others. To see whether it does, I shall chart out the possible combinations of primary and secondary motives in relation to permissible and obligatory actions.

(A) A permissible act done from a non-moral primary motive with duty as a secondary motive.
(B) A permissible act done from a non-moral primary motive and with a non-moral secondary motive.
(C) An obligatory act done from duty as a primary motive with duty as a secondary motive.
(D) An obligatory act done from duty as a primary motive and with a non-moral secondary motive.
(E) An obligatory act done from a non-moral primary motive with duty as a secondary motive.
(F) An obligatory act done from a non-moral primary motive with a non-moral secondary motive.

We do not need to consider (B), (D) and (F). For although these are possible combinations of primary and secondary motives, they are not options for a good-willed agent. A good-willed agent could not act in accordance with (B), for her action would have to be regulated by a concern for the lawfulness, or universal validity of her maxims, and hence by duty as a secondary motive. Similarly, the motivational pattern described in (F) is not a possibility for a good-willed agent, since duty plays no role at all.

It is less obvious that (D) is not a possibility on Kant's view. It is, nonetheless, ruled out. For the non-moral consideration that figures in the secondary motive will govern the types of action I will do from the primary motive of duty. I will do what I should, solely because I should, but only on the condition that my action meets the non-moral condition specified in the secondary motive. Suppose, for example, my secondary motive is sympathy, but my primary motive for Φ-ing is nothing other than duty. Sympathy functions as a secondary motive in the sense that it is a condition under which I will regard my primary motive, here the motive of duty, as sufficient. In the absence of sympathy for someone's plight, I will not help them from the primary motive of duty. But given that I have some sympathy for the plight of the person who would be helped by my act, I will Φ solely from (the primary motive of) duty. This is clearly contrary to Kant's view about the motivational structure of morally worthy acts, and with Herman's interpretation of this. For it would subordinate considerations of duty, to other considerations in the sense that it would make the former *conditional* upon the latter.[30] I shall, therefore, ignore (D), as well as (B) and (F).

I shall also ignore (A) as my concern is not with permissible actions, but with obligatory acts and why we should do them. This leaves us with (C) and (E). (C) does nothing to deal with the worry I have, since duty is at work at both levels. For, according to (C), the agent acts solely because the maxim of her action is lawlike (primary motive), and only on the condition that it is either lawlike or universally valid (secondary motive). Thus, the only way in which Herman's distinction between primary and secondary motives can support the account of acting from duty under consideration is in accordance with (E). For when one does some obligatory act, say, an act of helping someone in need, in accordance with (E) one would be acting from duty (as a secondary motive) while one's primary motive could involve thoughts about the other's situation. Thoughts about the lawlike nature of one's maxim would not then function as primary motives, but in a purely regulatory role.

But this impression is misleading. For, according to Herman, when duty functions only as a secondary motive, one is not acting from duty. 'It is', she writes, 'only in its function as a primary motive that one acts *from* the motive of duty at all.'[31] Thus, the Kantian good-willed agent cannot act in accordance with (E). She can, therefore, act only in accordance with (C); and this leaves the worry about the interpretation of acting from duty under consideration untouched. If I am morally required to do certain acts solely because my maxim is lawlike, then my primary motive cannot be, or include, a thought about the needs of the other person.

But perhaps a slightly modified understanding of the distinction between duty as a primary and as a secondary motive could address this problem. Marcia Baron conceives of duty as a secondary motive in a slightly different way from Barbara Herman, and wants to place more emphasis on duty in this role. I shall finish this section by briefly considering Baron's modified version of Herman's distinction. I shall argue that this understanding of the distinction fails to deal with the criticism of acting from duty understood as acting from respect for the moral law. I shall, however, try to develop her account in Chapter 4. But this will be possible only once it is freed from the constraint of the justificatory conception of the categorical imperative.

According to Baron, the secondary motive of duty does not have a merely regulative role, as it does for Herman, but also expresses the agent's commitment to morality, and is motivational 'with respect to proper attending, proper ordering of one's ends, and appropriate moral reflection'.[32] According to Baron, then, it seems that (E) is a real possibility on Kant's account of morally worthy actions. For, according to Baron, one *can* act *from* duty even if one's primary motive is not duty.[33] Moreover, she maintains that it is not duty as a primary motive, but the secondary motive of duty which is morally important. She writes:

> No premium is placed on the action being done from duty as a primary motive. What matters is that the action is in accord with duty and that *it is no accident that it is*: it accords with duty because the agent governs her conduct by a commitment to doing what is right.[34]

If (E) is a real possibility for a good-willed individual, then it seems as though one *can* act from duty while thoughts about the other person's condition act as the primary motive.[35] If this is correct, then acting from duty will not mean that the agent will be motivated solely by thoughts about the lawlike nature of her maxim to the exclusion of thoughts about the other person. Duty will be the sole secondary motive, but need not figure as a primary motive at all. If this is correct, then my objection will have been dealt with.

But I do not think that this is a real possibility for the Kantian conception of a good-willed individual, even if one accepts Baron's view that one will have acted from duty even if duty does not figure in the content of one's primary motivating thought. The key point about the moral worth of acting from duty as a secondary motive is that if one does the right act, '*it will be no accident that it is*' right. It will be no accident because, she claims, the action will be motivated, at the secondary level, by the agent's commitment to morality – that is, to doing what is right. The problem with this is that the agent's commitment to morality will only make the rightness of her actions non-accidental if the agent does the right thing for the right reason. For if one does the right act for the wrong reason, then the fact that one has done the right thing in this case will be accidental. It will be accidental for the same reason that the truth of some belief will be accidental if one does not come to hold it for the right reason. What are the right reasons? These will be the reasons why the relevant act ought to be done, i.e., the ground of duty. Thus, acting from duty at the secondary level is not sufficient for the rightness of one's action to be non-accidental. The rightness of one's act will only be non-accidental if duty functions as a secondary motive, while being motivated by thoughts (at the primary level), the content of which is the ground of duty. But according to the justificatory conception of the categorical imperative, the ground of duty is the lawlike nature of the agent's maxim. Thus, given the justificatory conception of the categorical imperative duty will not be able to function solely at the secondary level. It will have to function also as one's primary motive. In terms of the categorical imperative, this means that one will act from a commitment to doing those acts whose maxims are lawlike (secondary motive) and the lawlike nature of one's maxim will function as the sole primary motive also. If this is correct, then Marcia Baron's understanding of acting from duty does not deal with my particular worry.

The rejection of the justificatory conception of the categorical imperative

One could avoid all of the difficulties mentioned so far by rejecting either one, or all of the following views: (1) the symmetry thesis; (2) the view that a good-willed person would act, or tend to act, *solely* from duty; or (3) the view that for any duty there is only one ground, i.e., normative reason, which gives rise to it. But the options are limited. On the face of it, one could not, for example, reject (2) or (3) without also rejecting (1)[36] – although one could reject both (2) and (3) and hold (1). For if the symmetry thesis is correct, it could not be the case that a morally good person would tend to be motivated to do what she should by more than one consideration if only one consideration ever gives rise to an obligation. Similarly, we could not hold the view that a good-willed person would tend to be motivated to do what she should by only one moral consideration, if more than one consideration gives rise to these moral requirements, unless we abandoned the symmetry thesis. We could, however, stop short of rejecting all three theses if, for example, we rejected (1) and (3). We could then think of the good-willed agent as one who tends to do what she should solely from respect for the moral law while holding the view that specific obligations are, or at least can be, generated by a plurality of evidential moral considerations. The problem with this, however, is that we would then not be able to sustain the view that there is an essential and direct connection between morality and rationality. For we would have severed any essential connection between what it is in virtue of which an act has moral value and the normative reasons we have for performing that action. Things would be even worse if we held (3), but abandoned (1) and (2). For we would then not only be unable to hold the Kantian view that there is an essential and direct connection between morality and rationality, but will have given up the central Kantian view that a good-willed agent is one who acts solely from duty, i.e., from respect for the moral law.

We could, however, hold all three views by abandoning the justificatory conception of the categorical imperative. For if the categorical imperative is not the sole ground of duty, then morally good people will not be motivated to help others when they should, solely by thoughts about the lawlike nature of their maxims. Whether this will work, of course, will depend on the alternative account of acting from duty to the common-sense view rejected in Chapter 1 and the account of it as acting from respect for the moral law we would have to reject. It would also depend on what theory of normative moral reasons we use to fill the gap in Kant's theory left by the rejection of the justificatory conception of the categorical imperative. I will address these issues in Chapters 4 and 5. First, I want to consider whether there is reason to abandon the justificatory conception of the categorical imperative other than that it allows us to resolve these difficulties? I think there is.

The problem with this conception of the categorical imperative is that it quite clearly generates the wrong answers when it is regarded as the sole ground of duty. The problem I have in mind is not the fact, or supposed fact that the categorical imperative generates absolute side-constraints which are deeply implausible.[37] This would be a problem even if we thought of the categorical imperative as a necessary, but not the sole normative moral reason. The difficulty I have in mind stems from the combination of the justificatory conception of the categorical imperative with Kant's view that there can only be one ground of duty. The problem is that if I ought to do only those acts, the maxim of which is lawlike, and nothing else determines what it is I should do in a specific set of circumstances, then it will turn out that what I ought to do will always be to act in accordance with an imperative with disjunctive content. For there are many acts whose maxims cannot be conceived or willed as a universal law without contradiction, e.g., the act of lying from self-interest, of promise breaking, of indifference to others, and of failing to develop my talents. This means that there are many acts whose maxim is lawlike (as I am using this term), e.g., the act of telling the truth, of keeping my promise, of helping others, and of developing my talents. Thus, if I act from the maxim of any of these actions in any situation, I will have acted from a lawlike maxim – that is, from a maxim that can be conceived, or willed, as a universal law, and which the maxim of the contradictory act cannot. But if the lawlike nature of my maxim is sufficient to make my action morally right (which it must be if it is the sole ground of duty), then if I act in accordance with any of these maxims I will have done the right thing. If, therefore, the categorical imperative is the sole normative reason why we should do certain acts, then it will follow that we will have acted rightly if and only if we have acted in accordance with a duty either to tell the truth, or to keep our promise, or to help others or to cultivate our talents, etc. But it is clear that in many cases I will not have done what I should simply if I act in accordance with this disjunctive obligation. For example, in a situation in which I could save someone's life at little cost to myself I clearly would have failed to do what I should if I choose simply to tell someone some trivial truth. I will, however, have acted in accordance with the disjunctive duty, for telling the truth is one of its disjuncts. The same would be true if, say, I failed to keep a promise simply in order to practise playing the guitar. For once again I would have acted in accordance with the disjunctive duty, as one of its disjuncts is 'to cultivate my talents', and I would have done this to some extent by practising. For this reason we cannot plausibly think of the categorical imperative as the sole ground of duty.

We could then either abandon the view that it is a normative reason altogether, or the view that for any duty there is only one ground of duty. The latter option seems, at first sight, the more appealing, as it would enable Kant to hold the view that the categorical imperative is a normative reason why we should do certain acts, without the absurd view that we will have done what we should if we have acted in accordance with the above disjunctive duty. But, I think a more plausible account can be offered if we reject the justificatory conception of the categorical imperative. If we do this, however, we will have to offer an alternative account (a) of acting solely from duty which does not force us to reject the symmetry thesis; (b) of the ground of duty; and (c) of the role the categorical imperative has. It is to these tasks that I now turn.

4

AN ALTERNATIVE ACCOUNT OF ACTING FROM DUTY

Introduction

The two accounts of acting solely from duty considered so far both generate considerable difficulties for Kant's moral theory. According to the first account, to act solely from duty is to do what one should just because one should do that act. According to the second account, to act from duty is to act solely from respect for the moral law, or the mere universality of one's maxim. The problem with the first account is that, given the symmetry thesis, it generates the absurd conclusion that the only (normative) reason why we ought to do certain acts is because we ought to do them, which is no reason at all. This conclusion can be avoided only if the symmetry thesis – that is, the view that the reason why a morally good person will do an act and the reason why it ought to be done, will tend to be the same – is abandoned. But if we abandon this thesis, then Kant will no longer be able to hold onto his central view that there is an essential and direct connection between morality and rationality. For if we abandon the symmetry thesis, there need be no connection at all between what it is in virtue of which an action is morally good, and the normative reasons why it should be done. So despite the appeal of this account of acting from duty, we should not interpret Kant in this way unless we have to.

The second account of acting from duty gets around this problem. According to this view, to act from duty is to act from respect for the moral law, i.e., universality as such. Respect is a complex psychological state consisting in consciousness of the moral law and moral feeling, which may be termed the feeling of reverence (not to be confused with respect, which is the complex whole of which reverence is a part). Reverence should not, however, be understood merely as the effect of consciousness of the moral law, but as the sole way in which we can be aware of it. Thus understood, respect is a reverential awareness of the moral law. It is very difficult to untangle the various things Kant says about acting from respect for the moral law. Sometimes he says it is the affective aspect of respect (the feeling of reverence) which is the sole moral motive, while at other times he states that it is the cognitive aspect (consciousness of the moral law). But I think that he is best understood as holding the view that it is neither the consciousness of the moral law, nor the way in which we are conscious of it, but the moral law itself, which is the sole moral motive. If this is correct, then to act from respect for the moral law will be to act not from a reverential awareness of the moral law, but from what it is of which we are reverentially aware – the moral law itself. But if we are to act solely from the moral law, i.e., from mere universality as such, then we will have to act from a formulation of this principle which is capable of guiding action. Since in moral motivation Kant maintains that we must act from a purely formal principle, to act from respect for the moral law must be understood as acting from the categorical imperative as it is expressed in the formula of universal law. Only then will we be acting from a purely formal principle, i.e., one capable of conferring an unconditional value on the action done from it.

But although mere universality *can* be the normative reason why we ought to act in certain ways, and hence is not subject to the criticism levelled against the first account of acting from duty, it is vulnerable to other objections. The problem with this account is (a) that it means that a good-willed person cannot be motivated, or at least tend to be motivated, to do what she should by the needs of others; and (b) that it commits Kant to what I called the justificatory conception of the categorical imperative – that is, the conception of it as the sole ground of duty, the sole normative reason why we are morally required to do certain acts. These two difficulties make this account of acting from duty deeply implausible. The first means that a good-willed person will tend to be motivated to help others (when they are morally required to help others) not by facts about the other person, e.g., the fact that they are in need, or in distress, but solely by facts about themselves, about the lawlike nature of their maxims. The second means that for any situation I will have done what I should simply in so far as I act in accordance with the disjunctive duty either to tell the truth, or to keep my promise, or to help others, or to cultivate my talents, etc. But to act in accordance with this requirement I need only satisfy *any* one of its disjuncts; and this is plainly mistaken. I clearly have failed to do what I should in a situation in which I could help someone in distress at little or no cost to myself, if, for example, I tell someone some trivial truth. But I will have acted in accordance with the disjunctive duty.

I finished the last chapter by suggesting that we reject the justificatory conception of the categorical imperative. What is needed now is (a) an account of acting from duty that does not force us to reject the symmetry thesis; (b) an account of the role the categorical imperative has; and (c) an account of the ground of specific duties – that is, of normative moral reasons.

An alternative account of acting from duty

By distinguishing primary and secondary motives Marcia Baron's account of acting from duty offered the possibility of allowing the sort of specific considerations Aristotelians such as McDowell are keen to emphasise (the needs of others, my having promised to Φ, my being indebted to someone, etc.) to motivate a morally good person to do what she should while still acting from duty. For it makes it possible for duty, or the moral law, to act as a secondary motive while these specific considerations function as primary motives. This is because she maintains, following Herman, that what is important for Kant is that there be a non-accidental relation between the rightness of one's action and its motivation. In Chapter 3 I argued that this non-accidental relation between one's motivation, and the rightness of the resultant action, is only maintained if the content of one primary motivating thought is the normative reason why the relevant act should be done – that is, the ground of that duty. But given the justificatory conception of the categorical imperative, it follows that one should do the relevant act from the thought that one's maxim is lawlike; and this is equivalent to acting from duty as a primary motive. I argued, therefore, that given the justificatory conception of the categorical imperative, acting from duty, or respect for the moral law, as a secondary motive will require the agent to act from duty, or respect for the moral law, as a primary motive also. A different picture emerges, however, if we abandon the justificatory conception of the categorical imperative, as I think we should, and work with the idea that particular obligations are generated by the sort of concrete considerations in the situation, that McDowell is keen to emphasise, such as the other person's need, or my promise.

In criticising Baron's account of acting from duty I maintained that we could not hold onto the non-contingency of the rightness of the agent's action simply by acting from duty as a secondary motive. My commitment to do what is right is not sufficient to render the rightness of my action non-accidental unless I also do the right act from the right reason. The right reason is a motivating thought which has as its content whatever it is that makes the particular action obligatory. At present we have no account of what the ground of duty is, for we have rejected the idea that it is the categorical imperative. I shall, however, defer a discussion of this issue until the next chapter. Nonetheless, if we assume for the moment that what gives rise to particular obligations is concrete considerations, such as (but not only) the welfare of others, then to help someone who needs help, from duty, will be to do the obligatory act solely from the thought that he needs help (primary motive), with duty as a secondary motive. It is because duty is here functioning as a secondary motive that I regard the other person's need as sufficient once I see it as a consideration which gives rise to a moral requirement to help him. For to act from duty as a secondary motive is to regard myself as having sufficient reason to do some act (at the primary level) solely in so far as I judge that it is morally required.

This claim may seem to commit me to acting from duty as a primary motive as well as in its function as a secondary motive, but it does not. For it does not follow from the fact that I take myself to have sufficient reason to do some act solely in so far as I judge that it should be done, that I take this moral verdict to be the reason (or one of the reasons) I take to be sufficient. The reasons I take to be sufficient are the reasons why the particular action is morally required. When duty is my secondary motive I will regard these considerations as sufficient solely in so far as I judge them to give rise to an obligation, and I will regard them in this way *just because* they give rise to this obligation.[1] But the fact that some act is obligatory need not be one of the reasons I take to be sufficient. Indeed, we have seen that there is good reason to think that it is no reason to do the obligatory act at all.

It may be thought that this is incompatible with Kant's view that duty must be the sole and sufficient motive if one's action is to have moral worth. But although the account of acting from duty I am sketching means that we cannot understand the way in which duty is the sole and sufficient motive of moral actions in the way this is typically understood, there is an important sense in which one can act *solely* from duty on my account. To act from duty is to act from an unconditional commitment to morality (secondary motive) and to do what is required from the normative reasons (primary motive) why it is required. One's commitment to duty is unconditional only if one takes oneself to have sufficient reason to do some obligatory act irrespective of whether one is inclined to do it. One acts solely from duty if duty functions as a secondary motive, and if one is motivated at the primary level to do what one should by *nothing other than* the reasons why the act is morally required. The distinction between acting from duty and acting solely from duty will be determined, therefore, at the primary level. If one is motivated solely by (what one takes to be) the ground of duty, then one has acted solely from duty. If one is motivated at the primary level by this and by some inclination or need, then one has acted from duty, but not solely from duty.[2]

Does this account run together the motive of sympathy and that of duty in relation to beneficent actions? On my account if a good-willed individual is morally required to help someone in need, or relieve his distress simply because he is in distress, her primary motivation for helping will be nothing other than the fact that this person is in distress. But isn't this just what it is to act from sympathy rather than from duty? And isn't this in complete opposition to Kant's view?

Not according to the way in which Kant understands acting from sympathy. Sympathy, for Kant is the feeling of pleasure or pain at another's state of joy or sorrow.[3] To act from sympathy is, therefore, to be motivated by this type of feeling. It would not be to help someone just because he needs help, but to do so (at least partly) because one is pained by his condition, or because one gets pleasure from such acts.[4] But on my account of acting from duty such feelings function neither as a primary, nor as a secondary motive (which is not, of course, to suggest that the good-willed individual is not pained by the other's condition, or does not get pleasure from relieving their condition). One's primary reason will not be some painful feeling caused in one by the other's need, but simply the fact that he is in need, and one's secondary motive will be one's unconditional commitment to morality.

But it might be argued that sympathy could function as a secondary motive in a similar way to the way in which duty does – that is, in such a way that feelings of sympathy need not appear as primary motivating reasons. It is not clear to me how we should understand sympathy as a secondary motive, but perhaps it could be understood in analogy to duty as follows: sympathy functions as a secondary motive if the agent takes herself to have sufficient reason to help someone simply in so far as she judges that he needs help. According to this understanding of acting from sympathy in a case in which there is a moral requirement to help someone, and in which the reason why one should help them is just because they are in need, the primary motivating reasons of the good-willed individual will be the same as those of someone who acts from sympathy as a secondary motive in the specified sense. Both agents would help the other person just because he needs help.

There is, nonetheless, a sharp difference between the two. Unlike the good-willed person, the sympathetic individual will take herself to have sufficient reason to help others irrespective of whether such help is morally required. She will thus regard herself as having sufficient reason to help the other person even if, for some reason, the act of helping him is morally forbidden – perhaps because what he is doing is morally wrong, or because the only way she could help him would be by violating a perfect duty.[5] Consequently, her motivation will be such that if she does what she should, it will be purely accidental. This will not be true of someone who acts solely from duty as a secondary motive. For such a person will not take herself to have sufficient reason to act in a certain way simply in so far as she judges that someone needs help, but simply in so far as she judges that this act is morally required. She will not, therefore, regard herself as having sufficient reason to help the other person if this act is wrong (and recognised as such). There is, then, a clear difference between someone who acts from duty and from sympathy, on my account, even if one understands acting from sympathy along the lines that I have described acting from duty.

But even if I do not conflate acting from duty with acting from sympathy, it may be objected that I have made sympathy a necessary condition of morally worthy actions – how can the other person's need be sufficient to motivate me unless I have sympathy for their plight? But to make morality dependent on sympathy would be contrary to Kant's view. My account of acting solely from duty would certainly be inconsistent with Kant's if it implied that one's action can have moral worth only when one has sympathetic *inclinations*. For Kant clearly thinks that one's action can have moral worth in the absence of such inclinations.[6] But nothing I have said has this implication. It is not sympathetic inclinations, or even the feeling of sympathy which enables the good-willed individual to be motivated at the primary level solely by thoughts about the other's need, but (a) her respect for the moral law,[7] and (b) her commitment to morality. It may be that one's commitment to morality is not always sufficient for the agent's primary motivation to be nothing other than the need of the other person (when this need gives rise to a moral obligation), and that a sympathetic inclination is also needed as a primary motive. But then the individual will not be acting solely from duty. Duty may be their sole secondary motive, but their primary motivations will not be limited to the considerations which are the ground of duty – since in the situation described these considerations are not sufficient to motivate. They will also include some inclination. But to act *solely* from duty is to act solely from the secondary motive of an unconditional commitment to morality and solely from primary motivating thoughts which have as their content the reasons why the act ought to be done. My account of acting from duty is, therefore, consistent with what Kant says about the contrast between acting from duty and from sympathy.

But given what I have said so far, one might think that all that is needed for a right action to be morally good is for it to be motivated at the primary level by the normative reasons why it is right. If what determines whether or not an action is morally good is the motive from which it is done, and a morally good motive is one which is non-accidentally related to the rightness of the act done from it (if it is right), why think that any more is needed than that one's primary motives be the same as the normative reasons why the act is right? Why insist either on a distinction between primary and secondary motives, or, if one does, why think that duty must function as a secondary motive if someone, or some act is to be morally good?' If we can show that duty as a secondary motive is necessary if the alignment of the agent's motives and the rightness of their acts are to be non-accidental, then we will have answered not only the second question, but the first also. For then we will have shown that the distinction between primary and secondary motives is morally significant. We will have begun to show that duty as a secondary motive is necessary for the moral worth of actions if we can show that the relation between our motives and the rightness of our actions can be accidental, even though one did the right action from primary motives which are the same as the normative reasons why it is right. We will then have to show that duty as a secondary motive can make good this lack. But how, it may be asked, could the rightness of our action be only accidentally connected to the primary motives from which we do it, if these are the same as the normative reasons why it is right?

It would be merely accidental if I were such that I was only motivated to do the right thing by the normative reasons why it is right *on the condition that* it was in my interest to do so. As soon as I judge that it is *not* in my interest to do the right thing, the normative reasons which would otherwise motivate me to act, lose their grip on me. If the action I am considering is not in my interest, then prudential considerations will motivate me to do some other act. But so long as the right act *is* in my interest, prudence will have a purely regulative role. So long as the right act is in my interest, I shall be motivated to do it by the normative reasons why it is right.

If this sort of case is psychologically coherent, which I think it is, then we have a case in which I may be motivated to do the right thing, by the normative reasons why it is right, but in which the relation between my motives and the rightness of my action is purely accidental. It is accidental because, if circumstances had been such that the right act were not in my interest, I would not be motivated by these considerations to do this act, and it is not always the case that the right act is the one which is in my interest.

Can the distinction between primary and secondary motives make good this lack? I think it can. For here we seem to have a motivational structure which is captured very well by the distinction between primary and secondary motives. When the right act is in my interest, my primary motive for doing it will be the same as the normative reason why it is right. My secondary motive is not, however, duty but prudence. It is because prudence is here acting as a secondary motive that the relation between my motivational state and the rightness of my action is merely accidental. Acting from duty as a secondary motive would rectify this. For if one's secondary motive were an unconditional commitment to do what one should, and one's primary motive is the reason why one should act in this way, then it is difficult to see how the relation between one's motivation and the rightness of the act one is motivated to do could be merely accidental.

If all of this is right, then the moral worth of actions cannot be captured simply with reference to agents' primary motives, even if these are the same as the normative reasons why their action is right. We have to specify what their secondary motive is also. And this, by itself, gives us reason to think that the distinction between primary and secondary motives is both legitimate and useful for our understanding of moral worth.

The problem with the standard account of acting from duty is that, in conjunction with the symmetry thesis, it implies that we ought to Φ because we ought to Φ. Now although my account does not have this implication, it may seem to have an odd implication as the result of the symmetry thesis. For according to my account, to act solely from duty is to Φ solely from the reasons why one should Φ (primary motive), and from an unconditional commitment to treat these reasons as sufficient in so far as one judges that they give rise to the obligation to Φ. A morally good person will be one who tends to act from duty so understood. But given the symmetry thesis – that the reason why a relevantly informed good-willed agent will Φ will be identical with the normative reasons why she should Φ – it may seem to follow from this that one of the normative reasons why I should Φ will be my commitment to do the right thing. This would, however, be quite implausible. It is plausible to assume that I should help others when, and because, they are in need of help, but not that I should do so because they need help and because I am committed to doing the morally right thing.

One might argue that this commitment is a necessary condition of the possibility of paradigmatically moral considerations being normative reasons for me to act – that these considerations would not be normative reasons for me unless I were so committed.[8] But this is quite a different claim. Furthermore, it is one which is alien to Kant, as it would turn moral imperatives into hypothetical imperatives. For if moral considerations only constitute reason for me to act in certain ways if I care about the morality of my actions, then the obligations these considerations generate would be made conditional upon this concern. So if my account does imply that this commitment is a normative reason to act it will have implausible, and unKantian implications.

I do not, however, think it has these implications. The point of distinguishing between primary and secondary motives was to be sensitive to the very different ways in which deontic considerations can be motivationally relevant. Primary motives are considerations the agent would cite to explain her action, and typically in support of it also (at least in the absence of self-deception, and ignorance). Secondary motives do not function in this way. They are not considerations which the agent would cite to explain or support her action, but capture the conditions under which certain considerations can function as primary motives for the agent. Duty as a secondary motive functions as a negative condition of the salience of certain considerations for actions judged to be merely permissible. It acts as a negative condition in the sense that if I were to judge that some act is wrong, I would not regard myself as having reason to do it, and would regard myself as having reason *not* to do it. To put this another way, I would only regard myself as having reason to do the merely permissible on the condition that I judge this act to be permissible.

This does not, however, entail that one of my (primary) motivating thoughts for doing what I judge morally permissible is 'that it is morally permissible'. It does not even involve explicit deliberation about whether this act is morally permissible.[9] The mere fact that one is concerned to avoid the impermissible does not imply that one is constantly having the thought, 'is this permissible?'. One can be sensitive to the impermissible without having to be constantly worrying about it, just as when one is driving a car one can be sensitive, and responsive, to the brake lights of the car in front, without constantly thinking to oneself, 'is he about to brake?'. It is true that when one is a novice, one tends to have such self-conscious thoughts, but that is just because one is a novice. Typically the more competent one becomes, the more one will be responsive to such considerations without having constantly to be self-consciously on the look-out for them. I see no reason why this should not also be the case in morality.

The same point can be made in relation to actions which are recognised as morally required. For duty to function as a secondary motive is not for it to be a reason the agent would cite to explain why she did what she should, or to justify this. Rather, it is motivationally relevant in the sense that it explains why the considerations she would cite in support of her action have the distinctive motivational and deliberative salience they do for her. As a secondary motive, therefore, duty functions solely as a necessary condition for moral considerations to function as motives in the distinctive way they do for a morally good person, but is not itself a motive. It is motivationally relevant, but not a motive.

It does not, therefore, follow from the symmetry thesis that the agent's commitment to doing what is right for the right reason is a normative reason for doing what one should. The symmetry thesis relates solely to the good-willed agent's *primary* motives, not to their secondary motives also. The symmetry thesis does not, therefore, give rise to any problems for this account.

The transcendental conception of the moral law

It may, however, be said that although I can avoid the objection the second account of acting from duty was subject to by abandoning the justificatory conception of the moral law, this move is illegitimate because it ignores the many places where Kant states that it is the moral law itself which commands certain acts.These passages seem to suggest that Kant held the extreme and implausible view that the moral law is the one and only evidential consideration supporting the verdict that a certain act ought to be done in some specific situation. For, what one takes as necessitating some act is, at the same time, regarded as that in virtue of which the act ought to be done, i.e., as an evidential consideration. So Kant's view that it is the moral law which commands – that is, necessitates – certain acts, seems to commit him to the view that the moral law is the sole evidential consideration supporting the verdict that certain specific acts ought to be done – that is, that it is the sole normative reason why we ought to act in certain ways.

I do not, however, think that these passages were intended to express this implausible view. Despite the fact that his claim that specific moral laws, or duties, are 'derived from',[10] or 'grounded in'[11] the moral law are often taken as meaning that the moral law justifies these duties, the notions of 'grounding' and 'derivation' are not unambiguous. They may mean that particular obligations are justified by the moral law. If so, then the justificatory conception of the moral law will be correct. But the moral law may be understood as grounding particular obligations not in the sense that it justifies them, but in the sense that it acts as the condition of their possibility. To think of the moral law in this way is to think of it as the transcendental condition of the truth of our particular moral judgements. This may thus be called the *transcendental* conception of the moral law.

What, then, does the distinction between the justificatory and the transcendental conception of the moral law amount to? Is there really a difference between the question, 'why are we morally required to act in certain ways?', and the question, 'how is it possible that we are morally required to act in certain ways?'. These are, I believe, quite distinct questions, even if we can answer them both with reference to the same fact, or principle. For example, a necessary (albeit obvious and uninteresting) condition of my being morally required to do anything is that I am alive, but the fact that I am alive is seldom, if ever, a normative reason why I am morally required to act in certain ways. More controversially, the fact that I am *able* to act in certain ways may be thought to be a necessary condition for my being morally required to act in those ways, but need not always be a normative reason why I am required so to act. The fact that I am *able* to be honest to others is no more a reason why I ought to be honest than the fact that I am alive is. Nonetheless, one may think, as Kant did, that one could not be required to be honest unless one was able to. If this is accepted, then one's being alive, and one's being able to Φ will always be conditions of our being required to Φ, but will not always be normative reasons why we ought to Φ. And this is sufficient to show that there is a real distinction here.

This distinction can be further elucidated with reference to Kant's discussion of causality in the first *Critique*. It is clearly one thing to ask, 'what is the necessary condition of natural causality?', and quite another to ask 'why did some particular event occur?'. The first question requires a transcendental regressive analysis; the second requires a causal explanation. For Kant, the answer to the first question will be the principle of causality, and ultimately the transcendental unity of apperception, whereas the answer to the second will refer to previous events, but not to transcendental principles. If we conceive of the moral law according to the justificatory conception, we will conceive of it in analogy to a first cause, for I am suggesting that the normative reasons why we ought to act in certain ways be understood in analogy to causal reasons why certain events occur (although I am not suggesting that normative reasons are a species of causal reasons). If we go along this route we would then have to understand the moral law as analogous to the cause of some event, and the particular obligatory action as the analogue of the particular event caused. Note that on this analogy there is nothing on the moral side corresponding to transcendental principles.

To think of the moral law according to the transcendental conception, on the other hand, is to think of it in analogy to the principle of causality.[12] Whereas the justificatory conception of the relation of the moral law to particular obligations left us with nothing corresponding to the laws of nature and their conditions, the transcendental conception leaves us with nothing corresponding to the reason why some particular event occurred. On the moral side of the analogy this means that, according to the transcendental conception of the moral law, we have no account of the normative reasons why we ought to do certain actions.

The moral law can, therefore, be understood as answering at least two very different questions. According to the justificatory conception it is seen as answering the question, 'why am I morally obligated to Φ in circumstances C?': according to the transcendental conception it is thought of as answering the very different question, 'what is the condition under which Φ-ing can be represented as being obligatory?'.

To get a clearer perspective on what the transcendental conception of the moral law amounts to it is useful to develop the analogy with the principle of causality further. The concept of causality requires, Kant claims:

> That something, A, should be such that something else, B, follows from it *necessarily and in accordance with an absolutely universal rule*. Appearances do indeed present cases from which a rule can be obtained according to which something usually happens, but they never prove the sequence to be *necessary*. To the synthesis of cause and effect there belongs a dignity which cannot be empirically expressed, namely, that the effect not only succeeds upon the cause, but that it is posited *through* it and arises *out of* it.[13]

The category of causality is, Kant maintains, the only way in which we can explain the necessity with which one representation is experienced as following upon another – that is, it is the necessary condition for the representation of one event's causing another. But although the necessity with which event B is regarded as following from event A cannot be explained by means of empirical concepts, i.e., empirical rules, the type of event which is regarded as following necessarily upon another is determined empirically. For the content of the experience is determined by empirical laws which we can discover only by empirical investigation. But, Kant held, these particular causal laws are themselves only possible on the basis of the transcendental principle of causality, for it is only in virtue of this principle that they can acquire the strict universality they require as laws.[14] The idea here is not that the empirical causal laws of nature are in some way derived from the transcendental principle of causality. The principle of causality is too formal to allow this. Rather, as Friedman puts it:

> empirical laws are to be thought of as framed or nested, as it were, within a sequence of progressively more concrete and empirical instantiations or realizations of the transcendental principles . . . The notion of an *a priori* grounding is then expressed by the idea that, although purely empirical data play a necessary and unavoidable role in this procedure, the framing or nesting of such data within the transcendental concept of a nature in general is to result – at least in principle – in a unique and determinate description of the empirical world that thereby acquires a more than merely empirical status.[15]

The idea is that particular causal judgements, are possible only by subsuming some event under particular causal laws, and that these are possible only in so far as they are subsumed under transcendental principles.

What I am suggesting with the transcendental conception of the moral law is that Kant has something similar in mind in relation to the awareness of necessitation and what it is that is necessitated in relation to ethical experience. If we replace the experience of one event's being causally necessitated by another, with the experience of an action being necessitated in, or by, some set of circumstances, the transcendental conception of the connection between the moral law, on the one hand, and particular moral laws and their instances, on the other, should become perspicuous. According to this interpretation, the moral law is required to explain how any act can be experienced as practically necessary in some set of circumstances. What it is that is necessary is determined by specific moral laws and specific empirical considerations, which unlike the moral law cannot be known *a priori*. Particular moral laws and obligations would have the same peculiar hybrid nature Kant thinks laws of nature have. The awareness of necessitation is explained with reference to our taking ourselves as standing under an a priori law. What it is that is necessitated is explained by specific empirical considerations in the nature of the situation, which are related with practical necessity to certain actions by means of specific moral laws.

If this is right, then what Kant is doing with the moral law and specific moral laws is not describing a process we go through in practical deliberation – Kant would describe such a project as mere empirical psychology. Rather, what he is doing is stating what the transcendental conditions are for the sort of practical judgements we make when we make moral judgements. Kant could be right about this even if these principles do not, and ought not to, figure in our deliberation. For understood in this way, what he is claiming is not that the moral law is the implicit premise of our moral reasoning, but that it is presupposed by each of these particular judgements, for we can only judge that some act is necessary in the circumstances in so far as we subsume it under universally valid principles, which in turn are only possible in so far as they are subsumed under the *a priori* principle of universality as such. It is only on this assumption that our moral judgements are possible.

According to the transcendental conception of moral principles I am outlining, the moral law grounds the necessity implicit in particular obligations by grounding the lawlike nature of specific moral laws which provide the condition of the possibility of our particular moral judgements. According to this interpretation, the moral law is the highest principle of practical reason, not in the sense that it is the sole, or ultimate normative reason why certain acts ought to be done, but in the sense that it is the ground of the characteristic certain acts have of being practically necessary, i.e., obligatory. So when Kant states that it is the moral law that commands, he should not be taken as claiming that it is the moral law which necessitates some act. If the transcendental conception is correct, then Kant would no more think that this *a priori* principle necessitates some act than he thinks the category of causality necessitates some event. What it does is explain the necessity which this act is regarded as having when it is regarded as being obligatory.This transcendental conception of the moral law thus makes sense of the internal connection between acting from duty and acting from (respect for) the moral law, without implying that when someone acts from duty they are motivated solely by the moral law.

The argument for the transcendental conception

Why does Kant think that moral obligation can only be explained with reference to the moral law? His argument rests on the assumption that this necessity can be explained either by means of the material concept of the good, or by means of the formal principle of the will – the moral law – and that these options are exhaustive. Moral obligation cannot be explained with reference to the material concept of the good, according to Kant, for either the good is related to the will empirically, and thus contingently, or it has some compulsive power over the will as a natural cause, and thus undermines the freedom of the will. Either way, the necessity involved in moral obligation is left unexplained. Given that this necessity cannot be explained with reference to the material concept of the good, if it is explicable, it must be by means of the formal principle of the will – that is, by means of the moral law.

Kant argues for these claims in his exposition of the theorems in book one of the Analytic of the *Critique of Practical Reason*. He first considers the crude empiricist definition of the good as the object of desire. If this is how the good is defined, then one cannot explain the necessity involved in moral obligation, for the relation of the will to the good, so understood, can only ever be contingent. It can only be contingent because the will can only be determined to pursue this object on the basis of a felt pleasure associated with the idea of that object;[16] and we cannot know *a priori* that this object will be 'associated with pleasure, or displeasure or will be merely indifferent'.[17] Thus, Kant writes: 'All practical principles which presuppose an object (material) of the faculty of desire as the determining ground of the will are without exception empirical and can furnish no practical laws.'[18] A more refined empiricist definition of value attempts to get around this problem by distinguishing between the lower and higher faculty of desire. This distinction is based on the origin of the relevant pleasures. The pleasures of the lower faculty of desire are those of sense, whereas those of the higher faculty stem from the understanding. Given this distinction, it could be argued that one can get universality and necessity from material goods that are the object of the higher faculty of desire.

But Kant rejected this attempt to avoid his criticism. For even if the good is defined as the object of the higher faculty of desire, the good can still only be related to the will by means of some contingent felt pleasure in the anticipation of its reality, and whether or not this anticipation will evoke pleasure in the agent can never be known *a priori*. Since this pleasure could only be contingent, no progress is made in explaining the necessity involved in moral obligation by distinguishing the lower and higher faculty of desire, and defining the good in relation to the latter.

Kant's second theorem attacks the rationalist account of the good, and the attempt to explain moral obligation with reference to this. According to this account, the good is defined with reference to the rational idea of perfection. Since the good is here defined with reference to an idea of reason, it may not seem vulnerable to the criticism levelled against the empiricist account of value and obligation. Nonetheless, Kant maintained that this account is vulnerable to the very same criticism, and this can be seen when the idea of perfection in its practical sense is unpacked.

The idea of perfection can have no practical meaning until some end is given in terms of which perfection can be judged. For example, we cannot know whether a knife is a good one until we have an end by means of which to judge it. Once we know the appropriate end – in this case, cutting – we can then judge whether a particular knife is a good one, for this end will act as the criterion of perfection. But if the rationalist account of the good must be spelt out in terms of some end for man which acts as the criterion of perfection, then we need to know how the will is related to this end. And Kant maintains that the will can only be related to it by a contingent felt pleasure in the anticipation of the reality of this object. Since this pleasure can only be contingent, it leaves the necessity involved in moral obligation unexplained.

These arguments depend on the idea that the will can only be related to the good by means of a contingent desire and feeling of pleasure, and this assumption may be challenged. It may be said that the will can be determined to pursue some good not by a contingent desire, but by the nature of the good itself. If this is possible, then the good could be related to the will by law and with necessity. But Kant would maintain that this would still leave moral obligation unexplained. For on this view the good necessitates the will to action by 'forcing itself upon the will as the causal determinant of the will's action'.[19] But for Kant, the will must be free in the indeterminist sense of being an uncaused cause of action if moral agency is to be possible. Thus, if the good is related to the will as a causal determinant the concept of obligation and of the morality of the will cannot be explained.[20] The concept of obligation cannot be explained because consciousness of obligation presupposes the freedom of the will.[21] The concept of obligation cannot be explained, since one's acts can no longer be imputed to one, because one's will is no longer the ground of its own acts. So although this account of the relation of the good to the will can explain the categorical nature of moral imperatives, it cannot explain their obligatoriness. Although the will can be conceived of as necessitated by the good to act in a certain way it can no more be conceived of as obligated by the good than a stone can be conceived of as obligated by gravity to act in a certain way.

The will can only retain its freedom if it is not caused to act by any external cause including the good. But if we are to hold onto the will's freedom, then we are back where we started with a merely contingent relation of the will to the good and the possibility of moral obligation is still left unexplained. For if the good does not cause the will to pursue it, then the will must determine itself to pursue this end. But whether or not it does this will depend on whether the agent feels pleasure in the anticipation of the reality of the good; and this cannot be known *a priori*.

For these reasons Kant held that the necessity implicit in moral obligation could not be explained with reference to some material good. Given that he thinks there are only two options here, it follows that moral obligation can be explained only with reference to a formal principle of the will – the moral law.

The moral law and moral judgement

The moral law, as I understand it, has not only a transcendental role, but also acts as a criterion of moral judgement. Let us call this the criterial conception of the moral law. It is in its criterial role that the moral law is able to guide action. For the moral law to have this role is for it to be used as a reflective test of the permissibility of our maxims. A maxim is a subjective principle of action – that is, a principle on which the agent acts. One's maxim can be an objective principle also, but only when the principle from which the agent acts is the one from which she ought to act. To understand the moral law merely as a criterion, therefore, is to see it, not as a reason why we ought to act in certain ways, but solely as a test by means of which we can check that the principle from which we act is consistent with the requirements of morality.

In order to get clear about the distinction between the justificatory and criterial conceptions of the categorical imperative we need to distinguish three questions: (a) the question of *what it is* for a principle to be one in accordance with which we should act; (b) the question of *why* we ought to act in accordance with it; and (c) the question of how we can know that we have acted in accordance with objective principles, or how we can know that we have not acted on principles which are contrary to them. To answer the first question is to offer an analysis, or definition, of the concept of obligation, of what we mean when we say that some act is obligatory, or that acting in accordance with some principle is obligatory. To answer the second question is to state what the normative reasons are that give rise to some obligation. It is to state the ground of obligation rather than what the concept of obligation means. To answer the third question is to provide some sort of test by means of which one can assess one's moral judgement. This test may be either positive or negative. If it is positive, the test will enable us to tell which actions we ought to do, or which principles should inform our deliberation and action. If it is negative, it will only be able to tell us that either what we are doing, or the principle that informs our deliberation is impermissible. It would be able to tell us which principles should not inform our deliberation and action, but not which ones should.

Now whether or not I can sustain the view that the moral law can act as a criterion of moral judgement without being a normative reason to act in certain ways will depend upon whether I can keep the second and third questions distinct. Some might argue that these cannot be kept separate because whatever test we have for checking our moral judgements will, at the same time, be a reason for believing those judgements are correct. For example I may test my belief that I should not break my promise to A by applying the categorical imperative test to the maxim of this action. What I discover is that this maxim fails the test, that my maxim cannot be conceived as a universal law without contradiction. I discover, therefore that any action which falls under this maxim is wrong, and that the particular act of promise-breaking is thus wrong. But then it might be argued, the fact that this maxim fails this test is a reason for believing that this act is impermissible. Given this, it seems only a small step to concluding that the distinction between normative reasons for judging that we ought, or ought not to Φ and the criterion by means of which we can test these judgements collapses.

I think this distinction cannot be collapsed in this way. This distinction only appears to collapse because it focuses on epistemic, rather than practical reasons, i.e., on reasons for believing rather than reasons for acting.[22] Moral reasons are reasons why we ought to *act* in certain ways. They are reasons why I ought to keep my promise, to tell the truth, to help the needy, etc. The associated epistemic reasons will be the reasons for *believing* that I ought to keep my promise, tell the truth, help the needy, etc. Bearing this distinction in mind, my distinction between the justificatory and the criterial conception of the moral law can be sustained. For in making this distinction I am not denying that if some principle fails the test, this fact will give us a reason to *believe* that the act that falls under it is impermissible. All I am denying is the actions that fall under this principle are impermissible because their maxim fails the test. Failing the test can constitute a reason for believing that one ought, or ought not to Φ, but need not be a reason why we ought, or ought not, to Φ.[23]

I should add that there is nothing in what I have said so far that implies that one and the same consideration that is a practical reason cannot also be an epistemic reason. On the contrary, the consideration which is the practical reason will standardly also be an epistemic reason. Suppose, for example, I ought to Φ just because I promised A that I would, and that I know this. In such a case, the practical reason why I should Φ and my reason for believing that I should Φ will be the same – because I promised A that I would Φ. In so far as this fact is regarded as a practical reason it will be seen as supporting the act of Φ-ing. In so far as it is seen as an epistemic reason, it will be regarded as supporting the belief that I ought to Φ. I am not denying that practical reasons cannot also be epistemic reasons. All I am claiming is that something can be an epistemic reason without being a practical reason. This is all I need to sustain the distinction between the justificatory and the criterial conception of the moral law.

Given that we can distinguish a criterion, conceived of as a test by means of which we can assess our moral beliefs, and practical (normative) reasons, i.e., considerations in virtue of which certain actions ought to be done, we need to clarify what sort of criterion the categorical imperative is. Is it a positive or a negative criterion? Can it tell us which moral principles ought to inform our deliberation and action, or can it tell us only that certain maxims ought to be abandoned?

If the categorical imperative test works at all – that is, if it is not completely empty as many have claimed – then it can at least function as a negative criterion for moral judgement. For the principle which informs my deliberation and action, but ought not to, would show up as either inconceivable, or unwillable as a universal law. There is, however, a problem generated by Kant's scepticism about self-knowledge. He held that we can never know what our deepest maxims are,[24] and if this is correct, we will be unable to test them against the categorical imperative. But this will only be a problem for the categorical imperative procedure if we think of it as first apprehending our maxims by introspection, and then testing them. Maxims are *practical* principles and, as such, need not be known, or even knowable. They are rather 'to be lived up to'. For Kant, what is morally important is not knowing what our maxims are, but *trying* to act in accordance with certain principles;[25] and although we do not know what our maxims are, we do know how to live up to certain principles. What is tested, then, are the principles we try to live up to, and we do not need to have the sort of self-knowledge Kant denies we have in order to test these.

Can the categorical imperative function as a positive criterion? I see no reason why it should not if we draw on the procedure outlined in Chapter 3. I there argued that an action is morally required if its maxim is universalisable while the maxim of the contradictory act is not. This can easily be modified to work for maxims of actions, i.e., principles. So modified, it will follow that a principle is morally required if it is the contradictory of a maxim that cannot be conceived or willed as a universal law. So if I come to see that some principle cannot be universalised without contradiction I will not only be able to see that this principle ought to be abandoned, but that I ought to strive to live up to the contradictory of this principle. Thus, if I test the principle of indifference to the needs of others, and find that it ought to be abandoned, I can know that I ought to aspire to deliberate and act in accordance with the principle of beneficence. If the categorical imperative test works at all, therefore, it can be used not only as a negative criterion, but as a positive criterion also.

One surprising thing that follows if we reject the justificatory conception and adopt the criterial conception of the categorical imperative test is that use of this test is *not essential* for morally good action, or a morally good character, for Kant. What is essential is the moral law in its transcendental role. For the moral law must be presupposed as informing our thought in order to explain the distinctive form of necessity moral considerations are regarded as having for the good person. The criterial conception of the moral law, however, is a useful, but ultimately dispensable tool for the reflective moral agent. It would be important if it could be got to work, but if it didn't it would not be as devastating to Kant's ethics as many have thought.[26]

Summary

Let me summarise the account of acting from duty I have proposed, and the role of the moral law or the categorical imperative in respect to it. To act from duty is to act from a specific secondary and primary motive. One's secondary motive must be an unconditional commitment to morality. To have this commitment is to regard oneself as having sufficient reason to Φ in so far as one judges that one ought to Φ. This concern is unconditional if one regards these considerations as reasons to Φ independently of whether one is inclined to Φ, or whether Φ-ing is in one's interest. But although acting from this secondary motive is necessary to act from duty, it is not sufficient. For one must also act from primary motives which are the same as the ground of duty. Thus, the considerations one takes to be sufficient reason to Φ in so far as one judges that Φ-ing is morally required must act as primary motives, if one is to act from duty. One acts solely from duty if one's secondary motive is an unconditional commitment to morality and if one's primary motives are nothing other than the (normative) reasons why one should act.

When one acts from duty one acts from respect for the moral law, not in the sense that one regards the mere form of universality of one's maxim as the normative reason for acting, but in a transcendental sense. It functions transcendentally in the sense that it must be presupposed as the condition of the possibility of the necessity of morally obligatory actions. It is not the normative reason why some act is morally necessary, but explains how it is possible for that act, or any other, to be necessary. It is thus best understood in analogy to the category of causality. Just as the category of causality must be presupposed if we are to explain how one event can necessitate another, but is not itself a cause, so the moral law must be presupposed if we are to explain how considerations such as the needs of others can necessitate some action, but is not itself what necessitates this act. It is not a normative reason why we ought to Φ, but a transcendental ground of obligatory actions.

The moral law also has a criterial role on my interpretation. It offers a procedure by means of which we can test our moral judgement, but is not itself a normative reason why certain acts ought to be done. This means that it is a reason to believe that we ought, or ought not to do certain acts, but it is not a reason why we ought, or ought not to act in these ways. It is an epistemic, but not a practical reason. This criterial conception of the moral law also means that although it would be a useful guide to moral deliberation, applying the categorical imperative test is not essential to morally good action. The moral law, in its transcendental role, on the other hand is essential.

5

FILLING OUT THE DETAILS

Ross's theory of *Prima Facie* duties

Introduction

Given the interpretation of Kant's account of moral worth outlined in Chapter 4, I need to offer an account of normative moral reasons – that is, the reasons why we ought to perform certain actions. I have to do this because I have argued that there is an internal connection between the moral worth of actions and the normative reasons why they are right. This internal connection consists in the fact that a morally good action is one which, under favourable conditions, is done from (motivated by) the normative reason why it ought to be done. This internal connection is also expressed in the symmetry thesis. According to this thesis, a good-willed individual will be disposed to do the right act from the normative reasons why the act is right – that is, her primary motive for doing a right act will tend to be the normative reason why it is right. Some account of normative moral reasons is needed, therefore, in order to fill out the details of Kant's account of moral worth.

The contender for the role of the ground of duty in Kant's theory is the moral law. I have argued, however, that it should not be understood as occupying this role. Rather, it should be understood solely as playing a transcendental and criterial role. The moral law plays a purely transcendental role in so far as it explains the condition of the possibility of the representation of an action as necessary. In its criterial role it constitutes a test of the correctness of our verdictive moral judgements and the principles which inform these judgements. Neither of these roles tells us why we ought to do certain acts. We need, therefore, to look outside of Kant's theory for an account of normative moral reasons. In this chapter I argue that a Rossian theory of *prima facie* duties can fulfil this role, and can thus act as a necessary supplement to Kant's moral theory. I choose Ross's theory of *prima facie* duties to fill in the gap in Kant's account of moral worth because it, more than any other theory, allows different particular concrete facts to act as normative moral reasons while placing this within a context of strictly universal principles. In so far as it allows concrete facts, such as the simple fact that someone is in distress, to be the ultimate ground of duty, his theory allows morally good people to be motivated to do what they should by these concrete facts. In so far as this is placed within a context of strictly universal principles, it fits in with Kant's view that particular obligations are only possible in so far as they are subsumed under such principles. It is these considerations which make Ross's theory of *prima facie* duties suitable to fill the gap left by our rejection of the justificatory conception of the moral law in Kant's account of moral worth.

However, the claim that Ross's *prima facie* duties constitute basic normative reasons is controversial, and thus in need of justification. To many, Ross is simply stating *that* we ought to act in certain ways, and has no answer at all to the question of why we should so act. Christine Korsgaard expresses this view when she says that if you ask whether some claim on you is really justified, the intuitionist realist can only answer '"Yes". That is, all he can say is that it is *true* that this is what you ought to do.'[1] The worry here is that Ross, and other intuitionists, seem to present certain moral verdicts (those which express basic *prima facie* duties) as requiring no evidence, or justification, that we are just required to accept these verdicts unquestioningly. If a jury were to reach a verdict of guilt without any evidence for this verdict, we would certainly think that the procedure by which they reached this verdict was deficient in some way. If they went on to maintain that they do not *need* any evidence for their verdict, that they just *know* that the defendant is guilty, if they said 'just look at him, you can see he is guilty!', we would think them dogmatic, unenlightened and probably prejudiced. The worry Korsgaard expresses is that for the intuitionists certain moral verdicts, such as the verdict that I have a *prima facie* duty to keep my promise, or help others where I can, are just like this.

I think this criticism is based on, or at least made to appear compelling by, a misunderstanding of the notion of *prima facie* duties, as they are understood by Ross. This misunderstanding is not wholly the fault of Ross's commentators. Two features combine to add confusion. First, the term '*prima facie* duty' is, as Ross acknowledges, misleading, and second, his attempts to define this concept in *The Right and the Good* and in *The Foundations of Ethics* are unhelpful. What I want to do now is consider the various definitions of the notion of a *prima facie* duty in Ross. I argue that none of these offers a very good account, and then offer an alternative which articulates the idea Ross was trying to express. I maintain that Ross understood these principles as expressing not what we should do, but why we should act in certain ways.

Ross's notion of a *prima facie* duty

Ross contrasts the notion of a *prima facie* duty with that of 'duty proper' or 'actual duty'. He writes:

> I suggest '*prima facie* duty' or 'conditional duty' as a brief way of referring to the characteristic (quite distinct from that of being a duty proper) which an act has, in virtue of being of a certain kind (e.g. the keeping of a promise), of being an act which would be a duty proper if it

> were not at the same time of another kind which is morally significant. Whether an act is a duty proper or actual duty depends on *all* the morally significant kinds it is an instance of.[2]

Whether or not an action is our duty proper depends upon all of the morally relevant features of the action. The morally relevant features of the action are the particular ways in which it is *prima facie* right, or wrong. Thus, an action may be *prima facie* right in so far as it is an instance of beneficence, and *prima facie* wrong in so far as it is an instance of promise breaking, while the morally right thing to do, all things considered, i.e., our duty proper, may be either to keep our promise, or help someone. Our act will then be *prima facie* wrong (*qua* failing to help someone, or qua breaking of a promise), but actually right.

It cannot be emphasised enough that this does *not* mean that this act seems wrong but is not really. The term '*prima facie*' is not supposed to denote the characteristic an action may have of seeming to be a duty at first sight, but which may, on further investigation, turn out to be illusory. This term is not supposed to pick out a merely apparent moral aspect of actions, but a real one.[3]

> '*Prima facie*' suggests that one is speaking only of an appearance which a moral situation presents at first sight, and which may turn out to be illusory; whereas what I am speaking of is an objective fact involved in the nature of the situation, or more strictly in an element of its nature, though not, as duty proper does, arising from its *whole* nature.[4]

The distinction between a *prima facie* duty and a duty proper, or actual duty, should not be understood as one between an apparent and a real obligation. The term '*prima facie*' is not, however, arbitrary. For it is, Ross believes, only by first recognising each of the different morally relevant features of an action individually that we can come to make a judgement about whether or not it ought to be done. Knowledge of these individual features is, therefore, *prior to* our knowledge of whether or not the action (actually) should be done. It is this which justifies, or perhaps excuses, the use of the term '*prima facie*', for these features are what appears to us at first sight, *prima facie*.[5] One may or may not agree with Ross on this. What is clear, however, is that he did not understand the distinction between *prima facie* and actual duty as one between what seems to be, and what really is our duty.

This is important. For it is not uncommon for philosophers to claim that Ross's doctrine of *prima facie* duties is inadequate because it denies the possibility of real moral conflict. For example, John Searle writes:

> On this account *prima facie* obligations are contrasted with actual or real ones and the correct way to describe the conflict situation is to say that . . . I have no obligation at all to keep my promise. I do indeed *seem* to

> have an obligation, because promise-keeping, as Ross says, has a 'tendency to be our duty', but when all the facts are known it turns out that I have an obligation to help Jones, but none whatsoever to go to Smith's party . . . An immediate difficulty with [this description of the conflict situation] . . . is that on this view the promise in the conflict situation ends up counting for nothing. It is exactly as if I had never made a promise at all.[6]

This criticism is plainly based upon a misunderstanding of the notion of a *prima facie* duty. It clearly takes the contrast between *prima facie* and actual duty to be one between a merely apparent duty and a real one. Ross, however, is quite clear that the *prima facie* wrongness of a right act is not merely illusory. For example, in *The Foundations of Ethics*, he says:

> it remains a hard fact that an act of promise-breaking is morally unsuitable in so far as it is an act of promise-breaking, even when we decide that in spite of this it is the act that we ought to do.[7]

And in *The Right and the Good* he writes:

> When we think ourselves justified in breaking, and indeed morally obliged to break, a promise in order to relieve someone's distress, we do not for a moment cease to recognise a *prima facie* duty to keep our promise, and this leads us to feel, not indeed shame or repentance, but certainly compunction, for behaving as we do.[8]

We do not feel compunction because we recognise that our action appeared to be wrong but was not really. We feel compunction because we recognise that there really is some respect in which our action was morally deficient, and it is this real deficiency which the notion of a *prima facie* wrong aspect of a right act is supposed to capture.

In order to avoid the mistake that Searle and others make, many prefer the term 'pro tanto duty' to Ross's terminology.[9] For, unlike the term '*prima facie*' the term 'pro tanto duty' does not suggest an aspect of actions which appears to be, but isn't really, morally relevant. But this terminology is not without its problems. The main problem with this term is that it reinforces a more widespread, and insidious misunderstanding of Ross. For replacing the term '*prima facie* duty' with 'pro tanto duty' reinforces the impression that this notion is supposed to pick out a special kind of *duty*. It gives the impression that, for Ross, what is basic is a set of defeasible duties.[10]

What gives rise to this impression is that Ross's distinction looks like one between two types of duty: the *prima facie*, or pro tanto ones, and the actual ones. But the phrase '*prima facie* duty' is not supposed to pick out a distinctive type of duty at all, but something distinct from, yet related to duty. Thus, in *The Right and the Good* Ross says:

> The phrase '*prima facie* duty' must be apologized for, since . . . it suggests that what we are speaking of is a certain kind of duty, whereas it is in fact not a duty, but something related in a special way to duty.[11]

And in *The Foundations of Ethics* he writes, 'The phrase "*prima facie* obligation" . . . says too much; it seems to say that *prima facie* obligations are one kind of obligation, while they are in fact something different.[12] If *prima facie* duties are not a special kind of duty, yet are something related to duty in a certain way, we need to specify what the relation is between an action's being *prima facie* right[13] and its being actually right. In *The Right and the Good* and *The Foundations of Ethics* Ross offers a number of different accounts of the way in which the relation between *prima facie* and actual duty may be understood. I shall consider these in what follows. I argue that although these accounts shed some light on how the relation between *prima facie* duties and duty proper should be understood, Ross ultimately fails to offer a satisfactory account of this relation. But what he does say, and the context in which he says it, give us enough clues to propose an account which expresses the idea Ross was trying to articulate in his various formulations; which is that his theory of *prima facie* duties is a theory of basic normative reasons.

Three accounts of *prima facie* rightness

Ross offers three accounts of what it is for an act to be *prima facie* right, in contrast to being actually right. He defines *prima facie* rightness first in terms of a tendency to make an action actually right, second, in terms of the notion of 'fittingness', and third, with reference to the idea of responsibility.

There are, he maintains, no universal moral laws of the form, 'actions of type F are obligatory'.[14] There are, however, laws of the form 'actions of type F *tend* to be obligatory'. *Prima facie* duties are these laws. *Prima facie* duties are, he writes, 'laws stating the tendencies of actions to be obligatory in virtue of this characteristic or of that'.[15] The notion of a *tendency* to make actions right can, however, be understood in a number of different ways. It is sometimes understood probabilistically, as expressing the view that certain types of actions are *prima facie* right in the sense that most, or many of them are in fact right. According to this interpretation, to say that some characteristic is *prima facie* right is to say that most acts which have this characteristic are right. This account was initially ascribed to Ross by Peter Strawson who also raised a fatal objection to it. He points out that this sort of tendency is not a quality of particular acts at all, but of a class of acts.

> When we say of swans that they tend to be white, we are not ascribing a certain quality, namely 'tending to be white,' to each individual swan. We are saying that the number of swans which are white exceeds the

> number of those which are not, that if anything is a swan, the chances are that it will be white. When we say 'Welshman tend to be good singers,' we mean that most Welshman sing well; and when we say, of an *individual* Welshman, that *he* tends to sing well, we mean that he sings well more often than not. In all such cases, we are talking of a *class* of things or occasions or events; and saying, not that *all* members of the class have the property of *tending-to-have* a certain characteristic, but that *most* members of the class do in fact have that characteristic.[16]

If most swans are white, then it will be true of the class 'swans' that they tend to be white. It will not, however, be true of particular swans that they tend to be white. They will not *tend* to be either black or white, but will simply *be* either black or white. The same is true for the *prima facie* rightness of particular actions. We cannot understand the *prima facie* rightness of particular actions in terms of a tendency an act has to make this action actually right. Furthermore, if principles of *prima facie* rightness express such tendencies, then they will not be strictly universal. For the fact that beneficence is *prima facie* right will be a contingent, empirical fact. If as a matter of fact most beneficent acts were actually wrong, because considerations of beneficence were usually overridridden by some other moral consideration, then it would not be true that such actions are *prima facie* right. This would not be true because it would not be true of beneficent actions that the number of actually right ones exceeds the number of actually wrong, or merely permissible, ones.

The notion of a tendency to make actions right need not, however, be understood in this probabilistic manner. Indeed, Ross seems to have intended the notion of a tendency to make actions right to be understood non-probabilistically, in analogy to the way in which causal laws of nature tend to bring about certain effects.[17] Ross illustrates this point with the example of gravity. '*Qua* subject to the force of gravitation towards some other body, each body tends to move in a particular direction with a particular velocity; but its actual movement depends on *all* the forces to which it is subject.'[18] This illustration is instructive. The word 'tendency' is supposed to express a kind of force which always pulls in the same direction even when defeated by a greater, opposing force. Even when the gravitational force of one body on some object is defeated by that of some other body, the object is still tending to move in the direction of the first body. The object is still tending to move in the direction of the defeated force: it is just that, because of the greater opposing force, it *actually* moves in a different direction. When this notion of a tendency is applied to *prima facie* rightness and wrongness we get a view of them as what may be described as expressing a certain positive or negative 'deontic pull'. Any act which has the property of being *prima facie* right will be subject to this positive deontic pull, and any act which has the quality of being *prima facie* wrong will be subject to a negative deontic pull. Whether the act is actually right or wrong will be determined by the various deontic 'forces' to which it is subject, just as the movement of a body is determined by the various gravitational forces which act on it. Similarly, when a certain pull is defeated, it will still be effective, pulling the act in its deontic direction even though it is beaten by an opposing deontic pull.

But although this dispositional account seems to make sense of the *prima facie* rightness of an actually wrong act, as well as that of the universal principle which specifies that this type of act is *prima facie* right or wrong, it is difficult to unpack the metaphor of a 'deontic pull'. It is easy to make sense of what it is for a defeated gravitational force to continue pulling in a certain direction. If the victorious and the defeated forces are diametrically opposed – as they must be if the analogy is to be accurate – the defeated force will decrease the speed at which the object moves towards the body exerting the stronger pull. But a defeated deontic pull cannot be understood in this way. For rightness, unlike velocity, does not allow of degrees. In a particular situation one act cannot be slightly more right than some other possible act. In such a case the actual act would be right and the possible one wrong. There can of course be degrees of wrongness. In a certain situation act A could be more wrong than act B. But this cannot be translated by saying that act B is more right than act A. Being right is rather like hitting the bullseye in a game of darts. One can either hit the bullseye or miss it, but although one can miss it by a greater or lesser distance, one cannot hit it by a greater or lesser distance.[19] This is not to say that in any situation only one act can be right. All it implies is that if there is more than one right act each is right absolutely, and the doing of any other act would be wrong.

One could attempt to help Ross out here by maintaining that we can make sense of a negative deontic pull acting on a right act, if we understand it as reducing the value, or worth of the act. Value, unlike rightness, does allow of degrees, so if this suggestion were taken up by Ross, then he may be able to hold onto his dispositional account of *prima facie* duties. This suggestion, however, could not be taken up by Ross, as a central tenet of his position is that moral rightness and goodness are both distinct and independent notions.[20] Thus, for him, this proposed solution would rest on a confusion.

Sometimes Ross describes the notion of a *prima facie* duty counterfactually, and the notion of a tendency may be understood in this way. He writes:

> I suggest '*prima facie* duty' or 'conditional duty' as a brief way of referring to the characteristic (quite distinct from that of being a duty proper) which an act has, in virtue of being of a certain kind (e.g. the keeping of a promise), of being an act which would be a duty proper if it were not at the same time of another kind which is morally significant.[21]

According to this account of the *prima facie*, therefore, to say that a particular right act is *prima facie* wrong is simply to say that it would be actually wrong, in the absence of the other morally significant aspects which make it right. But although it is true that if an act is *prima facie* wrong, it would be actually wrong in the absence of some other *prima facie* consideration which makes it right, it is not clear that this tells us *what it is* for a right act to be *prima facie* wrong. The *prima facie* wrongness of a right act cannot consist simply in the fact that the act *would* be wrong *if* it were not for the other morally relevant features in virtue of which it is right. For this makes it sound as though there is only something morally deficient about the action in the counterfactual situation. This is not, however, Ross's view.

Furthermore, knowing that an act would be right in the absence of some other *prima facie* consideration that makes it wrong does not tell us what the relation is between *prima facie* and actual rightness. What we need to know is not that an act with a certain property F would be right in the absence of other properties that would make it wrong, but what the relation is between the property F and the actual rightness of the act in the counterfactual situation; and the counterfactual account is simply silent on this. In the end, then, the notion of a disposition to make actions actually right or wrong does not give us what we want from an account of *prima facie* rightness.

It may have been because Ross himself was unsatisfied with his account of *prima facie* rightness in *The Right and the Good* that he offered two new accounts in *The Foundations of Ethics*. The first of these stems from Ross's acceptance of C. D. Broad's definition of 'right'. In his *Five Types of Ethical Theory* Broad writes:

> It seems to me that when I speak of anything as 'right', I am always thinking of it as a factor in a certain wider total situation, and that I mean that it is 'appropriately' or 'fittingly' related to the rest of the situation . . . This relational character of rightness and wrongness tends to be disguised by the fact that some types of action are commonly thought to be wrong absolutely; but this, I think, means only that they are held to be unfitting to *all* situations.[22]

Ross agrees with this and adds only that 'being right' should be defined as 'being as fitting as possible to the total situation.[23] The property of being right cannot, he argues, be understood either as 'being *completely* fitting to the situation' or as 'being fitting *in some degree* to the situation'. For an act may be right despite the fact that it is not perfectly fitting, if, for example, it involves breaking a promise, or producing some evil. The same examples show that an act can be unfitting in some degree, but not wrong. So actual rightness should be understood neither as perfect fittingness, nor as fittingness in some degree, but as the quality of being as fitting as possible to the total situation.

It is during Ross's discussion of this point that he introduces his second definition of the *prima facie*. An act is *prima facie* right if it is fitting to *some aspect* of the total situation, and is *prima facie* wrong if it is unfitting to *some aspect* of the situation.[24] Ross thinks the notion of fittingness is indefinable, but nonetheless maintains that we can say something about it. In particular, we can distinguish different types of fittingness, and specify which is the appropriate type in ethics.

Ross distinguishes three types of fittingness: instrumental, aesthetic and moral. The first type of fittingness is the property something has of being well suited, or appropriate to some end. Instrumental fittingness can therefore, be understood as 'suitableness, or appropriateness for some purpose or other'.[25] But to say that an act is morally fitting to some responsibility the agent has, in virtue of being the fulfilling of this responsibility, is not to say that the fulfilling of this responsibility is well suited to some end the agent has in view. Moral fittingness is not a relation between an act and a desired end the agent has.

Aesthetic fittingness, like moral fittingness, is not instrumental, but is simply the distinctive way in which the parts of a beautiful whole relate to one another. Ross describes the distinctiveness of this relation in two ways. First, he states that a part of a beautiful whole is fittingly related to the other parts in the sense that it 'calls for' them.[26] Second, it is fittingly related to them in such a way as to give rise to a harmonious whole.[27]

Moral fittingness, he claims, has some affinity with both of these aesthetic characteristics: 'There seems to be something not altogether different in the way in which a situation calls for a certain act, and the way in which one part of a beautiful whole calls for the other parts.'[28] Further light is cast on the characteristic of being called for, by the second respect in which there is a family resemblance between moral and aesthetic fittingness: 'There is a direct harmony between the parts of the composition, as there is between a moral situation and the act which completes it.'[29] Ross's thought here seems to be that in seeing an act as called for by some aspect of the situation a morally sensitive agent recognises a certain disharmony, or incompleteness, in it and recognizes that the doing of a certain type of act will make good this lack. The idea seems to be that this recognition bears some resemblance to the way in which an artist recognises that a composition on which she is working calls for the final stroke which will complete it. In recognising some act as called for by some aspect of the situation, a morally sensitive person sees the situation as morally disharmonious, or incomplete, and, at the same time, recognises that the doing of this type of act will harmonise with, or complete this feature of the situation. In order to apprehend the fact that an act is *prima facie* right, therefore, one has to see the situation in a certain way, i.e., as morally disharmonious or lacking, and, at the same time, see this type of act as making good this lack.

This does not tell us what distinguishes moral from aesthetic fittingness, but Ross does not think anything can be said on this matter.[30] His view is that aesthetic and moral fittingness are two determinate types of the determinable 'fittingness', and we can no more describe that feature which distinguishes the one determinate form from the other, than we can describe what feature distinguishes the various determinate forms of the determinable 'being a colour'.[31] This inability does not reflect a philosophical failing, he maintains, but the fact that these determinate forms are not complex qualities sharing some aspects, and differing in others.

Nonetheless, one might think that the notion of fittingness is too much an aesthetic notion to play such a fundamental role in ethics.[32] The idea of one thing's being fitting to another, as Ross describes it, is essentially one of match. It means that the one 'goes with' the other, or enhances it in some aesthetically pleasing manner. For something to be unfitting to something else is for it to clash in some way, for example, in the way in which certain items of clothing, or colours, clash. It is not, however, clear to me that we can make sense of an aspect of an action failing to fit in with some aspect of a situation in this way. The idea is not that it clashes, or 'doesn't go' with this feature of the situation, but that it is in some way wrong without being actually wrong. Thus, I think that Ross's notion of disharmony is too much an aesthetic notion to be useful in understanding the relation of *prima facie* and actual rightness.

This brings me to the third and final attempt Ross makes to offer an account of *prima facie* rightness. I have already mentioned that in *The Right and the Good* Ross was dissatisfied with the phrase '*prima facie* duty', and preferred to use a different phrase rather than qualify the concept 'duty' with an adjective. In *The Foundations of Ethics* he replaces the phrase '*prima facie* duty' with the term 'responsibility'.[33] The substitution of 'responsibility' for '*prima facie* duty' has a number of advantages. It avoids the temptation to confuse duty with something distinct, yet related to duty, and means that the misleading term *prima facie* can be avoided.[34]

But the notion of responsibility does not apply neatly to all *prima facie* duties. It is not clear at all that I have a responsibility not to harm you, or to myself to make myself better, or to particular strangers who I could help. But even if we accept this account of the *prima facie*, it does not help us understand the relation between *prima facie* rightness and actual rightness. The notion of a responsibility does not describe the relation between some aspect of an action and its being right, but describes the relation between the agent, someone to whom the agent is responsible, and something, or someone, for which the agent is responsible. What we want to know, however, is what the relation is between the characteristic the action has of being the fulfilling of a responsibility and its being actually right. Knowing that all right actions have the characteristic of being the fulfilling of some responsibility tells us nothing about this. The account of *prima facie* duties as responsibilities does not, therefore, give us what we are looking for.

In the end, then, I think Ross fails to clarify what the relation is between *prima facie* and actual rightness.[35] Nonetheless, he gives us enough clues as to what he is getting at with this notion to allow us to offer such an account, and it is to this that I now turn.

Prima facie duties as principles of normative moral reasons

In *The Right and the Good* Ross introduces the notion of a *prima facie* duty in the context of his discussion of the question, 'What makes right acts right?'; and in *The Foundations of Ethics*, this notion appears at the end of his discussion of theories about the ground of rightness. This context suggests that he thinks of the relation between *prima facie* and actual duty as one of ground and consequent – that is, that he thinks of *prima facie* rightness as the reason why an act is actually right. This reading is also supported by the fact that he thinks of *prima facie* duties as that in virtue of which an act is right. This cannot, however, be the whole story, for Ross thinks that actions which are morally wrong can be *prima facie* right, but it cannot be said that such actions' *prima facie* rightness is understood as what makes the action right, as such actions are not right. Since the *prima facie* rightness of an act does not make the act right in all cases, this cannot be quite what Ross means by this term.

A better way of making the distinction Ross wants to make between *prima facie* duties and duties proper is with reference to Philippa Foot's distinction between verdictive and evidential moral considerations mentioned in Chapter 1. To remind ourselves, a verdictive moral consideration is the deontological status of some act. It corresponds to the content of an overall verdict about whether some act is morally right, wrong or permissible. Evidential considerations, on the other hand, are those which support, but do not constitute these verdictive considerations. Utilising this terminology we can elucidate Ross's distinction between *prima facie* duties and duty proper in the following way: a duty proper is a verdictive moral consideration, whereas *prima facie* duties are *evidential* moral considerations on the basis of which we reach, or ought to reach, an overall moral verdict, i.e., judge which verdictive moral consideration obtains. Such evidential moral considerations are not generalised verdictive moral considerations. Ross is not claiming that, in situations where one ought to keep one's promise, one should do so because one ought always to keep one's promise. Rather, *prima facie* duties are general evidential moral considerations. They describe general aspects of actions which are salient to moral deliberation and describe the way in which these aspects are salient. Thus, for example, the characteristic an act may have of being the keeping of a promise is salient to deliberation oriented towards reaching an overall moral verdict and always counts in favour of the act; whereas the characteristic an act may have of being the breaking of a promise is also salient to moral deliberation, but always counts against the act. Thus, we may talk of certain considerations having either positive or negative salience. For an aspect of an action to have positive salience is for this aspect to constitute a consideration in favour of doing the action. For an aspect to have negative moral salience is for it to be a consideration which counts against doing the act. We might describe this by saying that ways in which acts are *prima facie* right or wrong are moral aspects of the action which count for or against it. *Prima facie* duties then can be understood as principles which state evidential moral considerations, that is, which specify which types of considerations are morally salient, and how they are salient, to determining whether some action ought, or ought not to be done.

But if we are to say that for an aspect of an act to be *prima facie* right is for it to count in favour of that action, we have to say in what way that aspect favours it; and it seems the only answer we can give is that it favours it by providing a reason to do it. Thus, a *prima facie* wrong aspect of a right act can be understood as a moral reason against doing this action, which none the less ought to be done. Although this characteristic is not salient in the sense that it determines the deontic character of the action, it is salient in the sense that it picks out a way in which the act is morally deficient – that is, it picks out the fact that there is moral reason not to do it, an aspect in respect of which compunction is appropriate, despite the fact that the action as a whole is the right one. (This is the point Ross tried to articulate in terms of fittingness.) Similarly, a *prima facie* right aspect of a wrong action is an aspect of that action which gives us a moral reason to do the action, even though it ought not, all things considered, to be done. It is because this aspect constitutes a reason for doing the action even when defeated by stronger reasons on the other side, that it *would* make the action right in the absence of the considerations in virtue of which the act is *prima facie* wrong.[36] The idea here is simply that there is moral reason to do the act even though it ought not to be done, and this is no more problematic than the idea that there is some reason to believe that P, even though there is more reason to believe that not P. *Prima facie* duties then, do not express general verdictive moral considerations, but rather general evidential moral considerations. More precisely, they are principles of normative moral reasons specifying which considerations provide moral reasons, and whether these considerations give us reason to do, or not to do the action.

If we understand Ross's *prima facie* duties as expressing general evidential moral considerations, rather than as expressing some type of general verdictive moral considerations, the idea that his account constitutes a theory of normative moral reasons should not appear at all surprising. For, as we have seen, there is very little gap between the idea that some consideration is salient to determining what we should do, and the thought that it constitutes a reason why we ought to act in a certain way. What makes it seem otherwise is the verdictive terminology Ross uses, and the misleading accounts he gives of this notion. Once the terminology is abandoned and what Ross was getting at is clarified, there is good reason to think that his *prima facie* duties, that is, principles of moral salience, constitute principles of normative moral reasons, rather than principles of duty. As principles specifying which considerations are normative moral reasons, i.e., evidential moral considerations, these principles of moral salience can fill in the gap located at the end of Chapter 4. We now need to specify how Kant's account of moral worth looks once this hole is filled with a Rossian plug.

Filling in the hole

What I want to do now is fit Ross's account of normative moral reasons into the account of acting from duty outlined in Chapter 4. According to this account, to Φ from duty is to Φ from a specific secondary and primary motive. One's secondary motive must be duty. To say that duty functions as my secondary motive is to say that I regard myself as having sufficient reason (sufficient primary motivating reason, that is) to Φ solely in so far as I judge that Φ-ing is morally required. The fact that the act is required will not, however, be the (primary motivating) reason I take to be sufficient. This primary motivating reason will be the normative reason why Φ-ing is morally required, or, if my belief is false, the reason why I *believe* it is required.[37]

Since the moral law acts solely as the transcendental condition of obligation, and as a criterion of moral judgement it does not provide us with an account of normative moral reasons. But given Kant's account of moral worth some account of moral reasons is needed, for this account will specify what will act as the primary motives of morally good agents under favourable conditions. Since Ross's theory of *prima facie* duties is an account of normative moral reasons, this theory can be used to fill the hole in Kant's account of moral worth left by the rejection of the justificatory conception of the moral law. It is not, however, principles of *prima facie* duty which are the reasons why we ought to act in certain ways, but tokens of the types of consideration which fall under them. The principles are not themselves moral reasons, but specify what types of consideration are moral reasons. Nonetheless, the considerations they specify could not be moral reasons in the absence of these principles. For, it is only by falling under these principles, which in turn fall under the moral law, that they are able to acquire the strict universality which is necessary to give rise to a moral requirement.

What the moral reason is for acting in a certain way will depend upon the content of the obligation. If what I am morally required to do is to keep my promise, then the reason why I ought to do this will be determined by the principle of fidelity: I ought to Φ just because I promised A that I would. If my duty is one of beneficence, the reason why I ought to do this will be because I can alleviate someone's distress, or that I could make someone happy, or something of this sort. Given the symmetry thesis, this means that morally good actions will be done from primary motives which have as their content some concrete particular consideration in the nature of the situation specified by the relevant *prima facie* duty, such as the fact that I promised A to Φ, or that someone is in distress, or that someone did me a favour in the past, or something of this sort. But although it is a necessary condition of moral worth that an action be done from such primary motives, it is not sufficient. In order for an act to have moral worth it must also be done from a certain secondary motive. One's primary motive must be the normative reasons why the action is morally required, and one's secondary motive must be an unconditional commitment to the morality of one's actions. To act from such a secondary motive is not to act from some desire or other, but is simply to regard oneself as having sufficient reason to act in a certain way in so far as one judges that one ought to act in that way, and to regard oneself as having such reason independently of any need or desire we happen to have.

The advantage of utilising a Rossian account of normative moral reasons while giving a purely transcendental role to moral principles, from the principles of moral salience to the moral law itself, is that it allows concrete considerations such as the fact that I promised to do something, that someone needs help, that I owe someone a favour, etc., to motivate morally good people, without abandoning the idea that actions and moral deliberations of such people will be informed by a hierarchy of more and more abstract principles. It is thus not subject to the criticism levelled against the interpretation of acting from duty considered in Chapter 3. It also satisfies the requirement imposed by the symmetry thesis, unlike the standard interpretation of acting from duty.

Conclusion

In this chapter I have tried to provide the supplement Kant's account of moral worth needs, by drawing on Ross's account of *prima facie* duties. I have argued that these principles are not general verdictive moral considerations, but are general evidential moral considerations – that is, they do not specify *what* we ought to do, but *why* we ought to act in certain ways. Ross does not, therefore, merely offer a series of unsupported verdicts on what we should do, but provides the basic principles specifying what is salient to determining what we should do. No further moral justification can, or need, be offered for these principles. Nonetheless, we do not need to accept the moral verdicts they give rise to either on authority or by means of intuition. If someone cannot see that he ought to keep his promise just because he has made it, or that he ought to help someone just because they are in need, then the categorical imperative (in its role as criterion of moral judgement) can offer him reason to believe that he ought to do the acts these concrete considerations favour. For most of us, however, this will not be an issue. There is a great deal of disagreement about what we morally ought to do in certain circumstances, or types of circumstances (although moral philosophers tend to exaggerate the extent to which we do disagree). There is, however, a great deal of agreement about what is fundamentally morally salient, and how it is salient, to determining what we should do in these circumstances. For example, in the debate about abortion, most agree that the interests of the mother and the unborn child, as well as the value of human life, and autonomy are salient. What they tend to disagree about is the degree to which these very different and conflicting evidential moral considerations are salient, or about non-moral facts such as whether the foetus is a human, or a person. Nonetheless, disagreement can and does occur even at this fundamental level. The categorical imperative test cannot be used to get someone to see that some consideration gives them moral reason to act in a certain way, but it can be used to get them to see *that* they should act in that way. So even in cases where there is disagreement at a fundamental level about what is salient to how we should act, we are not reduced to mere assertion, or brute force. One could offer a justification for the moral verdict that we ought to Φ without alluding to the reasons why we ought to Φ.

6

ON THE VALUE OF ACTING FROM DUTY

Introduction

So far I have been concerned to get clear on what it is to act from duty. In this chapter I want to turn to the question of the value of acting from duty. Few would disagree with the point that Kant's example of the honest shopkeeper is supposed to illustrate, namely, that an action done from self-interest lacks any moral value even if it is, as in this case, the morally right thing to do. Indeed, many would be happy to go along with the claim that the second example of *Groundwork I* illustrates, namely, that the action of one who preserves his life from an immediate inclination to do so lacks any moral worth, even though this action accords with duty. But although one might concede that there is not a necessary link between actions done from immediate inclination, and morally worthy acts, one might nonetheless think that if one's immediate inclination were to do what one should, say, to help others, then one's action would be morally worthy. If I have only a *mediate* desire to help someone, then I desire this simply as a means, or way, of satisfying some other desire I have, such as the desire for praise, or honour. If on the other hand I desire to help someone for their own sake, rather than merely for the sake of some other end, then this desire is immediate. Kant's third example in *Groundwork I* is supposed to block the idea that the immediate desire to help others is morally good, and allow him to conclude that *only* the motive of duty has any moral worth. He writes:

> To help others where we can is a duty, and besides this there are many spirits of so sympathetic a temper that, without any further motive of vanity or self-interest, they find inner pleasure in spreading happiness around them and can take delight in the contentment of others as their own work. Yet I maintain that in such a case an action of this kind, however right and however amiable it may be, has still no genuinely moral worth.[1]

To emphasise his point, Kant goes on to ask us to imagine this friend of man overburdened with his own problems to such an extent that he has no inclination whatsoever to help others. If, in such a state, Kant claims, he could tear himself out of this deadly insensibility and help others 'without any inclination for the sake of duty alone; then for the first time his action has its genuine moral worth'.[2] His view is, then, that no inclination whatsoever has any moral worth. Only the motive of duty has this distinctive form of value, and thus can confer this value on the action done from it.

This view will appear to many to be false. Many will maintain that there is a plurality of motives that can be morally good. The motive of duty is one of them, but it is not the only one. Actions motivated by certain inclinations are also morally good.[3] In this chapter I want to defend Kant's view that only actions done from duty have moral worth. Before I attempt this, it will be useful to clear up some misunderstandings.

Some misunderstandings

The most obvious mistake is to see Kant as claiming that actions can only be morally good if we do not want to do them. This is how Schiller understood Kant and ridiculed him accordingly in the following well-known lines:

> Gladly I serve my friends, but alas I do it with pleasure.
> Hence I am plagued with doubt that I am not a virtuous person.
> To this the answer is given:
> Surely, your only resource is to try to despise them entirely,
> And then with aversion do what your duty enjoins you.[4]

Schiller clearly reads Kant as saying that our actions have moral worth only if we do not want to help others, and ridicules him accordingly. But this ridicule is undeserved. As many commentators have pointed out, Kant is not claiming that our actions only have moral worth if we do not want to do them. What he is claiming is that the question of whether we want to do what we should is irrelevant when we are considering whether these actions have any moral worth. Even when we want to do what we should, our actions only have moral worth when they are performed from the motive of duty. (Whether they have moral worth if they are done from duty *and* inclination is a different matter, to which I shall turn later.) Kant uses the example of someone who does not want to do what he ought to do not because he thinks that one's action only has moral worth if one does not want to do what morality requires, but because in cases where one wants to do what one ought to, it is not clear whether one's motive is inclination or duty.

In his later work Kant went even further, and came to believe that if one does not want to do what one should, this aversion would cast doubt on one's virtue. For example, in the *Religion within the Bounds of Reason Alone* he wrote the following:

> If one asks, What is the *aesthetic* character, the *temperament*, so to speak, *of virtue*, whether courageous and hence *joyous* or fear-ridden and

> dejected, an answer is hardly necessary. This latter slavish frame of mind can never occur without a hidden *hatred* of the [moral] law. And a heart which is happy in the *performance* of its duty (not merely complacent in the *recognition* thereof) is a mark of genuineness in the virtuous disposition.[5]

So Kant not only thinks that one's action can have moral worth if it is done with immediate inclination, but also expects that one would want to do what one ought if one were truly virtuous. We should, therefore, lay to rest the gross misinterpretation of Kant adopted by Schiller and others.

It may be thought that Kant held that the immediate inclination to help others lacks any value whatsoever, but this is also mistaken. Kant does not claim that the motive of spreading happiness is worthless: on the contrary, he describes it as 'amiable' and 'right', as well as deserving 'praise and encouragement'.[6] All he denies is that it has a distinctive form of value – that is, *moral* value. He denies it moral worth because he thinks that for something to be morally good it must be unconditionally good, i.e., good in all contexts, and, for reasons I will come to later, he thinks that the immediate inclination to help others is not good in the absence of a good will. But Kant's view that the immediate inclination to help others is not always good is compatible with the view that *when* it is good, it has genuine value, i.e., is praiseworthy. He certainly does not think that when the immediate inclination to help others is good it only has instrumental value. For Kant, being instrumentally good is not the same as being conditionally good. For him, instrumental value is just one form of conditional value. This is made clear in his discussion of the value of happiness. Kant thinks that happiness is a conditional good, and that its condition is the presence of a good will. But this does not mean that happiness is good only as a means of promoting a good will. Rather, it means that happiness is good if it is deserved, and it is deserved if one has a good will.[7] Kant thinks, therefore, that the immediate inclination to help others is praiseworthy, and is praiseworthy for its own sake. All he denies is that it is unconditionally good, and thus can be morally good.

But although Kant thinks that the inclination to spread happiness is praiseworthy *when* it is good, he also maintains that it 'stands on the same footing as other inclinations'. Now we know that he does not mean by this that the motive of spreading happiness is no better than some selfish inclination, for the latter inclination is never praiseworthy, whereas the former is. So to understand this remark we need to know *in what respect* the inclination to spread happiness is on the same footing as all other inclinations.

Non-accidental relation to rightness

Barbara Herman argues that all motives of inclination are unsuitable bearers of moral value because of their merely contingent relation to the rightness of the acts done from them. She considers the examples of the shopkeeper who is honest to his customers out of self-interest and the 'friend of man' who helps others from an immediate inclination to do so. The relevant point in both examples, she argues, is that the actions these motives give us reason to do may be right, but when they are this will be because of an accidental alignment of the agent's inclinations and circumstances.[8] If circumstances change so that it is in the shopkeeper's interest to lie to some of his customers the motive of self-interest gives him a reason to do this. Herman uses the same line of argument in relation to Kant's example of the 'friend of man'. She states that if one helps others just because one wants to, then one has a reason to help others to do what is wrong.[9] So if one is motivated solely by an immediate inclination to help others, then this inclination will give one a reason to do what is wrong. But a morally good motive cannot be one which gives the agent a reason to do what is wrong. Therefore, the immediate inclination to help others is not a suitable bearer of *moral* value.

Herman thus concludes that Kant's examples imply that he held that motives which incorporate inclinations, even the inclination to help others, have no moral worth because they are only contingently connected to the rightness of the acts which are done from them. Consequently, they fail to provide the agent with an interest in the morality of her actions.[10] This suggests, she argues, that a morally good motive must be one which gives the agent an interest in the rightness of her acts and 'therefore makes its being a right action the nonaccidental effect of the agent's concern'.[11] Only the motive of duty does this.

I think this account of what it is for a motive to have moral value is basically right, although the degree to which it is persuasive will depend on how we understand the idea of a motive's being *non-accidentally* related to the rightness of the act done from it. Herman seems to work with two distinct conceptions. The first is that a morally good motive will *guarantee* that the action done from it will be right. For example, she states that Kant's shopkeeper example 'suggests the need for a motive that will guarantee that the right action will be done'.[12] Here she clearly thinks that the motive of duty will provide such a guarantee. The second is that a morally good motive must be one that gives the agent an interest in the moral rightness of her actions. I reject the first understanding of the non-accidental relation of a motive and the rightness of the act done from it, and defend the second from a possible objection.

Although it is true that someone who acts from some inclination, even from the inclination to do one's duty, will not necessarily do what they ought to, this seems to be equally true of someone who acts from duty. For the rightness of my act does not depend solely on my motive, but also on the quality of my judgement and the truth of my beliefs. No matter how good my motive is, if my judgement is bad, or the beliefs on which I base my judgement are false, then it is not likely that I will do the right act.

This seems right even on my account of acting from duty. For according to this account, to act from duty is to regard oneself as having sufficient reason to Φ in so far as one judges that Φ-ing is right, and to be motivated to Φ by what one believes are the normative reasons why one ought to Φ. But the judgement that

Φ-ing is right in circumstances C, might be mistaken, as might one's beliefs about the normative moral reasons for Φ-ing. If my judgement that Φ-ing is right in the circumstances is mistaken, then if I act from duty, I will almost certainly fail to do the right thing. If my verdictive judgement is correct, but my beliefs about the normative reasons why I ought to Φ are mistaken, then I will do the right thing, but the fact that my act is right will be merely accidentally related to the primary motives from which I act. For if the reasons which are my primary motives are not the reasons why I ought to Φ, then it will simply be a matter of luck that I have correctly concluded that Φ-ing is right, and thus do the right thing. Consequently, if a morally good motive must be such that it guarantees that I do the right act, then no motive will be morally good.

Did Kant adhere to the implausible view that someone who acts out of duty *cannot* do a wrong act? A number of Kant scholars believe he did.[13] Paton, for example, cites a passage from *Groundwork II* where Kant states that motives other than duty sometimes issue in right actions and sometimes in wrong.[14] Paton claims that this passage implies that Kant held that the actions which follow from the motive of duty are always right. But this is very slim evidence for ascribing such an implausible view to Kant. The fact that Kant held that motives other than duty can result in wrong acts does not imply that he held that the motive of duty cannot.

One might think that the following passage supports Paton's interpretation:

> I shall here pass over all actions already recognized as contrary to duty, however, useful they may be with a view to this or that end; for about these the question does not even arise whether they could have been done *for the sake of duty* inasmuch as they are directly opposed to it.[15]

Here Kant appears to be claiming that someone who acts out of duty cannot do something which is contrary to duty. However, on closer inspection it can be seen that this is not the case. The crucial phrase is 'already recognized'. I take this to mean 'already recognized *by the agent*'. Understood in this way, Kant is not committed to the dubious assumption that one's motive guarantees the rightness of one's act. All he is saying is that an agent cannot do an act from the motive of duty which he has *already recognized* as being contrary to duty. This does not rule out the idea that one might do the wrong act from duty: all it rules out is the possibility of doing an act which one has recognised as being wrong from duty. There seems, therefore, to be no unambiguous support for the view that Kant thought that acting from duty guarantees the rightness of one's action.

What may lead commentators to ascribe such a view to Kant is his view that the moral worth of an act is independent of any result of willing it, and hence is independent of successfully achieving that result. But this is to confuse views Kant held about moral worth, or goodness, with views he held about moral rightness. He clearly held that the moral value of an act stems not from any result of our willing some end, but from the reasons from which we will that end. It is also clear that he held that an action has moral value only if it is done from duty. But Kant's distinction between acting in accordance with duty and acting from duty shows that he held that moral rightness is quite distinct from moral value. For to act in accordance with duty without acting from duty is to do the right action, but is not to do a morally good action. Since he held that moral rightness and moral goodness are quite distinct concepts, the mere fact that he holds that an action can have moral worth simply in virtue of willing in a certain way in no way shows that he held the same to be true of morally right acts.

If the motive of duty cannot be connected necessarily with the rightness of the agent's acts in the sense that this motive *guarantees* their rightness, in what sense are they non-contingently linked? Allison suggests that this necessary connection can be made by revising Kant's account so that for an action to have moral worth it should be both from and in accordance with duty.[16] But as Allison notes, although this would establish a necessary connection between moral goodness and right acts it would make Kant's claim trivial. Furthermore, if the motive of duty does not guarantee that one does the right act this leaves unexplained why Kant thought that this motive is morally good when it leads one to do the right act, but motives of inclination are not.

Why, then, does Kant deny that all inclinations are unsuitable bearers of moral worth? The second way of understanding Herman's claim seems to provide us with the answer. According to this understanding, what is distinctive of the motive of duty and which every inclination lacks, is the ability to give the agent an interest in the morality of her actions. This interest would no more guarantee that we do the right thing, than an interest in being prudent could guarantee that one always promotes one's self interest. But on this understanding of a morally good motive, what is important is not that the motive guarantees that the action is right, but that *when* it is right its being so is non-accidentally related to the motive from which it is done. On this interpretation, the rightness of one's act is non-accidentally related to the motive from which it is done because this motive gives the agent a non-derivative concern for the rightness of her actions. Actually, as I understand acting from duty, it is not that the motive of duty gives the agent an interest in the rightness of her action, but includes (as a secondary motive) an unconditional commitment to morality. It is because of this, and the fact that the agent's primary motivating reasons will be the same as the reason why the act is right, that make the fact that the act done from this motivational structure is right (when it is right) more than a merely lucky alignment of motivation and circumstances.

But if this is the way in which the motive of duty is non-accidentally related to the rightness of the actions that are done from it then it may look as though it fails to rule out all inclinations as bearers of moral worth. For although the immediate desire to help others fails to satisfy this criterion of moral worth, the immediate (*de dicto*) desire to do what is right seems to pass this test.[17] To have a *de dicto* desire to do the right thing is to be motivated to do whatever one believes is the right thing in the circumstances. So when one's moral belief is correct and one does the right act, its being right does seem to be non-accidentally related to the motive from which it is done. This is because if one is motivated by this *de dicto* desire then one will have a nonderivative concern for the rightness of one's actions. If this is correct, then at least this desire is a suitable bearer of moral worth.

It is tempting to respond to this by maintaining that if one acts from such a desire, then one is not really interested in the rightness of one's actions, but in satisfying one's desire. But this response distorts the way things are. What it is one is concerned about is determined by the content of one's desires, so the only way in which it could legitimately be said that someone who acts from a *de dicto* desire to do what is right is really concerned only about satisfying this desire would be if it could be maintained that this desire is really a desire to satisfy this very desire. But this would be to mistakenly treat a first-order desire (to do what is right) as a second-order desire (to satisfy this first-order desire). It may be true that we all have a second-order desire to satisfy our first-order desires, but it doesn't follow from this that we are not really concerned about the content of the first-order desires, and are only really concerned with the content of this second-order desire. Not only does this conclusion not follow, it seems false. Whether or not I am really concerned about the content of my desire has nothing to do with this second-order desire, but depends upon whether I desire this content for its own sake, or merely as a means of satisfying some other desire. But we could not say that the immediate *de dicto* desire to do the right thing is not really a desire to do what is right, for in so far as this desire is immediate it is a desire to do what is right for its own sake, rather than for the sake of satisfying some other desire we happen to have. Kant did not want to deny the possibility of an immediate desire to help others, but simply to deny that it has moral worth. I see no reason why he should think that a desire to do what is right could not be an *immediate* desire. If this is right, then this desire would express a nonderivative (immediate) concern, not for satisfying one's desires, but for the rightness of one's actions. It seems therefore that when one acts from a *de dicto* desire to do what is right, the rightness of one's actions will reflect the agent's genuine concern for the morality of her actions just as much as acting from duty does.

But although this desire would provide the right sort of link between the agent's motive and the rightness of the action done from it, it fails to fit in with another aspect of Kant's account of moral worth – what I have called the symmetry thesis. According to the symmetry thesis a morally good person's primary motives for doing what she should will tend to be the normative reasons why she should act in that way, and, conversely, the normative reasons why she should act in that way will tend to be her primary motive for so acting. The symmetry thesis ruled out the possibility that Kant understood acting from duty in the ordinary sense of doing the right thing just because it is right, for this would imply that some act is right just because it is right. The symmetry thesis also shows that a *de dicto* desire to do the right thing cannot be what will motivate a good-willed person. For if a good person were so motivated to do what she should, it will turn out that one of the normative reasons why she should act in that way is because she wants to. It is, however, seldom, if ever, the case that one of the normative reasons why certain actions are right is because we want to do what is right. The reason why I should help others is that they need help, not that they need help and I desire to do the right thing. Similarly, if I have promised A that I would Φ the reason why I should Φ is because I promised to, not because I promised to and because I desire to do the right thing. Consequently, even the immediate *de dicto* desire to do what is right cannot be a morally good motive. For although it will be non-accidentally related to the rightness of the action done from it when this act is right, it will not be non-accidentally related to rightness in the right way. The right way is the way generated by the symmetry thesis. The motive of duty, as I understand it, is non-accidentally related to rightness in the right way: no inclination is. Consequently, no inclination can have moral worth.

Overdetermined actions

We now need to turn to the issue deferred from Chapter 3 – that is, the question of whether overdetermined actions are morally good. It is useful in this context to distinguish two cases. The first is that of acting from duty and inclination where neither is sufficient by itself to motivate the dutiful action. Call these 'hybrid actions'.[18] The second case is that of acting from duty and inclination where both motives are sufficient for the action. Call these 'overdetermined actions'. Of course there are a number of cases which fall between these, but to include these would complicate things unnecessarily, so I ignore them.

The issue under consideration is easier in relation to hybrid actions than it is in relation to overdetermined actions, for Kant is clear that if an action is to have moral worth, the motive of duty must be sufficient to motivate the obligatory action.[19] And since for hybrid actions the motive of duty is not sufficient, they cannot have moral worth.

The reason why Kant insists that the motive of duty be sufficient is that if it is not, then the agent must seek out other reasons to do the action, and this is clear evidence that the agent does not regard moral considerations as decisive.[20] The main reason why he insists that the motive of duty should be sufficient is because when it is not, the agent makes dutiful action conditional upon the presence of an inclination. But this condition 'would destroy all moral worth just as surely as any admixture of anything empirical in geometrical axioms would destroy mathematical axioms'.[21] It is because we make dutiful action conditional upon the presence, and operation, of an inclination that hybrid actions have no moral worth. Can overdetermined actions have moral worth?

As we understand it, an overdetermined action is one which is motivated both by inclination and by duty where each of these is by itself sufficient to motivate the action. But what does it mean for each motive alone to be sufficient to motivate the action? One might maintain that for inclination to be sufficient is for it to suffice even if the agent judged the action wrong. But this will not do, for it would rob the motive of duty from any sufficiency worth having. As Baron points out:

> To say that inclination would suffice even if the agent saw the action to be wrong would be to say that in the event of a conflict between duty and inclination, inclination would win. But then what would it mean to say that duty suffices? Only that as long as there is no conflict between duty and inclination, duty will be a 'sufficient motive': it will 'win' as long as there is no contest. Clearly, to understand 'inclination would alone suffice' in this way robs the motive of duty of any sufficiency worth having.[22]

The problem is that with Baron's suggested alternative the motive of inclination is robbed of any sufficiency worth having. According to Baron, to say that an action is overdetermined is to say:

(1) that as long as I did not believe the action to be wrong, my inclination to do it would suffice to motivate me to perform the action (and would not need to be supplemented by additional motives, such as that this will pay off in the future, or that this is morally good to do, albeit not required); and
(2) that in the absence of cooperating inclinations the motive of duty would suffice; and
(3) that the action is determined by both motives (duty in its function as a primary motive, and inclination) operating separately, not by a happy marriage of the two (i.e., not through acquiring force by buttressing each other).[23]

The problem with this account is with (1). According to this, inclination is described as a sufficient motive to Φ only on the condition that I judge that Φ-ing is permissible (in the broad sense of permissible which includes the obligatory as well as the merely permissible). But this is just to say that if there were a perceived conflict between duty and inclination duty would win; and this still leaves it unclear what it means to say that inclination is a sufficient motive. Baron's reason for rejecting the alternative account of the sufficiency of inclination provides a good reason to reject her own account.

A better way of conceiving of overdetermined actions is as follows: an act of Φ-ing is overdetermined if and only if:

(1*) one would Φ (from inclination) in the absence of *any* moral judgement about the status of this act;
(2) in the absence of cooperating inclinations the motive of duty would suffice; and
(3) the action is determined by both motives (duty in its function as a primary motive, and inclination) operating separately, not by a happy marriage of the two.

It will not do to say that for inclination to be sufficient one would Φ even if one did not think that one should. For this is consistent with Φ-ing when one judges that this is wrong and, as Baron points out, this would rob the motive of duty of any sufficiency worth having. But by characterising overdetermined actions in the way I do in (1*) I avoid this. For if the counter-factual situation does not allow any moral judgement of the act, it rules out the judgement that it is wrong, and hence does not rob the motive of duty of any sufficiency worth having.[24]

When we apply this revised formulation of Baron's account of overdetermined actions to our account of acting from duty we get the following account. An action is overdetermined if and only if:

(a) one's secondary motive is an unconditional commitment to morality;
(b) one would Φ (from inclination as a primary motive) in the absence of *any* moral judgement about the status of this act;
(c) in the absence of cooperating inclinations the normative reasons why one ought to Φ would suffice (at the primary level) to motivate Φ-ing; and
(d) the action is determined by both primary motives (the ground of duty, and inclination) operating separately, not by a happy marriage of the two.

We will have to say more about the nature of overdetermined actions later. Before we do, however, I want to consider whether the very notion of an overdetermined action is incoherent.

Are overdetermined actions intelligible?

According to one line of thought, the very notion of an overdetermined action as we understand it does not make sense, or at least makes no sense within a Kantian context. Judith Baker, for example, argues that the idea that someone could do some act both because it is required and because it is appealing is unintelligible.[25] She illustrates this point with the example of someone who thinks that he should give a student a good grade because she deserves it, and who likes the student, and thus would like to give her a good grade anyway. Baker writes:

> Liking the student or liking to give good grades, one feels, cannot be an additional motive which helps the agent in determining the grade if he is to be credited with acting from a sense of fairness. It looks as if the requirements of fairness are what must exclusively determine the action, if it is done from a sense of fairness, and that the additional motives are not compatible with the idea of what fairness requires.[26]

She also considers a student who is committed to being a philosophy major, who finds that a certain appealing course is required by the department. 'It does not seem intelligible,' Baker writes, 'to say that the student takes the course both because it is required and because it is appealing.'[27]

But why should we think that someone who gives an essay a good grade or who chooses to do a required course from mixed motives is unintelligible? It might be that if we thought of these motives as causes of the teacher's action we would run into various difficulties, but Kant does not conceive of motives in this way, but as considerations which the agent regards as good reasons.[28] If, however, we think of motives as motivating, but non-causal reasons then it is by no means obvious that an overdetermined action would be unintelligible. We have no problem with the idea of someone believing that P on the basis of two arguments, each of which is regarded as offering sufficient reason to believe that P. Descartes seems to do this in the *Meditations*. In the third *Meditation* he concludes that God exists from his 'trademark argument', and later, in the fifth *Meditation* concludes that God exists from the ontological argument. Each of these arguments seems to be regarded by him as giving him sufficient reason to believe that God exists, and he seems to believe that God exists on the basis of both of them. Such an overdetermined belief appears intelligible. It might be possible for Descartes to say, 'I believe in the existence of God on the basis of the trademark argument; and although I think the ontological argument gives me sufficient reason to believe that God exists, I do not believe this for that reason.' But it seems equally possible, and intelligible, for him to say, 'I believe God exists on the basis of both the trademark argument and the ontological argument', even if he regarded each of these arguments as giving him sufficient reason to believe in God. But if the idea of an overdetermined belief is intelligible, why should we think that an overdetermined action is not? It is certainly possible that someone might think that some desire they have gives them sufficient reason to Φ, but to maintain that they did not Φ for that reason, but because of what they take to be the normative reasons why they ought to Φ. But this possibility by itself does not preclude Φ-ing from this desire as well as these moral reasons.

Baker's reason for thinking that such actions are unintelligible seems to be that they would be irrational.

> If an individual judges that the reasons he has so far considered are adequate to justify acting, then, in so far as he is rational, he acts on the basis of these reasons. To keep the door open, as it were, to other reasons when he has judged it is time for decision and action is irrational. But if one judges that there are moral considerations which justify doing something, one would be undermining one's own judgement and decision-making to welcome further motivation.[29]

The first point to make in response to this is that even if overdetermined actions are irrational, this does not entail that they are unintelligible. Second, it is not clear that overdetermined actions are irrational. It is clear that if one regards moral considerations as decisive, then once one comes to believe that there is sufficient moral reason to Φ one need not look for further reasons to Φ. To feel one *has* to look for further reasons would be to regard the moral reasons one already recognises as insufficient. But although one would not need to *look for* additional reasons to Φ, one may, nonetheless, *have* further reasons – reasons of inclination – and one might recognise that one does. In such a case it seems to me no more irrational to Φ both from the moral reasons one regards as sufficient as well as from the reason one's inclination provides, any more than it is irrational for Descartes to believe that God exists from one set of arguments he regards as sufficient proof *and* from reasons some other argument gives him to believe this.

Baker seems to think that overdetermined actions are not possible because this motivational structure would undermine one's own judgement and decision-making. But we need to distinguish two things here. The first is the reasons on the basis of which we judge that Φ-ing is required; the second is the reasons why we Φ. The fact that we want to Φ is never a reason why we ought morally to Φ. For example, the reasons why I ought to give some student's essay a good mark are that it is clearly written, imaginative, well-argued, shows understanding and a good knowledge of the literature, etc. I would not judge that I should give it this grade for these reasons *and* because I want to give it a good grade, or because I like this student. If I were to do this it might be thought that I would undermine my judgement, as Baker claims. For my moral judgement would not be arrived at by a consideration of purely moral reasons.

But although the inclination to Φ might not be able to figure as one of the reasons I have for judging that I ought to Φ, it could nonetheless, be a reason why I Φ. This is not irrational in the sense that it means that I am not motivated by the considerations which form the basis of my judgement that I ought to Φ, for if I am motivated by these moral considerations and by the fact that I want to Φ, then I am motivated by these moral considerations. The inclination does not stop these considerations motivating me – that is, being the reasons from which I act. All that follows in this case is that they are not the only considerations that motivate me to Φ – that is, my Φ-ing is overdetermined. It seems, therefore, that Baker offers no compelling argument for the view that the very idea of an overdetermined action is unintelligible, or irrational.

Henry Allison tries to circumvent the issue of whether overdetermined actions can have moral worth in a different way, with reference to Kant's theory of agency. Allison points out that for Kant an incentive can only determine the will if it is incorporated into the agent's maxim. Thus, in order to consider the issue of overdetermined actions we need to consider from what maxim the agent acts. If the action is really overdetermined, the maxim must be a complex one incorporating both incentives. Using Henson's example of Kant lecturing both from duty and inclination,[30] Allison claims the content of this maxim will be, 'I shall lecture whenever I am both obligated and feel inclined to do so.'[31] But, Allison argues, this will not do because it makes duty dependent on inclination.

He then considers whether the maxim can be described disjunctively. If it can, then the above criticism will not hold. But, Allison argues, such a disjunctive maxim is not a single maxim at all. 'It is rather a combination in one formula of two distinct maxims: I shall lecture whenever duty requires me to and I shall lecture whenever I have the opportunity and feel so inclined.'[32] But if these really are two maxims, we can ask on which one the agent acted; and although we cannot know the answer to this with certainty, this is still a meaningful question to ask in relation to the moral worth of an action. If the agent acted from inclination, his action has no moral worth. If he acted from duty, then it does. The point is that the notion of an overdetermined action disappears when it is so understood.[33] Thus, Allison writes, 'In the end . . . it would seem that the possibility of overdetermination . . . does not provide a cogent rejoinder to Kant's claim that being from duty alone is a necessary condition for the ascription of moral worth to an action.'[34] I do not wish to take issue with Allison's rejection of the conjunctive formulation of the maxim of supposedly overdetermined actions, as I think he is right to claim that Kant would deny that actions done from such a maxim would have moral worth. The problem with his attempt to dissolve the issue is with his discussion of the disjunctive maxim. There are two problems with this. The first is with his claim that a disjunctive maxim is really a combination in one formula of two maxims. There is a difference between a disjunctive maxim and two separate maxims, each of which has one disjunct for its content. For example, if, in a situation where I could either Φ or Ψ, I Φ from the disjunctive maxim 'I will either Φ or Ψ', then the fact that I have not Ψ-ed does not mean that I have failed to do something that I will. For what I will is not to Ψ, but either to Φ or Ψ, and in the absence of a separate maxim simply to Ψ, I will not have failed to do something that I will. If, however, I have two separate maxims, one to Φ and one to Ψ, and I Φ in a situation where I could either Φ or Ψ, then I would have failed to do something that I will, namely, to Ψ. Given that there is a difference between this and the two separate maxims, it might be that this disjunctive formulation of our two distinct maxims expresses better the nature of our motivation than either of the maxims which are its disjuncts by themselves. Since this might be true of the disjunctive account of an overdetermined action, it might be that we cannot split the disjuncts off into two separate maxims without distortion.

Second, Allison never explains why an agent cannot act from two different maxims at one and the same time. Those who claim that overdetermined actions are possible believe that one can act from two different motives at one and the same time. If, therefore, the discussion is to be shifted from motives to maxims, it would simply be question-begging to assert without argument that one couldn't act from more than one maxim. For, once we have shifted the focus to maxims, the question of whether we can act from more than one maxim at a time will be what is at issue.

I conclude, therefore, that both Allison and Baker fail to circumvent the issue of the moral worth of overdetermined actions. In the absence of some other argument to show that overdetermined actions are not possible we need, therefore, to address the issue of whether such actions have moral worth.

In Chapter 3 I claimed that there is some textual support for the view that Kant would not have thought that overdetermined actions have moral worth.[35] But I also noted that such passages cannot be regarded as decisive until we know why Kant thought that only the motive of duty can confer moral worth on actions. Once this is decided we can then see whether actions done from duty and inclination fulfil the criterion of moral worth. We have now specified what it is about the motive of duty that is distinctive, and in virtue of which it can confer moral worth on actions. We can now consider whether overdetermined actions can be morally good.

Are overdetermined actions morally good?

So far we have worked with the idea that the motive of duty is sufficient if and only if the agent would do the act she believes she should in the absence of any inclination to do the action. But the motive of duty can be understood as sufficient in a stronger sense. According to this strong sense of sufficiency, the motive of duty is sufficient if it could by itself motivate the agent to do the right act even if *conflicting* motives are present. Herman has argued that whether the sufficiency of the motive of duty is understood in the weak or strong sense, an overdetermined action cannot have moral worth. The problem with the weak notion of sufficiency is that counter-factual situations reveal that the connection between the agent's (overdetermined) motivation and the rightness of her action is merely accidental. The problem with the strong notion is that it generates implausible results. Since I am working with a different conception of the motive of duty I cannot simply help myself to the conclusion she reaches. Once I have summarised her argument, therefore, I shall see whether it works with the alternative account of acting from duty I outlined in Chapter 4.

Herman argues that if the sufficiency of the motive of duty is understood in the weak sense, it is possible that in different circumstances the non-moral motive might move the agent to do some act other than the one she should. For example, it might be that a shopkeeper is motivated to be honest both from duty and self-interest, and that the motive of duty is sufficient in the sense that he would be honest in the absence of the cooperating, non-moral motive. But the fact that he would be honest in the absence of the motive of self-interest is compatible with the possibility that he would not be honest if he came to have an aversion to being honest, because he came to think that honesty would not be in his interest. It may be that if the cost to him of being honest was not great he would act against his aversion from duty. Nonetheless, there is nothing about the weak notion of overdetermination that rules out the possibility that if the perceived cost to the agent was great, and his aversion to being honest strong enough, that he would act wrongly, even though the motive of duty would be sufficient by itself to move him to action in more favourable circumstances. This possibility casts doubt on whether the rightness of his action is really non-accidentally related to the motives from which it was done, even in the more favourable circumstances. For if in the counter-factual situation in which honesty is contrary to his interest he would not do the right thing, it looks as though the fact that he does the right thing *when* it is in his interest is merely the result of a contingent alignment of circumstances and his (overdetermined) motivation. If this is correct, then overdetermined actions, so understood, would lack moral worth.

This problem would be avoided if we think of the sufficiency of the motive of duty in the stronger sense – that is, where it is understood as sufficient in the sense that the agent would do the right thing even if some *opposing* inclination were present. The trouble with this interpretation, however, is that it is too strong, i.e., too demanding. As Herman puts it:

> While it seems reasonable to credit an action with moral worth if its performance does not depend on an accident of circumstances, it seems equally reasonable to allow that failure in different circumstances does not require denial of moral worth to the original performance.[36]

The worry here is that this account of the sufficiency of the motive of duty not only causes problems for overdetermined actions, but also for ones which are done solely from duty. It is overwhelmingly plausible to think that nothing more is needed for the motive of duty to be sufficient for the agent to Φ than that the agent Φ-ed *solely* from duty. But if we understand the sufficiency of the motive of duty according to the strong interpretation, something more than this is needed, namely, that it be the case that the agent would have done the right thing if some opposing inclination were present. If this is granted, then we would have to allow that it is possible that although the agent Φ-ed solely from duty, the motive of duty was not sufficient for her to Φ. It would not be sufficient if it is true that she would not Φ if she had some strong disinclination to Φ-ing for some reason. Suppose, for example, Kant's shopkeeper is honest solely from duty, but would not act in this way if being honest would lead to his ruin. According to the strong account of sufficiency we would have to say that although he was honest solely from duty, the motive of duty could not be sufficient, for if his honest action were to ruin him he would not do it. If this were correct, then many actions done solely from duty would turn out to lack moral worth, which is clearly not Kant's view. All that Kant requires is that the motive of duty be sufficient in the weak sense that it would motivate the action by itself, in the absence of any cooperating inclination. But, as we have seen, if the motive of duty is sufficient only in this weak sense, then when the overdetermined action is the morally right one, its being so will be the result of a merely accidental alignment of circumstances with the agent's motivation, and would thus lack moral worth.

It may seem that actions done solely from duty are subject to this same dialectic, but I do not think they are. What gets the dialectic going in the overdetermined case is the inclusion of inclination as a motive. It is because inclination is a motive in the overdetermined case that we have to ask what its relation is to the rightness of the act done from it, when it is right. We concluded that it is accidental because in different situations inclination would give us reason to do what is wrong. These counter-factual situations do not cast doubt on the non-accidental relation of the motive of duty when this is the sole motive, for since inclination is not here a motivating reason, we do not need to know whether in different situations it would give us different reasons. All we need to know is whether the motive of duty would give us reason to do the right thing in situations where doing what we should is contrary to our interests; and it is difficult to see how it could fail to do so. What is important is the sort of reasons this motive would give us in such situations, not whether we would, despite the cost to ourselves, succeed in doing the right thing.

Herman's argument is persuasive in relation to her understanding of acting from duty. But on her understanding an action can have moral worth if and only if duty is one's sole primary motive[37] – that is, if one does the right thing just because it is right. Only then is it the case that the rightness of the action is non-accidentally related to the motive from which it is done (*when* this act is right). I argued in Chapter 1 that we must reject this understanding of acting from duty because it does not fit with the symmetry thesis. I thus need to see whether Herman's argument against the moral value of overdetermined actions is applicable to my understanding of what it is to act from duty.

As I understand it, to Φ solely from duty is to Φ from primary motives which are the same as the normative reasons why one ought to Φ and from no other primary motives, and from an unconditional commitment to morality as a secondary motive. To regard oneself as having sufficient reason to Φ in so far as one judges that one ought to Φ is to regard moral reasons as unconditional. To treat moral reasons as unconditional is to regard moral considerations as *intrinsically* reason-giving. One would not regard moral reasons as unconditional if one only treats them as reason-giving on the condition, say, that they promote one's interest, or satisfy some desire one has.

Although there can be overdetermination at the secondary level, this is irrelevant to the question of the moral worth of one's actions. What is relevant is overdetermination of one's primary motives. For an action to be overdetermined at the primary level is: (a) for the primary motives to include reasons of inclination in addition to the normative reasons why the action ought to be done; (b) for the moral primary motives to be sufficient by themselves (in the absence of the cooperating inclination) for action; and (c) for the primary motives of inclination to be sufficient by themselves (in the absence of any judgement about the deontic status of the action).

In considering the value of overdetermined actions, so understood, we need to focus on what it is for (what I regard as) the normative reasons why I ought to Φ to be sufficient in overdetermined actions. At this point Herman's dialectic works in just the way it does with the ordinary notion of acting from duty. If we think of these reasons as sufficient in the sense that they would motivate me to Φ in the absence of reasons of inclination, this would leave open the possibility that I would not Φ in a situation in which some strong aversion to Φ-ing is present. This would mean that the whole, overdetermined motivational structure is only contingently related to the rightness of the action done from it. This can be avoided by working with a stronger sense of the sufficiency of the moral reasons, where this is understood as sufficient for action even if some opposing inclination were present. But this has the implausible implication of making the moral worth of my action here and now depend on how I would act in very different circumstances. This is implausible because if we work with a single notion of the sufficiency of the motive of duty we would have to apply this criterion to cases in which we act solely from duty. But this would have the implausible implication that the fact that we are motivated to do what we think right solely by duty is not enough for this motive to be sufficient for this act; and this would be like saying that the mere fact that A is the only cause of B is not enough for A to be the sufficient cause of B (because in some other circumstances A might not cause B). This means that we have to work with the weaker notion of the sufficiency of the motive of duty in overdetermined actions. But on this weaker notion, the relation between the rightness of one's action and the overdetermined motivational structure from which it was done will only be accidental. Such overdetermined acts cannot, therefore, have moral worth.

Imperfect duties

I want to finish this chapter by briefly considering moral worth in relation to actions that fall under imperfect duties. Imperfect duties introduce difficulties because actions that fall under them are not morally required. What is morally required is that we adopt certain maxims,[38] maxims of beneficence and self-improvement. Since the actions that fall under these principles are not required they cannot knowingly be done from duty, for one cannot knowingly do what is *not* morally required, from what one takes to be the normative reasons why it is morally required. But if such actions cannot be done from duty, they cannot have moral worth,[39] for on Kant's view, only actions done from duty can have moral worth.[40] Kant does not draw this conclusion, but what he says in the *Doctrine of Virtue* does commit him to the idea that beneficent actions cannot have moral worth.

The view that beneficent actions cannot have moral worth is not the view Kant held in the *Groundwork*. There he is quite clear that beneficent actions can be morally required and can thus be done from duty; and this seems the more plausible view to hold. Beneficent actions seem to be paradigm cases of morally good acts when they are done from morally good motives, and it seems that Kant can only accommodate this if he maintains that particular beneficent acts are morally required, which is just what he denies in the *Doctrine of Virtue*.

Why, then, should we agree with Kant that token beneficent actions are not morally required? He is committed to this view in the *Doctrine of Virtue* because he there maintains that imperfect duties require us only to adopt certain maxims, or principles.[41] But this simply raises the further question of why we should think that imperfect duties require only this of us. Kant does not explicitly answer this question, but his reason seems to be connected with the idea that there is latitude in relation to imperfect duties, whereas there is none (or at least less[42]) in relation to perfect duties.

But latitude could be accommodated without buying into the view that all we are required to do is adopt the principle of beneficence. One might think that in many situations where we are able to help others, and in which there is no one else around, there is no single specific act that we are required to do; for there will typically be very different ways in which we could help someone. Consider a situation in which I could help A either by Φ-ing or by Ψ-ing, but cannot do both. In such a situation there is no single act that I am required to do such that, if I fail to do it I do wrong. The reason for this seems to be that in this situation we have a categorical requirement with disjunctive content. What I am morally required to do here is either to Φ or Ψ. Consequently, I will have done what I should if I either Φ or Ψ. But although I will have done what I should if I Φ, it is not the case that Φ-ing is here morally required. If it were, then if I Ψ-ed I would have failed to do what I should. But as I have described the situation, if I Ψ I *will* have done what I should. This is because it is neither Φ-ing nor Ψ-ing that is morally required, nor are they both morally required. What is required is that *either* I Φ or I Ψ. We can capture all the latitude we want in this way by adding as disjuncts in the content of the obligation all the options between which we have latitude to choose. Latitude is here accommodated without recourse to the view that we are required only to embrace the principle of beneficence. For if I am required either to Φ or Ψ, I have latitude to choose either to Φ or Ψ.

Why prefer this way of accommodating latitude to Kant's way in the *Doctrine of Virtue*? The main reason for preferring it is that it allows particular beneficent actions to have moral worth even though the specific token action we do is neither morally required, nor believed to be. For I might correctly believe that what I should do in the circumstances is either Φ or Ψ, and Φ from what I take to be the normative reasons why I ought to Φ or Ψ (along with the appropriate secondary motive). Alternatively, since Φ-ing and Ψ-ing are simply determinate ways of helping, I might correctly believe that what I should do in the circumstances is either Φ or Ψ, and Φ from what I take to be the normative reasons why I ought to help. I see no reason why we cannot describe this act as being done solely from duty, even though the act of Φ-ing is not morally required. If this is right, then we can accommodate latitude while at the same time allowing Kant to maintain that beneficent actions can be morally good. For by allowing obligations to have disjunctive content we can allow that token actions that are not morally obligatory can be done from duty, even in the absence of false beliefs about what we should do, or why we should do it.[43]

Of course sometimes it will be the case that there is only one way in which I can help someone. In such cases we cannot claim that what duty requires is a disjunction of actions, and thus cannot accommodate latitude in this way. But I do not think this creates any special problems. For if I am the only one around who can help the other person, and there is only one way I can help, then I would be tempted to say that I have no latitude – that the specific action is morally required, and that if I fail to do it, I have failed to do what I should.

Conclusion

In this chapter I have attempted to defend Kant's claim that only actions done solely from duty can have moral worth. The reason Kant maintains this strong view is because he held that morally good actions acquire their value from the moral worth of the motives from which they are done, and a morally worthy motive is one that is (a) non-accidentally related to the rightness of the actions done from it, when it is right; and (b) subject to the symmetry thesis. If these two constraints are accepted, it will follow that no inclination can constitute a morally good motive, and Kant's controversial view will be vindicated. They not only explain Kant's view but show that although morally good motives and right actions are distinct, the former is, unsurprisingly, not independent of the latter. The converse is, however, not true. Despite the fact that many ascribe to Kant the view that the rightness of a right act is dependent on the goodness of the motive from which it is done, Kant clearly thought that an act could accord with duty without being done from duty, and thus that an act could be right without being morally good. Kant's view that no inclination can have moral worth does not, therefore, stem from his supposed contempt for inclination, but from a principled account of what it is for a motive to be morally good.

7

CONSTRUCTIVISM, AUTONOMY AND SIDE-CONSTRAINTS

Introduction

On the interpretation of Kant I have offered the moral law plays a transcendental and criterial role. In its transcendental role it constitutes the ultimate condition of the possibility of moral obligation. It does not tell us why we ought to act in certain ways, but simply tells us how it is possible that we could be obligated to act in any way whatsoever. Obligation needs explanation because to experience some act as obligatory in some situation is to experience it as practically necessary in that situation. This necessity cannot be explained with reference to any object of the will, or by any causal law, but must be explained by a formal principle of the will itself. This formal principle requires certain intermediate principles so that a specific action can be subsumed under it, but these intermediate principles are also best thought of not as normative reasons why we are morally required to do the relevant action, but solely as conditions of this action being morally required. The moral law does not, therefore, constitute a normative reason why we ought to do certain actions.

In its criterial role the moral law neither tells us what we have to do in a particular set of circumstances, nor why we ought to do that act in those circumstances. All it does is tell us whether our action falls under a maxim which is permissible. But an action can fall under a maxim which is permissible yet not be the one we ought to do in some particular set of circumstances. Acts of honesty fall under a permissible maxim, but in a situation in which I am the only person who could help someone in distress, I will not have done what I should merely by being honest. Furthermore, the categorical imperative does not tell us why we should act in certain ways. It is not the case that I should keep my promise, or help someone because the maxims of these actions can be willed without contradiction. My obligation to keep my promise, or to help someone, is not generated by some fact about my maxim, but by some concrete fact in the nature of the situation, such as the fact that I made a promise, or the fact that someone needs help. It is these concrete facts which are the grounds of particular obligations. What the categorical imperative test does is provide a criterion by which we can assess our moral judgements. By this I mean that it provides us with a reason to believe that our verdictive moral judgements are correct – that is, it gives us a reason to believe that we ought to act in certain ways. It can do this even though it does not give us reason to act in those ways, for the reasons we have for believing that we ought to Φ are far more abundant than the reasons why we ought to Φ, and in its criterial role the moral law provides us only with a reason for believing that we ought to Φ.

Neither the moral law nor the categorical imperative test provide us with reasons to do what we should. But given the symmetry thesis, we need some account of normative moral reasons to fill out the details of Kant's account of moral worth. Yet once the moral law is understood as having a purely transcendental and criterial role, there is nothing left in Kant's theory to tell us why we ought to do certain actions. We thus need some other theory of normative moral reasons to fill the gap in his account of moral worth. In Chapter 5 I suggested that Ross's account of *prima facie* duties can be used to fill this gap. This will not work if *prima facie* duties are thought of as verdictive moral principles, for such principles tell us what, in general, we ought to do, not why we ought to do these acts: but I argued that this is not how Ross understood them. Rather, he thought of them as what I call evidential moral principles, or better, principles of moral salience. These principles do not tell us what we should do, but specify which considerations are salient to determining what it is we should do, and how they are salient. This is just another way of saying that they are principles of normative moral reasons – that is, they are principles specifying which concrete considerations give us moral reason to act. Given that in acting from duty a morally good person will do what (she believes) she should from primary motives which have as their content (what she believes are) the normative reasons why she should do that action, she will be motivated to do what she should at the primary level by the type of concrete considerations specified by these principles.

This understanding of the moral law and moral worth, may seem to many to be incompatible with certain key aspects of Kant's moral theory. In this chapter I defend my account from three such charges. The first is that it is incompatible with Kant's constructivism. The second is that it is incompatible with his account of autonomy; and the third is that it is incompatible with his adherence to absolute side-constraints. I argue that my account is compatible with Kant's constructivism and his belief that morality and autonomy reciprocally imply each other – what I shall call, following Allison,[1] the 'reciprocity thesis'. In response to the third criticism I argue that although Ross's theory of *prima facie* duties could be modified to accommodate Kant's adherence to absolute side-constraints, Kant's account of moral worth is much more plausible if stringency is maintained without absolute side-constraints.

Kant's constructivism

The account of moral worth that I have offered may seem to be incompatible with the constructivist reading of Kant. According to constructivism, the only relevant moral facts are those pertaining to the procedure of construction.[2] Among the morally relevant facts are normative moral reasons, but on my account Kant's constructive procedure (the moral law in its criterial role) is not a normative moral reason at all. Such reasons are given, not by the categorical imperative procedure, but by concrete particular facts in the nature of the situation. Many will claim that this account of normative reasons works within a realist framework which is alien to Kant's constructivism.

One way to deal with this problem would simply be to reject the constructivist reading of Kant. But this response is too simple. There is clearly something in Kant's moral theory that makes a constructivist interpretation extremely plausible. Consequently, it would be inadequate simply to say that the constructivists are mistaken in their appropriation of Kant, because their interpretation does not fit with my reading of Kant's account of moral worth. What is needed, therefore, is first to specify the different ways in which Kant's constructivism may be understood, and second, to see whether my account is compatible with any of these.

As we shall see, whether my interpretation and emendation of Kant's account of moral worth is compatible with his constructivism will depend on how constructivism is understood. How, then, might Kant's constructivism be understood? I shall answer this question by considering how constructivism in general may be understood, and then in the light of this turn to Kant's constructive procedure. Unfortunately, constructivists do not distinguish the various ways in which their doctrine can be understood. It is, however, important for my purposes to do this. In distinguishing the different ways in which constructivism may be understood I do not intend simply to list the various forms of constructivism that are about, but to try to pick out what is common to them all, and, more importantly, consider the various ways in which this core element of the doctrine can be understood.

Central to the constructivist project is the attempt to steer a path between various forms of relativism and subjectivism, on the one hand, and moral realism, on the other. The central aim is, therefore, to retain objectivity in ethics without recourse to moral realism.[3] Essentially, constructivism is the view that the moral principles determining what we should do are established by means of what it is reasonable to choose, and that what it is reasonable to choose is what we would choose if we were to carry out a certain procedure. Different constructivists offer different procedures,[4] but what makes them constructivists is that answers to practical questions are to be determined in some way by a distinctive constructive procedure.

One issue constructivists should be clear on is the nature of their claim that the basic principles of ethics, or justice, are determined by what would be chosen, or agreed, by agents carrying out the relevant procedure. They may be understood as claiming that for a principle to be correct and for it to be constructed by means of the relevant procedure are one and the same thing. According to this understanding of constructivism, the fact that we ought to adopt some set of principles is identical with the fact that they would be chosen by agents carrying out the appropriate procedure. Let us call this 'reductive constructivism'. Reductive constructivists may be either analytic or non-analytic. If they are analytic reductivists then they will be claiming that what we *mean* when we say that we ought to do some act, or adopt some principle, is that this act or principle would be chosen by agents carrying out the relevant procedure. Non-analytic reductive constructivists deny that this is what we mean when we say that we ought to act in a certain way, or adopt a certain principle, but nonetheless insist that the property of being a principle that we ought to adopt, and that of being a principle we would choose if we carried out the relevant procedure are one and the same.

Constructivists need not be reductive, however. They may leave aside the question of what it is for a practical principle to be required, or legitimate, and claim only that we ought to act in accordance with these principles *because* they would be chosen by agents carrying out a certain procedure. Let us call this 'justificatory constructivism' for now. Here the constructive procedure is not understood as telling us what it is for us to be required to act in certain ways, but as telling us why we should act in those ways.

Justificatory constructivism can take two forms. It may be understood as expressing the view that the constructive procedure gives us a *reason to act* in certain ways or adopt certain principles, or as giving us a *reason to believe* that we ought to act in certain ways, or adopt certain principles. Since this distinction is simply the application of the distinction made in Chapter 4 between the justificatory and the criterial conception of the categorical imperative test, I shall henceforth reserve the term 'justificatory constructivism' for the view that the constructive procedure gives us a reason to act in certain ways, and use the term 'criterial constructivism' for the view that the constructive procedure gives us a reason to believe that we ought to act in certain ways.

The sorts of claim many constructivists make frequently make them look like reductive constructivists.[5] But this form of constructivism is not, I believe, the best form the theory can take. As an analytical claim, reductive constructivism is deeply implausible. The claim that we ought to adopt certain principles, because, say, they would be chosen by agents in the original position, may be true, but if it is true, it is an important and substantive truth, not an analytical one. Of course, analytical truths need not be obvious at first sight, but that is not the point. If this is what we mean when we say that someone ought to adopt a certain principle, then once the analysis has been put forward we should recognise it for what it is. This may require careful reflection, but I think it is highly improbable that those who deny that this is what they mean have all failed to reflect carefully enough on what they believe when they believe that some act ought to be done. The cause of their disagreement is not a failure to understand what it is they are saying, but a disagreement about the nature of some property, the justification of claims about principles we ought to adopt, or about whether the constructive procedure at issue is a reliable criterion of moral judgement.

Non-analytical reductive constructivism is not vulnerable to the above criticisms, for it does not involve a claim about what we mean, but about the nature of the world, about the nature of the property of being a principle that ought to be adopted. But although this form of constructivism is better than the analytical variety in this respect, it does not fit well with other distinctive aspects of constructivism. For one of the things constructivists want to avoid is the sort of meta-ethical issues that would be constitutive of this form of constructivism.[6] Furthermore, constructivists see themselves as offering a position which is distinct from moral realism and relativism. Yet reductive non-analytical constructivism fails to do this, as it is a form of moral realism.[7] If constructivism turns out to be a form of moral realism, therefore, it would lose much of what is distinctive of it.

Given these difficulties with reductive constructivism, it seems that the best form of constructivism is either justificatory or criterial. Indeed, these forms of constructivism seem appropriate to constructivists' concern with justification, especially with justification to others.[8] One of the things constructivists dislike about realism and relativism in ethics is that these views limit the authority of moral verdicts.[9] Authority is limited within relativism because the verdicts will be valid only if certain contingent facts hold. These facts may be social or personal. They may be a shared tradition, religion, culture, desire, or concern. The point is that the moral verdicts generated within these contingent frameworks will be recognised as valid only for those who share the tradition, religion, concern, etc. If I do not share in some religion, then the fact that its sacred text prescribes a certain course of action will not be regarded by me as a reason to perform that action. If I do not live in a liberal society and share liberal values, the fact that some act is illiberal may not be seen by me as a reason not to do it.

The moral realist is no better off than the relativist in this respect, according to constructivists. For if someone does not 'see' the property some act has of being wrong, then appeal to this property in no way helps them to see that they have reason not to do it.[10] Indeed, if a certain sort of upbringing is necessary to be sensitive to this property, and one has not had that sort of upbringing, one may be unable to detect it. But if the constructivist procedure is merely formal – that is, makes no reference to traditions, faiths, or moral properties – then the justification it offers will not be restricted in its scope in the way that relativist and realist justifications are.[11] This is because it makes no reference to particular desires, properties, or traditions.

The best form of constructivism is, therefore, either justificatory or criterial constructivism. Consequently, if Kant is to be seen as a constructivist, he should be understood in accordance with one of these two forms of constructivism. To understand his ethics as a form of justificatory constructivism is to see the categorical imperative as a procedure which provides us with normative moral reasons why we ought to act in accordance with certain more specific moral principles. According to this view, the categorical imperative test tells us why we ought to act in accordance with principles of fidelity, beneficence, self-improvement, gratitude, and so on.

If we regard Kant's ethics as a form of criterial constructivism, then the categorical imperative test will be thought of as a procedure by means of which we can check our verdictive moral judgements. If the principle which the action falls under can be willed as a universal law without contradiction, then that gives us reason to believe that our judgement that we ought to do that act is correct. If the principle which the action falls under cannot be willed as a universal law without contradiction, then this gives us reason to believe that our judgement that we should not do that act is correct.

Does my account of Kant's ethics allow for either form of constructivism? Since I have rejected the justificatory conception of the moral law my interpretation is incompatible with the view that Kant is this sort of constructivist. For on my understanding of Kant, the categorical imperative does not tell us why we ought to act in certain ways, and this clearly contradicts the justificatory constructivist reading of Kant. But since I maintain that the moral law can act as a criterion of moral judgement, my account is quite compatible with a criterial constructivist reading of Kant. Indeed, my account is a criterial constructivist account. This form of constructivism allows us to capture everything constructivists wish to say about Kant's moral philosophy so long as it is construed solely in terms of reasons for believing that we ought, or ought not to Φ, rather than as providing us with reasons why we ought, or ought not to Φ. Once we have distinguished these different forms of constructivism we can see that my interpretation of Kant's theory of moral worth does not mean that we have to jettison a constructivist reading of Kant. All that must be jettisoned are certain forms of constructivism. But it cannot be a constraint on interpretation and modification of Kant's moral theory that it be compatible with all forms of constructivism.

But although I do not have to jettison Kant's constructivism, I have to concede that as I understand his account of moral worth the constructivist aspect of his view loses its centrality. As I pointed out at the end of Chapter 4, use of the categorical imperative test has no essential role to play in morally good action, or a morally good character, for Kant. It is a useful, but ultimately dispensable tool for the reflective moral agent. Thus, although it would be good if it could be got to work, if it did not it would not be as devastating to Kant's account of moral worth as many have thought. This is not to say that the moral law does not play an essential role in morality. For in its transcendental role this principle underpins the very possibility of morality, and hence of moral worth. But this (transcendental) understanding of the moral law is not a distinctively constructivist understanding.

Does the fact that my reading of Kant's account of moral worth means that his constructivism is a useful, but not the distinctive aspect of his account, cast doubt on my interpretation? I do not think it does. Kant is often seen as concerned primarily with the attempt to refute various forms of scepticism. In the first *Critique* he is seen as arguing primarily against those who deny that we can have knowledge of the external world, and in the *Groundwork* and the second *Critique* as arguing against the moral sceptic who asks for a reason to do what morality requires. Now it would be wrong to claim that Kant was completely unconcerned with addressing these sceptics in the first and second *Critiques*. But I think it is equally wrong to regard this concern as his central aim in his critical work. In the first *Critique* Kant's main concern was not with providing us with reasons for believing in causality and the external world, but with showing how such knowledge is possible; and in the *Groundwork* and the second *Critique* his prime concern was not with providing everyone with reasons for doing what they should – as if they somehow previously lacked such reasons[12] – but with showing how morality is possible. What is distinctive about Kant in these fields was not the justification of certain important beliefs we have but with showing how it is *possible* for those beliefs to be true. His prime concern was not with justification, but with a transcendental grounding of knowledge and morality. It is this that is distinctive and new in Kant. He does not simply provide us with new answers to the old question: 'How can we have objective knowledge?', or 'Why should we be moral?', but introduces a new question – 'How is objective knowledge possible?', 'How is morality possible?' It is the answers to these new questions, not to the tired old sceptical questions, that are distinctive of Kant's philosophy, and it is this distinctive approach that I have tried to capture with the transcendental conception of the moral law.

His answers to these questions do have implications for sceptical worries. To begin with, if we can have objective knowledge, and morality is possible, then the sceptic cannot maintain the strong thesis that we *cannot* have objective knowledge, or that morality *cannot* be unconditionally binding on us. In epistemology the sceptic would be pushed to the much weaker claim that we *might* not have objective knowledge, but then his worries would have lost a lot of their urgency, and importance. Similarly, if morality can be unconditionally binding, all the sceptic can say is that for all we know it might not be unconditionally binding. But once again, this worry will have lost most of its bite.

This is not to say that Kant was unconcerned with justification; he was not. All I am claiming is that this is not central to his philosophy. What is central is showing that objective knowledge and morality are possible. If this is right, then what is important to his ethical theory is the moral law in its transcendental role. The moral law in its criterial role may be a useful constructive tool for testing our own and others' moral verdicts, but it is not, I think, central to Kant's account of moral worth.

Autonomy

A second objection that might be raised against my account of Kant's theory of moral worth relates to the connection between morality and autonomy in Kant. This worry relates to my rejection of the justificatory conception of the moral law, and to the alternative account of normative reasons I use to fill the gap left by this treatment of the moral law in Kant's account of moral worth. For it may be argued that it is only if the moral law is the ground of duty that the will will be bound only by its own principle when we do what we should. This is because it would be this principle that makes obligatory acts practically necessary – that is, binding on the will. If, on the other hand, it is certain concrete facts in the nature of the situation which ultimately (in the justificatory sense of 'ultimately') make actions obligatory, then the will will be bound not by its own principle, but by facts about the external world. If the will is bound only by its own principle, then it is autonomous. If it is bound by facts about the external world, then it is constrained by something external, and is thus heteronomous. Since I want to say that the normative moral reasons why we ought to act in certain ways are concrete facts about the world, rather than the moral law, it seems that my revised account of Kant's theory of moral worth is incompatible with his view about the relation of morality and autonomy.

It will help in addressing this issue to specify what it is for one to act autonomously, as Kant understands it, and to distinguish this from spontaneous (negatively free) action.[13] It is also useful to note to what these distinct notions of freedom are contrasted. For once we get clear about Kant's conception of autonomous action we will be able to see that we do not need the justificatory conception of the moral law to capture the reciprocity thesis. All we need is the transcendental conception. How, then, does Kant understand sponaneity and autonomy?

Spontaneity is the property the will has of 'being able to work independently of *determination* by alien causes'.[14] This is only possible if the various incentives do not cause (determine) us to act, but can lead to action only by being incorporated into our maxim, or subjective principle of action. Since we do not merely *have* maxims, but *make* certain considerations our maxim,[15] spontaneity is the capacity to determine oneself to act on the basis of *self-imposed* principles. This means that certain considerations can lead to action only by being recognised as providing good reason to act, and to think of these considerations as providing good reason is to subsume them under freely chosen maxims. To say that maxims are freely chosen is not to say that they are adopted randomly. It is, rather, to deny that we are caused to adopt them by our character traits, dispositions, or environment, and to maintain that we adopt them because we think they are legitimate. To think of ourselves as negatively free is thus to think of ourselves as subject, not to the natural order of causes, but to the normative order of reasons. To think of ourselves as negatively unfree is to regard ourselves as subject only to the natural causal order.

Autonomy, or positive freedom, is 'the property the will has of being a law to itself (independently of every property belonging to objects of volition)',[16] and is contrasted to heteronomy where this is understood as the object of volition giving the will the law in virtue of its relation to the will.[17] But what does it mean for the will to be a law to itself? The most natural way of understanding this is as the capacity the will has to act on the basis of self-imposed principles. But this cannot be right, for then the concept of autonomy would not be distinct from that of spontaneity. Kant must, therefore, understand this sense of being a law to itself in a more restricted way. According to this more restricted sense, the will is a law to itself if it acts not only on the basis of self-imposed principles (spontaneity), but on the basis of self-imposed principles that are 'independent of every property belonging to the object of volition'.[18] This means that we exercise our autonomy only when the good reasons we recognise are not based on some desire or need we have. If we treat some consideration as giving us a reason to act because it will satisfy some desire, we will be exercising our spontaneity (we will not be caused to act in this way by this desire), but will not be exercising out autonomy. We will not be exercising our autonomy even though we will have acted on the basis of a self-imposed principle, because this consideration is regarded as reason-giving only in so far as it can be related to an object of volition. The self-imposed law in accordance with which we act is not, therefore, independent of every property belonging to the object of volition, and thus the will will not be a law to itself in the specified sense.

Since considerations do not acquire their status as reasons from the object, or material, of the agent's maxim when the agent exercises her autonomy, they can only acquire their reason-giving force from the lawlike form of the agent's maxim, according to Kant. He thus identifies the will's being a law to itself with 'the principle of acting on no maxim other than one which can have for its object itself as at the same time a universal law', which is just the formula of universal law. It is for this reason that Kant maintains that acting morally and acting autonomously are one and the same thing.[19]

Many have found the argument for this identification unpersuasive. My aim here is not to respond to Kant's critics by defending his claim that acting morally and acting autonomously are one and the same, or at least reciprocally imply each other. For whether or not Kant has a good argument for this identification, what is clear is that the reciprocity thesis is central to his moral theory. What I aim to do here is show that my understanding and emendation of his account of moral worth are compatible with this crucial aspect of his moral theory.

The cause of the problem is my claim that the moral law should be understood according to the transcendental, but not the justificatory conception. The lawlike nature of the principle under which some action falls does not give me a normative reason to do that act, but is a condition of the possibility of some consideration being a *moral* reason – that is, of its being able to generate a *categorical* imperative. The reasons why we ought to act in certain ways are given by concrete considerations in the nature of the situation, such as the fact that someone needs help, or the fact that I have made a promise. Because these considerations are the normative reasons why we ought to act, they will be the (primary) motivating reasons of moral agents, for the symmetry thesis states that (under favourable conditions) morally good agents will do what they should from the moral reasons why they should do that act.

Does this mean that morally good agents will act heteronomously, as Kant understands this? I do not see how it does. For to act heteronomously, for Kant, is for the agent to treat considerations as reasons only if they can be connected up with some desire or need the agent happens to have. But nothing I have said about normative moral reasons, and moral motivation suggests that. My view is that what motivates good people, what they regard as a good reason for action, is not their inclination to do this or that, but things like the needs of others, and the promises they have made. Furthermore, these concrete considerations are not regarded as reasons because they satisfy some contingent desire or need, but because they are subsumed under principles of moral salience, which in turn are subsumed under the moral law. Certain concrete considerations are regarded as having a special reason-giving force – can only be regarded as having such reason-giving force – because they are subsumed by the agent under the moral law. The 'because' here is not a justificatory 'because', but a transcendental one, but that doesn't make any difference in relation to whether one's action is heteronomous or not. All that is essential is whether the considerations that are regarded as reason-giving are so regarded only because they are related in some way to contingent desires of the agent. Since my account of moral worth does not imply this, it does not constitute a heteronomous account of moral worth – something Kant would regard as an oxymoron.

Nonetheless, the worry may remain that my account does not seem to constitute an autonomous account of moral worth either. For although my account means that a good person will not appeal to any contingent desire or need she happens to have in justifying her action, she will also not appeal to the moral law, or categorical imperative. This is because the moral law does not function as a normative moral reason on my reading of Kant's account of moral worth. Yet if Kant's claim that acting autonomously is one and the same thing as acting morally is to be maintained, it seems that the moral law must act as the ultimate justification of a good person's action. If no desire or need can provide the ultimate reason for autonomous action, the question arises of what can provide the required ultimate reason; and Kant's answer seems to be 'the moral law'. It is for this reason that he thinks that morality and autonomy are the same. But if the moral law is the ultimate reason for doing what we should, then, given the symmetry thesis, it would be one of the primary motives of a good agent – which I have denied.

But given what I have said above, it would be odd if my account of moral worth in Kant were not one which is compatible with his theory of autonomy. For it would mean that someone who acted from duty as I understand this would be acting neither heteronomously (because the considerations that motivate them are not regarded as reasons simply because they further some desire the agent has) nor autonomously. This would suggest that Kant's conception of heteronomy, autonomy, or both was too limited, or that there is some third option. I do not, however, think we have to regard Kant's account of autonomy and heteronomy as overly restricted in this way. What is important in regard to autonomy as Kant understands it is that the reason-giving force certain considerations are regarded as having stem not from some contingent desire or need, but from the moral law. Another way of putting this is that normativity should stem from the moral law rather than some desire or need. It is tempting to think that we must trace the source of the normativity some consideration is regarded as having by looking for further justificatory reasons. But normativity need not be traced back along this route. It can be traced back along a transcendental rather than a justificatory route, and, as we have seen, these routes need not cover the same territory. If the sort of concrete considerations which I claim will motivate good people can only acquire the distinctive normative force they are regarded as having when they are regarded as giving rise to a moral obligation by being subsumed under absolutely universal principles of moral salience (*prima facie* duties) which in turn must be subsumed under the moral law, then the distinctive form of normativity these considerations possess will ultimately stem from the moral law, even though the moral law is not the ultimate reason why we ought to do the relevant act. The authority these considerations are regarded as having when they figure in morally good motives must be traced back to the moral law. Since actions are autonomous if and only if the normative force of the reasons from which they are done can be traced back to the moral law, then in so far as one acts from duty as I understand it one can be understood as acting autonomously. What makes it look otherwise is the thought that the reason-giving status of some consideration can only be traced back to the moral law along a series of more and more abstract justificatory reasons. Once we abandon this view, and recognise that reason-giving status can be traced along a series of transcendental conditions, we can see that the fact that the moral law functions as a transcendental condition, but not as a justificatory reason why we ought to act in certain ways, is quite compatible with Kant's reciprocity thesis.

Absolute side-constraints

The third objection to my account of Kant and moral worth focuses on the use of Ross's theory of *prima facie* duties to fill the hole in Kant's account of moral worth left by the rejection of the justificatory conception of the moral law. One of the distinctive aspects of Kant's moral theory is the inclusion of absolute side-constraints. He clearly held that certain ways of promoting good outcomes are always ruled out. If, for example, we could only help someone by telling a lie then we cannot help.[20] But Ross's theory of *prima facie* duties leaves no room for the idea of absolute side-constraints. According to this theory, *any* consideration can override any other. So considerations of beneficence can override considerations of fidelity, or truthfulness. In this respect, then, Ross's theory seems incompatible with Kant's views, and thus, it may be argued, cannot be used to supplement Kant's account of moral worth.

The first thing to say in response to this objection is that, although Ross thought that considerations falling under one principle could be overridden by considerations falling under any other, he did not think that all moral considerations were equally weighty. For example, he clearly thought that the principles of non-maleficence,[21] fidelity,[22] and gratitude[23] are more stringent than that of beneficence. Given that this stringency does not mean that considerations of fidelity will always beat those of beneficence, it is difficult to spell out what being more stringent means here. We can talk of considerations of fidelity as being *weightier* than those of beneficence, but it is hard to unpack this metaphor. We can, however, at least say that if considerations of fidelity are weightier than those of beneficence, then the practical reason our promise gives us cannot be overridden by the fact that breaking it would enable us to make another person very slightly better off than she otherwise would have been. The benefits to others must be considerable before these considerations can override that of fidelity, although I doubt that we can spell out how considerable they have to be in any useful way. All we can say is that considerations of fidelity, non-maleficence and gratitude give us stronger, or more compelling moral reasons than those of beneficence, although they are not so strong, or compelling that they always win out in a conflict with beneficence. There is, then, a hierarchy of stringency built into Ross's theory of *prima facie* duties.

But the fact that this theory allows certain considerations to be weightier than others still falls short of Kant's view that certain considerations always win out when they conflict with others. Kant not only thought that considerations of truthfulness were more stringent than those of beneficence simply in the sense that the former considerations carry more normative weight than the latter. He also thought that they are more stringent in the sense that they always win out in a conflict.[24] It is this that Ross's theory of *prima facie* duties seems unable to accommodate. But although Ross did not believe in absolute side-constraints, there is nothing about the theory of *prima facie* duties which stops considerations being stringent in the strong sense that they are *essentially* overriding. I do not see why one could not hold that *prima facie* duties of fidelity are such that they always override those of beneficence when they conflict. If this is right, then we could simply modify Ross's theory of *prima facie* duties to fit in with Kant's adherence to absolute side-constraints.

It may be thought that in doing this we no longer have a theory of *prima facie* duties, that what is distinctive of this theory is that no one principle could be said always to override any other, and thus that any principle is overridable by any other. As I have noted, this was certainly part of Ross's theory of *prima facie* duties, but I do not think it is essential to the theory as such. What is distinctive of the theory as such is that it constitutes principles not of verdictive moral considerations, but of evidential moral considerations. The principles do not tell us what we ought or ought not to do, but what is salient to determining what we should or should not do – that is, they constitute a theory of normative moral reasons. On this view what is salient to determining what we should do is not certain principles stating that we should do acts of the relevant type – that would be uninformative – but concrete considerations that fall under the principles of salience. What is salient is the fact that I made a promise, or that I could make someone better off, or repay a service, etc. These concrete facts would not give us moral reasons unless they fell under principles of moral salience, but these principles do not give us further reasons to act in certain ways. Rather, like the moral law, they function as transcendental conditions of these concrete facts being moral reasons for us. If a theory of *prima facie* duties is understood in this way – as a theory of principles of normative moral reasons rather than principles of verdictive moral considerations – then this theory is compatible with the view that some concrete considerations are such that they always win out in a moral conflict. If this is correct, then we can capture Kant's absolutism within the theory of *prima facie* duties which is being used to supplement his theory of moral worth.

But although we can accommodate Kant's adherence to absolute side-constraints within a theory of *prima facie* duties, I do not think we should. I, like many others, think that at least some absolute side-constraints, such as truthfulness,[25] are deeply implausible. There are few things of which we are certain in ethics, but barring exceptional circumstances, I think we can be sure that Kant was mistaken in believing that it would be wrong to lie to a murderer who asks about the whereabouts of his intended victim.

But not all side-constraints are as implausible as this. One might think that although it is sometimes right to lie, it is never right to kill innocent people. Of course defenders of this side-constraint would have to specify what is to count as being innocent, but even if this is done, I think that this side-constraint would remain implausible if we think of it as absolute – that is, as unoverridable. Certainly, the life of an innocent is among the most weighty of moral considerations, and in all but the most extreme situations it will be wrong to take an innocent's life, even if it is the only way of producing some great good. But those who believe that this consideration constitutes an absolute side-constraint go further and claim that nothing whatsoever *could* be such as to make it the case that we ought to take the life of an innocent. It is this that I think is implausible. I think that, after reflection, most of us would agree that there is some possible set of circumstances in which the good that can be obtained only by killing an innocent person, or the evil to be avoided, is so great that it could outweigh the reason against this act introduced by the value of the innocent person's life. We may disagree about what would be sufficient to outweigh this serious moral consideration, but most would, I think, agree that at some point considerations on the other side could be such as to make killing the right thing to do, especially if the person to be killed heroically agreed that we should do this and asked us to do it.

This is not, of course, to say that if we ought to kill an innocent there is nothing about which we should feel compunction. But we should not feel compunction because we have done wrong, but because we recognise that the overridden consideration does not stop being a very weighty moral consideration even when it has been overridden. Being overridden is not being annihilated, but simply outweighed, and something does not lose the moral weight it has simply because there is something weightier on the other side of the moral scales.[26]

The idea that it is always wrong to kill an innocent person is not only implausible, it is not supported by either the formula of universal law or the formula of the end in itself. If I wanted to test my judgement that it is sometimes right to kill an innocent person to save many other innocent people, I could ask myself whether my maxim could be willed as a universal law without contradiction. A possible world in which everyone has the maxim of killing an innocent person to save many others is quite conceivable. It need not be a world in which everyone goes around killing innocents, for there may not be many situations in which this maxim would be relevant. If this possible world is just like the actual one apart from the fact that everyone has this maxim, then the vast majority of us would *never* be in a situation relevant to this maxim.

Do we transgress the requirement never to treat others merely as a means when we kill an innocent to save the lives of others? To treat someone in this way is certainly to treat them as a means, namely, as a means of saving the lives of others, but the issue is not whether we treat someone as a means to an end, but whether we treat them solely in this way. What, then, does it mean to treat someone merely as a means? One way is to treat them in ways to which they could not consent.[27] If we coerce or deceive someone we treat them in ways to which they could not consent, and thus treat them merely as a means. But do we treat them in this way if we kill them to save other innocent lives? I do not see that we do. For although someone might not agree to being killed for the sake of the greater good, this is something they could agree to, and is thus an end they *could* share. The idea that we should never treat others as mere means does not proscribe killing innocent people for the sake of some greater good, and thus does not support this absolute side-constraint. It does support the view that coercion and deception are always wrong, but there is, I believe, very little plausibility to the view that coercion and deception are always wrong. The fact that my act is one of coercion, or deception, certainly gives me reason not to do it, and this may be because these are ways of treating others as mere means. What cannot plausibly be maintained, however, is that we can know *a priori* that the reasons against doing the action these considerations give us are such that they must override any other feature of our action that gives us reason to do it.

My view is then that rather than modify Ross's theory of *prima facie* duties to make room for Kant's adherence to absolute side-constraints, we should abandon Kant's adherence to this doctrine. The task would then be to show that the categorical imperative test does not generate absolute side-constraints – that although Kant believed in absolute side-constraints, there is nothing in his theory that commits him to them. There are many who have attempted this with varying degrees of success.[28] My view is that whether or not this strategy can be made to work, it is the strategy that we should adopt.

It should be noted that the abandonment of absolute side-constraints in no way turns Kant into a consequentialist.[29] Consequentialists maintain that the right act is always the one that produces the most good. One does not need to have recourse to absolute side-constraints in order to deny this. All one needs is (a) the view that good outcomes are not the only consideration that are salient to determining what is and is not morally right, and are thus not the only things that can make actions right; and (b) the view that certain considerations, such as those of fidelity and truthfulness, are not automatically overridden by the fact that one could bring about a small increase in overall well-being by breaking one's promise, or by lying. I want to abandon the doctrine of absolute side-constraints, but do not reject (a) or (b). My account of moral worth in Kant does not, therefore, turn Kant into a consequentialist. It allows for the view that considerations of fidelity and truthfulness are *intrinsically* reason-giving – that is, reason-giving independently of their standing in some causal relation to a good outcome – and allows that these considerations are more stringent than than those of beneficence. All I have rejected is the extreme view that it is always wrong to lie, or break a promise, or even to kill, no matter what the circumstances.

Summary

In this chapter I have argued that once we keep certain distinctions in mind, primarily, between practical reasons (why we ought to Φ) and epistemic reasons (for believing that we ought to Φ), and between the transcendental and the justificatory conception of the moral law, we can see that the way in which I understand and develop Kant's theory of moral worth is compatible with other key aspects of his moral theory.

It is compatible with his constructivism if this is understood as what I call 'criterial constructivism'; for although the categorical imperative test is not understood as giving us a reason to do certain actions, it can give us reason to believe that we ought to do certain acts, and thus can provide a constructive procedure for checking, or rejecting our moral verdicts.

I have argued that my understanding of moral worth is compatible with Kant's view that there is a reciprocal relation between morality and autonomy. Morally good actions as I understand them are not heteronomous, because in morally good action the agent does not regard certain concrete considerations as reason-giving simply on the condition that they are instrumental to the satisfaction of some contingent desire, or need. Moral action is autonomous action if and only if the will gives the law to itself, and the will gives the law to itself if and only if the normative force of its reasons can be traced back to the principle of the will – the purely formal moral law. Once we recognise that this 'tracing back' need not move along a series of more and more fundamental normative reasons, but may move along a series of more and more fundamental transcendental conditions, the fact that the moral law is not the ultimate reason why we ought to act in certain ways does not mean that we have to abandon the reciprocal connection between morality and autonomy in Kant.

Finally, I have tried to develop Kant's account of moral worth by utilising Ross's theory of *prima facie* duties understood as a theory of normative reasons. But this has meant that we have to abandon Kant's adherence to absolute side-constraints. I have argued that the best way to deal with this problem is to attempt to show that the categorical imperative test does not generate such constraints, and thus allow his general normative theory to be more context sensitive, while retaining the idea that certain considerations carry more normative weight than others.

8

CONCLUSION

Absolutely universal principles and context sensitivity

Introduction

What I have been keen to do in the account of moral worth I have outlined is to find an essential role for strictly universal moral principles without committing myself to the view that these principles must figure, explicitly or implicity, in the moral deliberation of good agents. In this way I wanted to accommodate the idea that good agent's are responsive to concrete particular considerations such as the fact that someone is in need, or in distress, or the fact that I have made a promise, without mediating thoughts about principles, while also insisting that strictly universal principles have a necessary role in morality. The Kantian assumption that the motivating reasons why good people do what they should will be identical with the normative reasons why they should do those actions allows us to do this if we assume that certain concrete considerations constitute the ultimate ground of particular duties. But we have to reject the justificatory conception of the moral law and adopt something like Ross's theory of *prima facie* duties, understood as a theory of normative moral reasons – that is, as principles which specify which concrete, particular considerations are normative moral reasons. Rather than think of the moral law according to the justificatory conception, we should think of it and the *prima facie* principles that fall under it as transcendental conditions of an action being obligatory. Without subsuming some action under these strictly universal principles we could not experience an action as necessary in some set of circumstances, for it is only by subsuming the action under such principles that such an experience is possible. The moral law and principles of *prima facie* duty thus function in a way that is analogous to the category of causality and particular natural laws in Kant. These moral principles are not themselves moral reasons why we should act in certain ways, but are necessary conditions of *something else* – some concrete consideration – being a moral reason why we should act in some way. Such principles thus have an essential role in morality, but do not figure as motivating thoughts in morally good actions, for they do not have a justificatory role. The content of the motivating thoughts of good agents will be either the normative reasons why the obligatory action ought to be done, or what the agent believes are the normative reasons why she should act.

Saving the moral phenomenology

This account of the role of the moral law seems to me not only to present us with a better account of morally worthy actions, but also presents us with a phenomenologically more plausible account of the role of the moral law than the alternative justificatory conception. Nobody deliberates from anything like the moral law to particular moral laws and then to some specific moral verdict in their everyday deliberation. In concrete situations, say, where someone is in need and I can help him, or where I have made a promise, or where I could show gratitude, I neither need, nor typically do deliberate from the moral law to the particular moral verdict that I ought to help, or keep my promise, or show gratitude. Indeed, the specific verdicts I reach in such situations seem often to be based solely on particular concrete facts, such as the fact that someone needs help, or the fact that I have made a promise, or that someone has benefited me in some way.

In response to this Kantians tend to maintain that although we do not have self-conscious thoughts about the moral law, when we deliberate, such thoughts nonetheless must figure as *implicit* premises in our reasoning. But this response raises the question of why these premises are so self-effacing; and a phenomenologically plausible answer is that this is because they are not playing this sort of role. The transcendental conception of the moral law allows us to do this, and thus allows things to be the way they typically appear to be.

This seems to me to be the way Kantians should respond to the charge that their moral theory is abstract. Often this charge is based simply on confusion or highly suspect assumptions.[1] But there is, I think, something behind this type of objection, and it is something like the thought that there is something artificial about the way in which the Kantian typically portrays moral deliberation – that is, in accordance with the justificatory conception of the moral law. This justificatory account of the role of such moral principles is artificial because none of us deliberates like this, or at best do not think that we do, and *we cannot get ourselves to believe that we should*. Kantians typically respond to this dismissively, maintaining that the phenomenology, or common sense, has no authority against what can be known by pure reason. This sort of dismissal of our ordinary, everyday understanding is a persistent temptation in philosophy which can be traced back to Plato's image of the cave. To give in to this temptation is, furthermore, a persistent and serious philosophical vice. This temptation is, therefore, to be resisted. What makes Kantians succumb to it is, I would suggest, a failure to distinguish the justificatory from the transcendental conception of the moral law and moral principles. If they had recognised this distinction, they would recognise that a perfectly legitimate, and distinctively Kantian, response to the charge of abstraction is to abandon the justificatory conception of the moral law and moral principles and embrace the transcendental conception. Since on this picture the moral law and moral laws do not play the role of normative moral reasons, they can let this space in their moral theory be filled by the sort of concrete considerations we ordinarily and quite naturally think of as filling it. The transcendental conception of the moral law thus means that Kantians do not need to insist that although the moral law and moral principles generally do not seem to figure in our moral deliberation they really do. They can allow things to be just the way they appear to be in this respect – and this is a good thing.

The transcendental conception of the moral law and particularism

A second advantage of the transcendental over the justificatory conception of moral principles is that this conception enables the Kantian to defend the idea that principles have an *essential* role to play in moral theory. Particularists deny this. According to particularists moral principles neither play nor need to play any significant role in our moral thinking. All that is needed, they maintain, are particular considerations in particular concrete situations. It is these particular considerations rather than moral principles that give us moral reasons to act in certain ways. Furthermore, they maintain that there is no lawlike connection between properties, such as the property of helping someone in distress, or of promoting well-being, on the one hand, and thin moral or normative properties, such as the property of being good, required, or a reason to act, on the other. What this means is that we cannot conclude that because some property is good, or reason-giving in one situation, that it will be good or reason-giving every time it is instantiated.

Those who wish to defend moral principles tend to take issue with particularists on these two points. They tend to argue that moral principles do play an important role in our deliberation, albeit for the most part implicitly, and they defend the idea that there are certain principled relations between natural and moral properties. We have seen that if we think of moral principles as having a transcendental role, rather than a justificatory one, we can concede to the particularist that the moral law plays no significant role in moral deliberation, and even that when it does figure in our deliberation, it may distort it – making us less sensitive to context and competing considerations. We can concede this because we think of moral principles as having a transcendental rather than a justificatory role in morality. This leaves the principled ethicist having to battle it out with the particularist on the particular moral principles they deny.

But this is a rather unsatisfactory way of engaging with particularism, for the best form of particularism does not argue merely by means of counter-examples to particular moral principles to the view that there are none.[2] Rather, the best form of particularism has a principled objection to the very possibility of moral principles – namely, Moore's doctrine of organic wholes. If this doctrine is correct, as some particularists maintain, then there cannot be a principled relation between certain natural and moral properties; or at least, if there is, it can only be by some sort of world historical chance. For according to this doctrine, the value an instance of some property will have, or whether it will have any value at all, will depend on which other properties are instantiated with it. In some cases the part may make the whole better, in other cases worse, in yet others it will make no evaluative contribution at all. Its value-conferring nature will be dependent on the other properties of the whole of which it is a part. This holism means that there can be no principled connection between instances of natural properties and instances of moral properties.

Moore would deny that his doctrine has this implication. He held that one could embrace holism about value as well as principled relations between instances of certain natural and evaluative properties, by distinguishing intrinsic from contributive value.[3] For Moore, intrinsic value is a non-relational form of value that is determined wholly by the non-evaluative intrinsic nature of the intrinsically good thing. Contributive value, on the other hand, is a relational form of value. It is the value that some part confers on the whole of which it is a part. For something to have contributive value is for it to stand in a 'better-making' relation to the whole of which it is a part. Moore thought that the doctrine of organic wholes relates solely to contributive value. It is the doctrine that the value something contributes to the whole varies, because this contribution is conditioned by the other parts of that whole. But since contributive value is different from intrinsic value, this view is consistent with the view that the intrinsic value of the part does not change from context to context. For example, pleasure may be intrinsically good. That means that it is always good wherever it is instantiated. But the value that an instance of pleasure contributes to some enjoyment will vary. If one takes pleasure in the well-being of others, then one's pleasure will be not only intrinsically good but also contributively good. The presence of this pleasure makes things better. If, however, one takes pleasure in the suffering of others, then the fact that one gets pleasure from this will make this enjoyment worse. The fact that one gets pleasure from other people's suffering is not a redeeming feature of the situation, but actually makes things worse. Nonetheless, Moore would maintain that although the contributive value of the pleasure has changed, its intrinsic value remains unaltered. The pleasure itself remains intrinsically good even though the situation is made worse by its presence.

If Moore's view is sustainable, then holism would not seem to wreck moral principles as some particularists claim. For the principled relations would still obtain between natural properties and intrinsic value even though they would not obtain between these same natural properties and contributive value. Unfortunately this attempt to have one's holistic cake and eat it cannot be sustained. It cannot be sustained because it cuts off intrinsic value from any reason-giving relation, and hence denies its essentially practical nature. On this Moorean picture the reasons we have to act, or respond in certain ways are determined wholly by contributive value. If something is contributively good, then we have reason to pursue it, promote it, endorse it, or welcome it. If something is contributively bad, then we have reason to regret it, abolish it, condemn it, or avoid it. The fact that the same thing might be *intrinsically* good or bad does not seem to imply that we have any further reason to welcome or avoid it. Suppose, to use my earlier example, we think that pleasure is intrinsically good, and that when it is pleasure in other people's suffering it is contributively bad (it makes things worse). If there is some connection between intrinsic value and practical reasons then in such a situation we would have to say that the fact that this instance of pleasure is contributively bad means that we have reason to disapprove of it, but the fact that it is intrinsically good means that we have reason to welcome it. But there seems no reason whatsoever to welcome this pleasure. To think that there is is to think that the fact that the agent feels pleasure is a redeeming feature of the situation, but this thought seems to be ruled out by the fact that its presence makes things worse – that it is contributively bad. One can only hold onto moral principles within a holistic framework, therefore, at the cost of severing the connection between intrinsic value and practical reasons. This is, I think, too great a cost to pay. Given that it is, if organic holism is true then there could be no principled relations between natural and moral properties.

One cannot, therefore, attack particularists simply by defending the particular principles to which they offer counter-examples. One must attack the doctrine that is doing the real damage, namely, the doctrine of organic wholes. The transcendental conception of the moral law and moral laws provides us with a way of doing this. For according to this understanding of moral principles the focus shifts away from moral deliberation (where particularists are understandably happy to engage with their opponents) to the practical necessity actions must possess if they are morally required. According to the transcendental account of the moral law, our moral experience can only be explained with reference to strictly universal principles, which in turn must be explained with reference to the purely formal principle of universal law as such – that is the moral law. Consequently, there must be strictly universal moral principles. Given that if the doctrine of organic wholes is true, there would be no strictly universal moral principles, if there are such principles then this doctrine, as well as the particularism it sustains, must be false.

For these reasons, and for the reasons mentioned in Chapter 4, I believe that the best way to think of the relation between the moral law, moral laws and particular moral obligations is in accordance with the transcendental conception. It may be that the best way is not good enough. If it is not, then at least it will have brought to light an interesting and underexplored issue in ethics – that is, the issue of the nature and possibility of practical necessity. What I hope to have done in this book is persuade the reader that the transcendental conception of the moral law and the account of moral worth that goes with it not only provides us with an interesting theoretical possibility, but constitutes the most plausible picture of moral worth and the role of moral principles.

NOTES

Introduction

1 This is not to deny that there is an internal relation between an action's being one that ought to be done and our having good reason to do it. It is just to deny that the fact that it ought to be done is one of those good reasons.
2 See Chapter 1 for an account of this distinction.
3 That is, assuming that the agent knows the relevant facts, that their judgement is good, that they are not weak-willed, or in some other way practically irrational, and that they are able to act in this way.
4 For the sake of brevity I shall omit the reference to what we believe in what follows, and talk simply of doing the right thing just because it is right.
5 The symmetry thesis also makes this an untenable account of moral worth. For if good people are motivated to do what they should by a certain psychological state, then this psychological state will be the normative reason why they should do that act. But it seems mistaken to think that the reason why an act, say, of promise-keeping, or beneficence, is morally required is just because the agent is in a certain psychological state.
6 See, for example, J. McDowell, 'Values and Secondary Qualities', in T. Honderich (ed.) *Morality and Objectivity: A Tribute to J. L. Mackie*, London, Routledge and Kegan Paul, 1985, pp. 110–29, and J. Dancy, *Moral Reasons*, Oxford, Blackwell, 1993.

1 Doing the right thing just because it is right

1 See, e.g., C. Korsgaard, 'Kant's Analysis of Obligation: The Argument of *Groundwork I*', in *Creating the Kingdom of Ends*, Cambridge, Cambridge University Press, 1996, Chapter 2, Barbara Herman, 'On the Value of Acting from the Motive of Duty', in *The Practice of Moral Judgment*, Cambridge, MA, Harvard University Press, 1993, Chapter 1, and D. Cummiskey, *Kantian Consequentialism*, Oxford, Oxford University Press, 1996, Chapter 2.
2 The arguments of this chapter do not assume that Kant held that an action has moral worth if and only if it is done *solely* from duty. I shall, however, address this issue in Chapters 3 and 6.
3 See, for example, W. D. Ross, *The Right and the Good*, Indianapolis, Hackett, 1988, p. 158.
4 The relevant belief–desire pair would be the desire to do what is right, and the belief that this act is right.
5 There are actually two claims which sound distinctively Humean: the first is that a desire is a necessary motive, and the second is that whenever one is motivated, a desire is present. It is the first claim with which I have little sympathy. The second is consistent with the view that a desire need not be a motive.

6 See, for example, J. McDowell, 'Are Moral Requirements Hypothetical Imperatives?', *Proceedings of the Aristotelian Society*, vol. 52 (suppl.), 1978, pp. 13–29, T. Nagel, *The Possibility of Altruism*, Princeton, NJ, Princeton University Press, 1979, M. Smith, 'The Humean Theory of Motivation', *Mind*, 1987, vol. 96, pp. 36–61, D. McNaughton, *Moral Vision*, Oxford, Blackwell, 1988, Chapter 7, J. Dancy, op. cit., and T. Scanlon, *What We Owe to Each Other*, Cambridge, MA, Harvard University Press, 1998, Chapter 1.

7 See P. Foot, 'Morality as a System of Hypothetical Imperatives', in *Virtues and Vices*, Oxford, Blackwell, 1978, pp. 157–73 and M. Smith, *The Moral Problem*, Oxford, Blackwell, 1994, pp. 77–84.

8 '"Ought" and Motivation', in W. Sellars and J. Hospers (eds), *Readings in Ethical Theory*, New York, Appleton-Century-Crofts, 1952, p. 503. Because he identifies practical reasons with motives, Falk thinks that this internal analysis of 'ought' entails what he calls the motivational analysis, according to which 'I ought to Φ' means 'I have a compelling motive to Φ'. But these two analyses are quite independent of each other, and one can accept the first without accepting the second.

9 Ibid.

10 Ibid.

11 P. Foot, 'Are Moral Considerations Overriding?', in *Virtues and Vices*, Oxford, Blackwell, 1978, p. 182.

12 S. Scheffler, *Human Morality*, Oxford, Oxford University Press, 1992, p. 30.

13 'Kant's Analysis of Obligation', p. 60.

14 Michael Smith seems to adhere to something like this principle in his 'The Argument for Internalism: Reply to Miller', *Analysis*, 1996, vol. 56, no. 3, pp. 182–3.

15 This is not to say that an action would fail to be rational if it was not done from the reason why it ought to be done. I agree with T. Scanlon that rationality 'involves systematic connections between a person's judgements and his or her subsequent attitudes' (*What We Owe to Each Other*, op. cit., p. 33). One's action is rational, therefore, if it accords, or at least does not conflict, with one's beliefs about what one has reason to do. All that is needed for there to be an essential connection between the morality and rationality of action is a necessary connection between beliefs about why one ought to act in a certain way and the moral worth of our actions. Nonetheless, it would still be odd if this necessary connection was cut off from the reasons why we ought to act in a certain way. It would be better to see the connection as one between perceived reasons to act and the morality of one's action. But if there is to be a necessary connection between these, then there would have to be a necessary connection between the reasons why we ought to Φ and the reason why Φ-ing is morally good.

16 I thank André Gallois for this example.

17 *Ak* IV, 421n/*Gr*, 89n. In Chapter 7 I shall argue that Kant's moral theory looks more plausible if we interpret the categorical imperative test in such a way that it does not generate this sort of absolute side-constraint.

18 It is generally agreed that someone need not be able to change necessary truths if they are to be omnipotent. If there are perfect duties, then it will follow that the claim that acts which fall under them are obligatory will amount to a necessary truth. For example, if keeping one's promise is a perfect duty it will follow that whenever anyone keeps their promise they will have done the right thing. The fact that, if there were such duties, an omnipotent demon would be unable to do anything about the deontological status of the relevant act would not undermine his omnipotence.

19 Those who have argued this include H. J. Paton, 'An Alleged Right to Lie: A Problem in Kantian Ethics', *Kant-Studien*, 1953–54, vol. 45, pp. 190–203 and C. Korsgaard, 'The Right to Lie: Kant on Dealing with Evil' in *Creating the Kingdom of Ends*, Chapter 5.

20 There is, of course, a disanalogy here. For, in the case of happiness, whatever *makes* one happy *causes* one to be happy. But whatever makes an action right does not cause it to be right. This raises the difficult question of what this 'making' relation is. This is, however, a question I do not intend to address here.
21 Jonathan Dancy criticises Michael Smith along these lines in his, 'Why There is Really No Such Thing as the Theory of Motivation', *Proceedings of the Aristotelian Society*, 1994–5, vol. 95, pp. 1–18.
22 W. D. Falk, '"Ought" and Motivation', and Bernard Williams, 'Internal and External Reasons', in *Moral Luck: Philosophical Papers 1973–1980*, Cambridge, Cambridge University Press, 1981, pp. 101–13.
23 (2) is distinct from (1), for it does not follow from the fact that one does not judge an act wrong, that one judges that it is either morally required or merely permissible. One might simply fail to form any judgement whatsoever about the deontological status of one's action.
24 The idea here is that in cases of conflict acts which would normally be regarded as wrong may be morally required. If, for example, one could only help someone by telling a lie, one might judge that here the act of lying is morally required. But because lying is normally wrong, it is reasonable to assume that if a good person judges that in some such situation she should lie, she would not lie unless she thought that it was morally required.
25 The distinction between something's being a motive and its being motivationally relevant also has the advantage that it provides a better explanation of people's motives than the alternative in non-moral cases. For example, if we fail to make this distinction we would have to say of someone who believed that brushing her teeth would not be fatal, and who would not brush her teeth if she thought this would kill her, that this belief was one of her motivating reasons for brushing her teeth. It is far more plausible to say that her belief that brushing her teeth is not fatal is motivationally relevant, but not one of her motives. Her motivating reasons would probably be something like the belief that brushing her teeth would be a good way of looking after them, or perhaps this belief plus a desire to look after them.
26 'Reason and Motivation', *Proceedings of the Aristotelian Society*, 1997, p. 139.
27 *Some Problems in Ethics*, Oxford, Clarendon Press, 1931, p. 47.
28 'The Right and the Good', *Philosophia*, 1992, vol. 21, pp. 235–56.
29 Op. cit., pp. 501–2.
30 Ibid, pp. 503–4.
31 Ibid, p. 504.
32 'Reasons and Motivation', in *Proceedings of the Aristotelian Society*, 1997, vol. 71 (suppl.), pp. 99–130.
33 My view is that there is. For an argument in defence of this view see Elijah Millgram, 'Williams' argument against external reasons', *Nous*, 1996, vol. 30, pp. 354–88.
34 *The Moral Problem*, pp. 151–77. Smith's analysis is actually of the concept of a normative reason. But since he thinks that 'to say that someone has a normative reason to Φ is to say that there is some normative requirement that she Φ' (p. 95), his analysis of a normative reason will, *ipso facto*, function as an analysis of a normative requirement, and hence of a moral requirement.
35 Ibid, p. 95.

2 Repect and moral motivation

1 *Ak* V, 73/*CPrR*, 76. Cf., also *Ak* V, 75/78, 76/79, 78/81, and 79/81–2.
2 *Ak* IV, 401n/*Gr*, 69n.
3 This changes in the *Metaphysics of Morals* where he takes respect as one moral feeling among others. I shall return to this later.

4 *Ak* IV, 401n/*Gr*, 69n, and *Ak* V/*CPrR*, Chapter 3.
5 Paul Guyer, however, goes too far in the opposite direction when he claims that:

> the feeling of respect is thus a complex but ultimately pleasurable state of feeling produced by our decision to adhere to the moral law, grounded, like other feelings of pleasure, in the recognition of the possibility of the realization of our own objectives but reflecting in its very complexity the fact that not all of our objectives are conjointly satisfiable.
>
> (1997, p. 360)

Furthermore, Kant never states that respect is pleasurable but that it can be understood in analogy to pleasure.
6 *Ak* IV, 400/*Gr*, 68. See also *Ak* IV, 401n/*Gr*, 69n.
7 *Ak* IV, 436/*Gr*, 103.
8 *Ak* IV, 440/*Gr*, 107.
9 *Ak* V, 76/*CPrR*, 79.
10 I here follow A. Broadie's and E. Pybus' discussion of this point in 'Kant's Concept of "Respect"', *Kant-Studien*, 1975, vol. 66, pp. 58–64, especially in pp. 59–60.
11 *Ak* IV, 432/*Gr*, 99.
12 *Ak* IV, 401n/*Gr*, 69n.
13 *Ak* V, 73/*CPrR*, 76.
14 Kant describes *a priori* judgements, concepts, or principles, as those which are necessary and universally valid (*CPR*, B4–5). Thus, an *a priori* principle is one which is 'indispensable for the possibility of experience' (*CPR*, A2/B5).
15 A. Broadie and E. Pybus make this point lucidly, op. cit., pp. 61–2n.
16 *Ak* V, 76/*CPrR*, 79.
17 Moral Feeling is 'the susceptibility to feel pleasure or displeasure merely from being aware that our actions are consistent with or contrary to the law of duty', *Ak* VI, 399/*MM*, 201.
18 *Ak* VI, 399/*MM*, 200.
19 *Ak* VI, 402/*MM*, 203.
20 *Ak* IV, 401n/*Gr*, 69n.
21 Ibid.
22 *Ak* VI, 464/*MM*, 256.
23 '*Achtung* in the *Grundlegung*', in Ottfried Höffe (ed.) *Grundlegung zur Metaphysik der Sitten: Ein Kooperativer Kommentar*, Frankfurt am Main, Vittorio Klostermann, 1993, pp. 97–116.
24 It is for this reason that Walker says that 'what Kant says about *Achtung* in the *Grundlegung* is confused' (1993, p. 98).
25 *Ak* VI, 464/*MM*, 256 (my emphasis).
26 If the determination of the will occurs in accordance with the moral law but only by means of a feeling of any kind whatsoever, which must be presupposed in order that the law may become a determining ground of the will, and if the action thus occurs not for the sake of the law, it has legality but not morality.

(*Ak* V, 71/*CPrR*, 74).

27 'Motivation and Moral Choice in Kant's Theory of Rational Agency', *Kant-Studien*, 1994, vol. 85, pp. 15–31. He writes that respect is a 'motivational attitude with two aspects, one cognitive, the other affective' (ibid., p. 25). 'The moral feeling of respect is effected by moral judgements of the understanding, which are themselves impotent in the relevant respect' (ibid., p. 24). McCarty is not, however, the only one to interpret respect as a complex mental state. Broadie and Pybus (op. cit.), A. Reath ('Kant's

Theory of Moral Sensibility: Respect for the Moral Law and the Influence of Inclination', *Kant-Studien*, 1989, vol. 80, pp. 284–302), and H. Allison (*Kant's Theory of Freedom*, Cambridge, Cambridge University Press, 1990, p. 123) also hold this view.

28 Op. cit., pp. 21–3.
29 Ibid., p. 24.
30 This interpretation is adopted by Andrews Reath, 'Kant's Theory of Moral Sensibility', pp. 287 ff.
31 It should be noted that this difficulty is not peculiar to the interpretation of respect we are considering, but applies also to the view that respect is simply a feeling caused by our consciousness of the moral law.
32 *Laws of Freedom*, Oxford, Oxford University Press, 1963, p. 181n.
33 *Ak* VI, 402/*MM*, 204.
34 *Ak* IV, 400/*Gr*, 68.
35 *Ak* IV, 412/*Gr*, 80.
36 *Ak* IV, 414/*Gr*, 81.
37 *Ak* IV, 412/*Gr*, 80.
38 *Ak* IV, 413/*Gr*, 80.
39 *Ak* IV, 413/*Gr*, 81.
40 *Ak* VI, 222/*MM*, 49.
41 This is a common reading of Kant which can be found in both Hegel and Ross.
42 I argue for this in 'In Defence of the Abstract', *Bulletin of the Hegel Society of Great Britain*, vol. 33, 1996, pp. 42–53.
43 *Ak* IV, 401n/*Gr*, 67.
44 *Ak* IV, 419/*Gr*, 87.
45 *Ak* V, 71/*CPrR*, 74.
46 *Ak* V, 72/*CPrR*, 74. Kant also states that the moral law is the moral incentive at a number of other places in the *Critique of Practical Reason*, e.g., pp. 72/75, 75/78, 78/81, 79/82 and 88/91.
47 L. W. Beck, *A Commentary on Kant's Critique of Practical Reason*, Chicago, University of Chicago Press, 1960, p. 221.
48 See C. Korsgaard, 'Kant's Analysis of Obligation: The Argument of *Groundwork I*', p. 57, Andrews Reath, 'The Categorical Imperative and Kant's Conception of Practical Rationality', *The Monist*, 1989, vol. 72, pp. 384–410, Barbara Herman, 'On the Value of Acting from the Motive of Duty', in *The Practice of Moral Judgment*, Cambridge, MA, Harvard University Press, 1993, p. 11 and Marcia Baron, *Kantian Ethics Almost without Apology*, Ithaca, NY, Cornell University Press, 1995, pp. 188–93.
49 *Ak* VI, 23–4/*Rel*, 19.
50 *Ak* IV, 400/*Gr*, 68–9.
51 *Ak* IV, 421n/*Gr*, 88n.
52 *Ak* V, 75f/*CPrR*, 78f.
53 H. J. Paton suggests this strategy, but dismisses it (*The Categorical Imperative: A Study in Kant's Moral Philosophy*, London, Hutchinson's University Library, 1947, p. 66.
54 *Ak* V, 72/*CPrR*, 74–5.
55 *Ak* IV, 419/*Gr*, 87.
56 *Ak* IV, 401n/*Gr*, 69n.
57 *Ak* IV, 460n/*Gr*, 128n.
58 *Ak* V, 72/*CPrR*, 74.
59 *Ak* IV, 401n/*Gr*, 69n.
60 *Ak* IV, 401n/*Gr*, 69n.
61 *Ak* IV, 401n/*Gr*, 69n.
62 This view was originally formulated by W. D. Falk, '"Ought" and Motivation', in W. Sellars and J. Hospers (eds) *Readings in Ethical Theory*, New York, Appleton-Century-Crofts, 1952, pp. 492–510, but see also W. Frankena, 'Obligation and Motivation in

Recent Moral Philosophy', in A. I. Melden (ed.) *Essays in Moral Philosophy*, Washington, DC, University of Washington Press, 1958, pp. 40–81, C. Korsgaard, 'Skepticism about Practical Reason', in *Creating the Kingdom of Ends*, 1996, pp. 311–34, and M. Smith, *The Moral Problem*, Oxford, Blackwell, 1994. I use Smith's formulation here (op. cit., p. 61). For arguments against internalism see D. Brink, 'Externalist Moral Realism', *Southern Journal of Philosophy*, 1986, vol. 24, *Supplement*, pp. 23–42.

63 *The Moral Problem*, p. 60.

3 Acting from respect for the moral law

1 This was argued in Chapter 2.

2 There is great disagreement about how many formulations of the moral law Kant lists. For a discussion of the literature see my 'Formulating Categorical Imperatives', *Kant-Studien*, 1993, vol. 83, pp. 317–40.

3 *Ak* IV, 436/*Gr*, 103–4.

4 See C. Korsgaard, 'Kant's Formula of Humanity' in *Creating the Kingdom of Ends*, Cambridge, Cambridge University Press, 1996, pp. 106–32, and P. Guyer 'The Possibility of the Categorical Imperative', *Philosophical Review*, 1995, vol. 104, pp. 353–85.

5 *Ak* IV, 400/*Gr*, 68.

6 H. Paton, for example, sometimes talks in this way. See *The Categorical Imperative: A Study in Kant's Moral Philosophy*, London, Hutchinson's University Library, 1947, pp. 61–2.

7 *Ak* IV, 400/*Gr*, 68.

8 *Ak* IV, 436–7/*Gr*. 104.

9 Hegel, and Hegelians, often criticise Kant for separating in thought what is not, or cannot be separated in reality when he claims that a moral motive is one which makes no reference to an end. For, it is argued, we cannot separate the end of an action from the act, since every act has an end. See for example, *Phenomenology of Spirit*, trans. A. V. Miller, Oxford, Oxford University Press, 1977, pp. 386–7 and p. 377. But Kant's point is not that morally good actions lack an end, but that they are only good on the condition that this end does not motivate.

10 In the *Critique of Practical Reason* he says, 'it is certainly undeniable that every volition must have an object and therefore a material' (*Ak* V, 34/*CPrR*, 34), and in the *Metaphysics of Morals* that 'there can be no action without an end' (*Ak* VI, 385/*MM*, 190).

11 *Ak* IV, 403/*Gr*. 71 (my emphasis).

12 *Ak* IV, 421/*Gr*, 88. See also *Ak* VI, 392/*MM*, 196.

13 *Ak* IV, 400–1/*Gr*, 68–9. See also, *Ak* V, 72/*CPrR*, 74.

14 See, e.g., *Ak* IV, 400/*Gr*, 68–9, *Ak* V, 72 /*CPrR*, 74–5 and *Ak* V, 72/*CPrR*, 75.

15 *Ak* VI, 403/*MM*, 204.

16 See *Ak* VI, 421ff/*MM*, 218ff.

17 See, for example, Onora Nell (O'Neill), *Acting on Principle: An Essay on Kantian Ethics*, New York, Columbia University Press, 1975, and Nancy Sherman, *Making a Necessity of Virtue: Aristotle and Kant on Virtue*, Cambridge, Cambridge University Press, 1997, Chapter 7.

18 It is partly for this reason that A. R. C. Duncan (*Practical Reason and Morality*, London, Thomas Nelson and Sons, 1957), H. J. Paton ('The Aim and Structure of Kant's *Grundlegung*', *Philosophical Quarterly*, 1958, vol. VIII, pp. 121–5) and T. C. Williams (*The Concept of the Categorical Imperative*, Oxford, Clarendon Press, 1968, Chapter 7) reject this view of the categorical imperative as prescribing what rational agents must do. Duncan goes so far as to claim that the categorical imperative is merely descriptive.

Paton and Williams, however, do not go that far. They hold that it is prescriptive, but not in the strong sense that commentators such as Broad understand it to be.

19 C. D. Broad (*Five Types of Ethical Theory*, London, Routledge & Kegan Paul, 1930, Chapter 5) and Alistair MacIntyre (*After Virtue: A Study in Moral Theory*, London, Duckworth, 1981, Chapter 4) are among those who have criticised Kant along these lines.

20 Sometimes he seems to conceive of the categorical imperative as a principle which specifies what duty, or obligation is. See, for example, *Ak* V, 8n/*CPrR*, 8n, and *Ak* VI, 225/*MM*, 51. See also *Ak* IV, 412/*Gr*, 80, *Ak* IV, 420/*Gr*, 88, and *Ak* IV, 439/*Gr*, 107. At other times he understands it as constituting the sole *ground* of duty (*Ak* IV, 403/*Gr*, 71), while, at other times he understands it in the way Duncan, and others interpret it, i.e., merely as a test, or criterion.

21 Cf. e.g., Michael Stocker, 'The Schizophrenia of Modern Ethical Theories', *Journal of Philosophy*, 1976, vol. 73, pp. 453–66, Susan Wolf, 'Morality and Partiality', *Philosophical Perspectives*, 1992, vol. 6, pp. 243–59, and Bernard Williams, 'Persons, Character and Morality', in *Moral Luck*, Cambridge, Cambridge University Press, 1981, pp. 14–19.

22 I deal with Judith Baker's and Henry Allison's claim that this notion is unintelligible in Chapter 6.

23 *Ak* V, 72/*CPrR*, 74–5.

24 My point here is not that on this account of acting from duty morally good agents will help others from selfish motives. It does not seem right to describe someone who helps others solely from a thought about the lawlike nature of her maxim as acting selfishly. My point is simply that thinking of moral motivation in this way fails to capture the common-sense idea that morally good people will be motivated in such situations by thoughts about the other person.

25 Barbara Herman, 'On the Value of Acting from the Motive of Duty', in *The Practice of Moral Judgment*, Cambridge, MA, Harvard University Press, 1993, pp. 1–22, and Marcia Baron, *Kantian Ethics Almost Without Apology*, Ithaca, NY, Cornell University Press, 1995, Chapter 4.

26 It might be thought that aiming at actions which promote or are consistent with the agency of others is distinctive of morally good actions. But it is a key element of Kant's argument in *Groundwork I* that the moral worth of actions does not stem from any end whatsoever, but from the reason from which one aims at some end. If one aimed at actions which promoted and were consistent with the agency of others from some self-interested, or empirical motive, one's action would lack any moral worth.

27 This assumes, of course, that one's belief is true. One could be motivated to act otherwise than as one should from the *false* belief that this is what one should do. But this presupposes that it is the belief, rather than the fact, that one ought to act in a certain way which is the moral motive. I rejected this view in Chapter 2.

28 'On the Value of Acting from the Motive of Duty', op. cit. p. 16.

29 In this way, Herman claims, she can 'preserve the sense in which, for Kant, the motive of duty is ubiquitous – without having to accept the view that all our actions must be seen as matters of duty' (Ibid., p. 17).

30 Cf. *Ak* VI, 36/*Rel*, 31.

31 'On the Value of Acting from the Motive of Duty', p. 17.

32 *Kantian Ethics Almost Without Apology*, op. cit.

33 Ibid., p. 134.

34 Ibid., p. 131.

35 Baron's view is that duty need only function as a primary motive where the agent is disinclined to do what she should.

36 I say 'on the face of it' because I shall offer an account of acting solely from duty which enables one to reject (3) without rejecting either (1) or (2).

37 Those who argue this have in mind Kant's infamous views about the supposed right to lie from altruistic motives. For a defence of Kant, see Christine Korsgaard, 'The Right to Lie: Kant on Dealing with Evil', in *Creating the Kingdom of Ends*, Cambridge, Cambridge University Press, 1996, pp. 133–58, and H. J. Paton, 'An Alleged Right to Lie: A Problem in Kantian Ethics', *Kant-Studien*, 1953–54, vol. 45, pp. 190–203.

4 An alternative account of acting from duty

1 If this is correct, we can see not only *that* the standard interpretation of acting from duty is mistaken, but why it is so commonly assumed. The mistake is illegitimately to move from the fact that a good-willed person regards herself as having sufficient reason to do what she ought simply in so far as she recognises what her duty is, to the thesis that she regards duty *as being* this sufficient reason.

2 My account allows actions to be overdetermined in more ways than this, since one's action could be overdetermined at the secondary level as well as the primary one. But what makes the moral difference is overdetermination at the primary level, so this is all I consider here. I return to the issue of overdetermined actions in Chapter 6.

3 *Ak* VI, 456/*MM*, 250.

4 *Ak* IV, 398/*Gr*, 66.

5 Barbara Herman makes this point well. 'Suppose', she writes, 'I see someone struggling, late at night, with a heavy burden at the back door of the Museum of Fine Arts. Because of my sympathetic temper I feel the immediate inclination to help him out. We need not pursue the example to see its point' ('On the Value of Acting from the Motive of Duty', in *The Practice of Moral Judgment*, Cambridge, MA, Harvard University Press, 1993, p. 5).

6 *Ak* IV, 398–9/*Gr*, 66.

7 In Chapter 2 I argued that respect for the moral law is the necessary condition of our being motivated to act in accordance with its dictates, but is not, for Kant, the moral motive. I shall say more about the relation between the moral law and moral motivation later on in this chapter.

8 One may, for example, think that these are reasons only for those who care about them, or that they are reasons only for those who participate in the practice.

9 This sort of criticism was made by Bernard Williams in his 'Persons, Character and Morality', in *Moral Luck: Philosophical Papers 1973–1980*, Cambridge, Cambridge University Press, 1981, p. 18.

10 *Ak* IV, 421/*Gr*, 88.

11 *Ak* IV, 403/*Gr*, 71.

12 Or perhaps the transcendental unity of apperception.

13 *CPR*, A91–2/B123–4.

14 See M. Friedman, 'Causal Laws and the Foundations of Natural Science', in P. Guyer (ed.), *The Cambridge Companion to Kant*, Cambridge, Cambridge University Press, 1992, p. 171.

15 Ibid., pp. 185–6.

16 *Ak* V, 21/*CPrR*, 19.

17 *Ak* V, 22/*CPrR*, 20.

18 *Ak* V, 21/*CPrR*, 19.

19 J. Silber, 'The Copernican Revolution in Ethics: The Good Reexamined', in Robert Paul Wolff (ed.), *Kant: A Collection of Critical Essays*, Notre Dame, University of Notre Dame Press, 1968, p. 277.

20 *Ak* V, 33/*CPrR*, 33.

21 *Ak* V, 29–30/*CPrR*, 29.

22 This distinction tracks closely Kant's distinction between the theoretical and practical use of reason. I think we have to find a place for practical reasons which is distinct from

epistemic ones, otherwise practical reason will only be intelligible as reasons which support the belief that we ought, or ought not, to act in certain ways. But then we will not be able to explain what is irrational about someone who forms beliefs about what he should do on the basis of the reasons which support these beliefs, but never *acts* in accordance with them.

23 This point can be illustrated with an analogous distinction within the theoretical realm between the reason why something has a certain property, and the reason for believing that it has this property. For example, my reason for believing that the water is hot may be because, when I place a thermometer in it, it registers one hundred degrees centigrade. But this can hardly be said to imply that the reason why the water is hot is because the thermometer registers one hundred degrees. The reason why it is hot is, say, because it was left on the hot plate. There is, of course, the disanalogy that the reason why the water is hot can be expressed in causal terms which can be discovered by means of empirical investigation, whereas the reason why some action is right is neither causal nor discoverable by empirical investigation. But my point was just that there is an analogous distinction to be made within theoretical reason to the one I am making between practical reasons and criteria. I am not claiming that the analogy runs very deep.

24 See, for example, *Ak* IV, 407–8/*Gr*, 75 and *Ak* VI, 20/*Rel*, 16.

25 Cf. O. O'Neill, 'Consistency in Action', in *Constructions of Reason: Explorations of Kant's Practical Philosophy*, Cambridge, Cambridge University Press, 1989, pp. 81–104.

26 My conclusion here may seem to be incompatible with Kant's contructivism. I deal with this objection in Chapter 7.

5 Filling out the details

1 Christine Korsgaard, *The Sources of Normativity*, Cambridge, Cambridge University Press, 1996, p. 38.

2 *The Right and the Good*, Indianapolis, Hackett, 1988, pp. 19–20.

3 Ibid., p. 20.

4 Ibid.

5 *The Foundations of Ethics*, Oxford, Clarendon Press, 1939, p. 84. Because of this, it is easy to be so impressed with some respect in which an act is right that we assume straight off that it must be the one we are bound to do (Ibid.).

6 John Searle, '*Prima Facie* Obligations', in J. Raz (ed.) *Practical Reasoning*, Oxford, Oxford University Press, 1978, p. 82.

7 *The Foundations of Ethics*, p. 85.

8 *The Right and the Good*, p. 28.

9 See, e.g., S. Kagan, *The Limits of Morality*, Oxford, Clarendon Press, 1989, p. 17, B. Hooker, 'Ross-style Pluralism versus Rule-consequentialism', *Mind*, 1996, vol. 105, p. 534n, and J. Dancy, *Moral Reasons*, Oxford, Blackwell, 1993, p. 180.

10 Thus, for example, Hooker writes that Ross's foundational principles

> enumerate general duties such as the duty not to injure others, not to steal, not to break one's promises, not to tell lies, and the duties to be just, to show gratitude for kindness received, and generally to do good for others . . . These general duties are *prima facie* in the sense that none is absolute – that is, each is capable of being overridden by the others.
>
> (1996, p. 534)

11 *The Right and the Good*, p. 20.

12 *The Foundations of Ethics*, pp. 84–5.

13 Ross uses the phrases '*prima facie* obligatory', '*prima facie* duty' and '*prima facie* right' interchangeably. This is because he holds that, subject to a minor qualification (*The Right and the Good*, p. 3), the terms 'ought to be done', 'duty', 'obligatory', and 'right' pick out one and the same quality of actions (Ibid., p. 4). I have some doubts about this, but will follow Ross's practice here.
14 There are, therefore, no absolute prohibitions, side-constraints, or perfect duties, according to Ross.
15 *The Foundations of Ethics*, p. 86. See also *The Right and the Good*, p. 28.
16 'Ethical Intuitionism', in *Readings in Ethical Theory*, W. Sellars and J. Hospers (eds), New York, Appleton-Century-Crofts, 1952, p. 256. This view is also ascribed to Ross by J. Searle ('*Prima Facie* Obligations', in J. Raz (ed.), *Practical Reasoning*, Oxford, Oxford University Press, 1978, Chapter 5) and J. Dancy ('Ethical Particularism and Morally Relevant Properties', *Mind*, 1983, vol. 92, pp. 530–47).
17 This point was first made in response to Strawson by A. C. Ewing (*Second Thoughts in Moral Philosophy*, London, Routledge & Kegan Paul, 1959, p. 109). It has since been made by R. Gay ('Ethical Pluralism: A Reply to Jonathan Dancy', *Mind*, 1985, vol. 94, pp. 250–62), and P. Pietroski ('*Prima Facie* Obligations, Ceteris Paribus Laws in Moral Theory', *Ethics*, 1993, vol. 103, pp. 489–515). Ewing and Pietroski, however, understand the analogy with causal laws as expressing a *ceteris paribus* clause. This is different from the analogy I am considering here, but I will consider this account when I consider the counter-factual definition of *prima facie* rightness.
18 *The Right and the Good*, pp. 28–9. And in *The Foundations of Ethics* he writes:

> We cannot say, for instance, that a certain force impinging on a body of a certain mass will always cause it to move with a certain velocity in the line of the force; for if the body is acted on by an equal and opposite force, it actually remains at rest; and if it is acted on by a force operating in some third direction, it will move in a line which is oblique to the lines of both forces. We can only say that any force *tends* to make the body move in the line of the force.
>
> (p. 86)

19 Williams is wrong in understanding the work of a defeated *prima facie* duty as reducing the rightness of a right act ('Ethical Consistency', *Proceedings of the Aristotelian Society*, 1965, supp. vol. 39, pp. 103–24).
20 This is the central argument of *The Right and the Good*. See, e.g., pp. 3–4.
21 *The Right and the Good*, p. 19.
22 *Five Types of Ethical Theory*, pp. 164–5.
23 *The Foundations of Ethics*, p. 53.
24 Ibid., pp. 52–3.
25 Ross states that it is always suitableness for a purpose someone has, but although this type of fittingness always involves a reference to some purpose, it need not be to one which someone has. A car may be a suitable, or appropriate means of getting from A to B irrespective of whether someone wants to get from A to B. Ross's point does, however, hold in relation to fittingness as it is applied to acts. If an act is instrumentally fitting, it is always fitting for some purpose the agent has.
26 *The Foundations of Ethics*, p. 54.
27 Ibid.
28 Ibid.
29 Ibid.
30 Ibid.
31 Ibid., pp. 54–5.
32 Ewing abandons the notion of fittingness for this reason (*Second Thoughts in Moral Philosophy*, p. 94).

33 *The Foundations of Ethics*, p. 85. This term was suggested to him by Carritt.
34 This definition requires modification. Ross held that *prima facie* duties are qualities of actions, but a responsibility is not a characteristic of an act. Consequently, the notion of a *prima facie* duty cannot be understood as a responsibility, but should be understood as picking out the characteristic an act has of *fulfilling* a responsibility. On this account, then, to say that an act is *prima facie* right in some respect is just to say that it fulfils some responsibility the agent has, and to say that it is *prima facie* wrong means that there is some responsibility which it leaves unfulfilled.
35 This is not to say that we do not learn many things about this notion from what he says. Among other things, we have learnt that all of the ways in which an action can be *prima facie* right share the characteristic of being the fulfilling of a responsibility, that this characteristic is a real feature of actions and not merely something apparent, and that the actual rightness of right actions is determined by their *prima facie* rightness.
36 Since it is the fact that some aspect of the action is always morally salient in the same way which makes the counter-factual claim that the *prima facie* duty would make the action actually right if the other opposing evidential moral considerations were absent true, this counter-factual claim cannot be basic, as Ross sometimes suggests.
37 In what follows I ignore cases where my moral beliefs are false. This is not to avoid any difficulty such cases might introduce – I do not believe they introduce any – but is simply for brevity's sake.

6 On the value of acting from duty

1 *Ak* IV, 398/*Gr*, 66.
2 *Ak* IV, 398/*Gr*, 66.
3 This is, for example, W. D. Ross's view in *The Right and the Good*, Indianapolis, Hackett, 1988, Chapter 7.
4 This version is taken from H. Paton, *The Categorical Imperative: A Study in Kant's Moral Philosophy*, London, Hutchinson, 1947, p. 249.
5 *Ak* VI, 23–4n/*Rel*, 19n.
6 *Ak* IV, 398/*Gr*, 66.
7 For an excellent account of these issues see C. Korsgaard, 'Two Distinctions in Goodness', in *Creating the Kingdom of Ends*, Cambridge, Cambridge University Press, 1996, Chapter 9.
8 'On the Value of Acting from the Motive of Duty', in *The Practice of Moral Judgment*, Cambridge, MA, Harvard University Press, 1993, pp. 3–6.
9 'Suppose', she asks,

> I see someone struggling, late at night, with a heavy burden at the back door of the Museum of Fine Arts. Because of my sympathetic temper I feel the immediate inclination to help him out. We need not pursue the example to see its point.
>
> (Ibid., p. 5)

10 Ibid.
11 Ibid., p. 6.
12 Ibid., p. 4.
13 Cf., for example, H. Paton, *The Categorical Imperative*, p. 40 and H. Allison, *Kant's Theory of Freedom*, Cambridge, Cambridge University Press, 1990, p. 109.
14 *Ak* IV, 411/*Gr*, 79.
15 *Ak* IV, 397/*Gr*, 65.
16 *Kant's Theory of Freedom*, p. 113.
17 The distinction between a *de dicto* and a *de re* desire to do what is right is, roughly, a

distinction between a desire to do what is right *as such* and a desire to do those acts which are right (acts of fidelity, beneficence, gratitude, etc.). The distinction can be specified more accurately as follows. Construed *de dicto* 'I want to do what is right' means 'I want that: I do what is right'. Construed *de re* this means 'there is a right act of which I want that: I do it'. See W. V. O. Quine 'Quantifiers and Propositional Attitudes', in L. Linsky (ed.) *Reference and Modality*, Oxford, Oxford University Press, 1971, p. 101.

18 I here follow Marcia Baron's terminology, *Kantian Ethics Almost Without Apology*, Ithaca, NY, Cornell University Press, 1995, p. 151.

19 See, e.g., *Ak* V, 71/*CPrR*, 74, and M. Baron, op. cit., pp. 152–3.

20 See M. Baron, op. cit., pp. 154–5.

21 *Ak* V, 93/*CPrR*, 96–7.

22 M. Baron, op. cit., p. 156.

23 M. Baron, op. cit., pp. 156–7.

24 I shall have more to say about what it means for duty to be a sufficient motive later.

25 'Do One's Motives Have to be Pure?', in Richard Grandy and Richard Warner (eds) *Philosophical Grounds of Rationality: Intentions, Categories, Ends*, Oxford, Clarendon Press, 1986, pp. 457–73.

26 Some of Baker's other examples illustrate hybrid actions, and so can be ignored for our purposes. Quotation taken from ibid., p. 466.

27 Ibid., p. 467.

28 *Kantian Ethics Almost Without Apology*, pp. 188–93.

29 'Do One's Motives Have to be Pure?', p. 467.

30 In 'What Kant Might Have Said: Moral Worth and the Overdetermination of Dutiful Action', *Philosophical Review*, 1979, vol. 88, pp. 39–54.

31 *Kant's Theory of Freedom*, p. 117.

32 Ibid., pp. 117–18.

33 Allison does not want to deny the possibility of disjunctive maxims altogether. But in the legitimate ones the disjunction will express a number of conditions for adopting an end. Ibid., p. 118.

34 Op. cit., p. 118.

35 *Ak* V, 72/*CPrR*, 74–5.

36 'On the Value of Acting from the Motive of Duty', p. 10. Henry Allison illustrates this point nicely when he says, 'we would hardly deny moral worth to the action of a person who heroically resisted torture for two hours on the grounds that the person would have succumbed had the torture been continued an hour longer' (*Kant's Theory of Freedom*, p. 115).

37 When it functions solely as a secondary motive the actions it regulates will not be regarded as morally required, and could not have moral worth, according to Herman ('On the Value of Acting From the Motive of Duty', p. 16).

38 *Ak* VI, 389/*MM*, 193 and *Ak* VI, 393/*MM*, 196.

39 Marcia Baron makes this point in *Kantian Ethics Almost Without Apology*, p. 165.

40 This did not seem to be Kant's view in the *Groundwork* as there he claims that beneficent actions can be done from duty (*Ak* IV, 398/*Gr*, 66). But given the way in which he defines imperfect duties in the *Metaphysics of Morals*, he is committed to the view that beneficent actions cannot be morally good.

41 In the *Doctrine of Right* Kant puts forward a different account of the content of imperfect duties. There he maintains that what these duties require of us is that a certain action be done from a certain incentive, the moral law (*Ak* VI, 214/*MM*, 42 and *Ak* VI, 218/*MM*, 46). But this view undermines the distinction between acting in accordance with duty and acting from duty. For if such duties require us to perform beneficent acts from duty, then simply to act in accordance with this duty is already to act *from* duty.

42 I say 'at least less' for one might think that there are different ways of, say, keeping a promise. If I promise to pay you £10.00 I could do this either by writing a cheque, or by giving you cash, and I could do either of these this morning, this afternoon, or this evening. Given that each of these options is no better than any of the others as a way of keeping my promise, and thus of doing my duty, I can simply choose how I fulfil my (perfect) obligation.

43 This way of accommodating latitude may seem to collapse Kant's distinction between Right and Virtue as these are described in the *Metaphysics of Morals*, but Kant does not need this distinction to get what he wants – which is a distinction between mere external conformity with duty and virtue. All he needs for this is his distinction between acting in accordance with duty and and from duty. Actions which accord with duty, but are not done from duty, are those which have mere external legality, and are thus subject to an external law-giving. Virtuous action, on the other hand, is that which is done from duty, from a free adoption of certain maxims and principles, and this is not subject to any form of external law-giving. It is subject only to the free self-legislation of the subject.

7 Constructivism, autonomy and side-constraints

1 H. Allison, *Kant's Theory of Freedom*, Cambridge, Cambridge University Press, 1990, p. 7.

2 J. Rawls, 'Kantian Constructivism in Moral Theory', *Journal of Philosophy*, 1980, vol. 77, p. 519.

3 O. O'Neill, 'Constructivism in Ethics', in *Constructions of Reason*, Cambridge, Cambridge University Press, 1989, p. 206.

4 In Rawls the procedure is a suitably constructed social point of view that all can accept ('Kantian Constructivism in Moral Theory', p. 519), whereas in Scanlon we must ask ourselves whether our actions could be justified to others on grounds they could not reasonably reject ('Contractualism and Utilitarianism', in A. Sen and Bernard Williams (eds) *Utilitarianism and Beyond*, Cambridge, Cambridge University Press, 1982, p. 116).

5 Sometimes Rawls makes a more modest claim that the procedure is simply a device to make explicit basic moral convictions we already have (*A Theory of Justice*, Oxford, Oxford University Press, 1972, pp. 18–19, and p. 21).

6 See S. Darwall, A. Gibbard and P. Railton 'Towards *Fin de Siècle* Ethics', *Philosophical Review*, 1992, vol. 101, pp. 137–44.

7 It need not, however, be a form of non-naturalistic moral realism that invokes the sort of queer moral properties, or Platonism, which many constructivists think is a non-starter.

8 See, for example, Onora O'Neill's constructivism in *Constructions of Reason*, and T. Scanlon's in *What We Owe to Each Other*, Cambridge, MA, Harvard University Press, 1998.

9 See, e.g., Onora O'Neill, 'The Public Use of Reason', op. cit., Chapter 2, and Christine Korsgaard, *The Sources of Normativity*, Cambridge, Cambridge University Press, 1996, especially Lecture 1.

10 See Korsgaard, *The Sources of Normativity*, pp. 32–3. I actually think this misrepresents the realist position, but that is another matter.

11 Of course, the success of this enterprise will rest on whether such a formal procedure can generate any real practical conclusions, or at least constraints on practical conclusions. But this is a quite general worry about the viability of the categorical imperative test which is not limited to a constructivist reading of Kant.

12 'A critic who wished to say something against that work [the *Groundwork*] really did better than he intended when he said that there was no new principle of morality in it but only a new formula. Who would want to introduce a new principle of morality and,

as it were, be its inventor, as if the world had hitherto been ignorant of what duty is or had been thoroughly wrong about it?' (*Ak* V, 8n/*CPrR*, 8n).

13 As L. W. Beck points out, there are actually five different notions of freedom in Kant ('Five Concepts of Freedom in Kant', in J. T. J. Srzednick (ed.) *Philosophical Analysis and Reconstruction: A Festschrift to Stephan Körner*, Dordrecht, Martinus Nijhoff, 1987, pp. 35–51), but spontaneity and autonomy are the only relevant conceptions for our purposes.

14 *Ak* IV, 446/*Gr*, 114.

15 See H. Allison, *Kant's Theory of Freedom*, p. 88.

16 *Ak* IV, 440/*Gr*, 108.

17 *Ak* IV, 441/*Gr*, 108.

18 *Ak* IV, 440/*Gr*, 108.

19 *Ak* IV, 447/*Gr*, 114.

20 'On the Supposed Right to Lie from Altruistic Motives', in *Immanuel Kant: Critique of Practical Reason and Other Writings in Moral Philosophy*, trans. L. W. Beck, Chicago, University of Chicago Press, 1949.

21

> When we have come to recognise the duty of beneficence, it appears to me that the duty of non-maleficence is recognised as a distinct one, and as *prima facie* more binding. We should not in general consider it justifiable to kill one person in order to keep another alive, or to steal from one in order to give alms to another.
>
> (Hackett, 1988, *The Right and the Good*, Indianapolis, p. 22)

22 Op. cit., p. 35.

23 Op. cit., p. 30.

24 One of the ways in which Kant distinguishes perfect from imperfect duties is with reference to exceptions. Perfect duties, he writes, 'allow of no exception in the interest of inclination' (*Ak* IV, 421n/*Gr*, 89n), with the implication that imperfect duties do allow such exceptions. I take this to mean that whenever we fail to act in accordance with a perfect duty we do wrong, whereas we do not when we fail to act in accordance with an imperfect duty. If I fail to tell the truth, then I have done wrong, but I can fail to help someone when I can yet do no wrong.

25 The most implausible side-constraint is that of honesty. Kant thought that in a conflict between honesty and beneficence, honesty would always win. This is seen in his notorious example of someone being asked by a murderer where his potential victim had sought refuge. Kant thought that if we could not remain silent we should, in such a situation, tell the murderer where his victim is. If there is anything we are certain of in ethics, it is that Kant is deeply mistaken in thinking that in such a situation we should tell the truth. It may be that certain considerations do constitute absolute side-constraints on how we may be beneficent, but considerations of truthfulness, though important, are not important enough to outweigh the reason the pointless death of an innocent gives us to lie.

26 Ross is often unjustly accused of being unable to cope with moral conflict. But this criticism rests solely on a rather crude misunderstanding of the notion of a *prima facie* duty. (see Chapter 5).

27 I here Follow O. O'Neill's account of treating others merely as means. See 'Between Consenting Adults', in *Constructions of Reason*, Chapter 6.

28 H. Paton, for example, notes that Kant only claims that perfect duties allow of no exceptions *in the interest of inclination* – that is, they allow of no *arbitrary* exceptions. This leaves open the possibility that they do allow, what Paton calls, *necessary* exceptions, namely, exceptions made, not in the interests of inclination, but because of some overriding duty. This overriding duty need not be a perfect duty, but may, Paton argues, be an imperfect duty ('An Alleged Right to Lie: A Problem in Kantian Ethics',

Kant-Studien, 1953–54, vol. 45, p. 192). More recently, C. Korsgaard has attempted to argue that (rightfully) lying to the murderer is consistent with Kant's ethical theory ('The Right to Lie: Kant on Dealing with Evil', in *Creating the Kingdom of Ends*, Chapter 5.). For a very different approach see David Cummiskey's *Kantian Consequentialism*, Oxford, Oxford University Press, 1996.

29 I mention this because some think that Ross is a kind of consequentialist.

8 Conclusion

1 See my 'In Defence of the Abstract', *Bulletin of the Hegel Society of Great Britain*, 1996, vol. 33, pp. 42–53.

2 I have in mind here the particularism put forward by Jonathan Dancy ('An Unprincipled Morality', unpublished).

3 Moore makes this distinction in *Ethics*, London, Oxford University Press, 1966, p. 130. The term 'contributive value' is, however, not Moore's, but W. D. Ross's (*The Right and the Good*, Indianapolis, Hackett, 1988, p. 72).

BIBLIOGRAPHY

Allison, A., *Kant's Theory of Freedom*, Cambridge, Cambridge University Press, 1990.

——, *Idealism and Freedom: Essays on Kant's Theoretical and Practical Philosophy*, Cambridge, Cambridge University Press, 1996.

Ameriks, K., 'Kant on the Good Will', Ottfried Höffe (ed.) *Grundlegung zur Metaphysik der Sitten: Ein Kooperativer Kommentar*, Frankfurt am Main, Vittorio Klostermann, 1993, pp. 45–65.

Aune, B., *Kant's Theory of Morals*, Princeton, NJ, Princeton Univerity Press, 1979.

Baker, J., 'Do One's Motives Have to be Pure?', in Richard Grandy and Richard Warner (eds) *Philosophical Grounds of Rationality: Intentions, Categories, Ends*, Oxford, Clarendon Press, 1986, pp. 457–73.

Baron, M., *Kantian Ethics Almost without Apology*, Ithaca, NY, Cornell University Press, 1995.

Beck, L. W., *A Commentary on Kant's Critique of Practical Reason*, Chicago, University of Chicago Press, 1960.

——, 'Five Concepts of Freedom in Kant', in J. T. J. Srzednick (ed.) *Philosophical Analysis and Reconstruction: A Festschrift to Stephan Körner*, Dordrecht, Martinus Nijhoff, 1987, pp. 35–51.

Benson, P., 'Moral Worth', *Philosophical Studies*, 1987, vol. 51, pp. 365–82.

Bittner, R., 'Maximen', in G. Funke and J. Kopper (eds) *Akten des 4. Internationalen Kant-Kongresses, Mainz, 6–10 April 1974*, 1974, pp. 485–98.

Blum, L., *Friendship, Altruism and Morality*, London, Routledge & Kegan Paul, 1980.

Brink, D., 'Externalist Moral Realism', *Southern Journal of Philosophy*, 1986, vol. 24, Supplement, pp. 23–42.

Broad, C. D., *Five Types of Ethical Theory*, London, Routledge & Kegan Paul, 1930.

Broadie A. and Pybus, E., 'Kant's Concept of "Respect"', *Kant-Studien*, 1975, vol. 66, pp. 58–64.

Broome, J., 'Reason and Motivation', *Proceedings of the Aristotelian Society*, 1997, vol. 71 (suppl.), pp. 131–46.

Carnois, B., *The Coherence of Kant's Doctrine of Freedom*, trans. D. Booth, Chicago, University of Chicago Press, 1987.

Cummiskey, D., *Kantian Consequentialism*, Oxford, Oxford University Press, 1996.

Dancy, J. 'Ethical Particularism and Morally Relevant Properties', *Mind*, 1983, vol. 92, pp. 530–47.

——, *Moral Reasons*, Oxford, Blackwell, 1993.

——, 'Why There is Really No Such Thing as the Theory of Motivation', *Proceedings of the Aristotelian Society*, 1994–5, vol. 95, pp. 1–18.
——, 'An Unprincipled Morality', unpublished paper.
Darwall, S., Gibbard A. and Railton, P., 'Towards *Fin de Siècle* Ethics', *Philosophical Review*, 1992, vol. 101, pp. 115–89.
Dietrichson, P., 'What does Kant Mean by "Acting from Duty"?', in R. P. Wolff, (ed.) *Kant: A Collection of Critical Essays*, Notre Dame, University of Notre Dame Press, 1968, pp. 315–30.
Duncan, A. R. C., *Practical Reason and Morality*, London, Thomas Nelson and Sons, 1957.
Ewing, A. C., *Second Thoughts in Moral Philosophy*, London, Routledge & Kegan Paul, 1959.
Falk, W. D., '"Ought" and Motivation', in W. Sellars and J. Hospers (eds), *Readings in Ethical Theory*, New York, Appleton-Century-Crofts, 1952, pp. 492–510.
Foot, P., 'Morality as a System of Hypothetical Imperatives', in *Virtues and Vices*, Oxford, Blackwell, 1978a.
——, 'Are Moral Considerations Overriding?', in *Virtues and Vices*, Oxford, Blackwell, 1978b.
Förster, E. (ed.) *Kant's Transcendental Deductions: The Three Critiques and the 'Opus Postumum'*, Stanford, CA, Stanford University Press, 1989.
Frankena, W., 'Obligation and Motivation in Recent Moral Philosophy', in A. I. Melden (ed.), *Essays in Moral Philosophy*, Washington, DC, University of Washington Press, 1958.
Friedman, M., 'Causal Laws and the Foundations of Natural Science', in P. Guyer (ed.) *The Cambridge Companion to Kant*, Cambridge, Cambridge University Press, 1992, pp. 161–99.
Funke, G., and Kopper, J. (eds) *Akten des 4. Internationalen Kant-Kongresses, Mainz, 6–10 April 1974*, Berlin, de Gruyter, 1974.
Garcia, J. L. A., 'The Right and the Good', *Philosophia*, 1992, vol. 21, pp. 235–56.
Gay, R., 'Ethical Pluralism: A Reply to Jonathan Dancy', *Mind*, 1985, vol. 94, pp. 250–62.
Gregor, M., *Laws of Freedom*, Oxford, Oxford University Press, 1963.
Guyer, P., *The Cambridge Companion to Kant*, Cambridge, Cambridge University Press, 1992.
——, 'The Possibility of the Categorical Imperative', *Philosophical Review*, 1995, vol. 104, pp. 353–85.
——, *Kant and the Experience of Freedom*, Cambridge, Cambridge University Press, 1997.
Harbison, W. G., 'The Good Will', *Kant-Studien*, 1980, vol. 71, pp. 47–59.
Hegel, G. W. F., *Phenomenology of Spirit*, trans. A. V. Miller, Oxford, Oxford University Press, 1977.
Henson, R., 'What Kant Might Have Said: Moral Worth and the Overdetermination of Dutiful Action', *Philosophical Review*, 1979, vol. 88, pp. 39–54.
Herman, B., *The Practice of Moral Judgment*, Cambridge, MA, Harvard University Press, 1993.
——, 'On the Value of Acting from the Motive of Duty', in *The Practice of Moral Judgement*, Cambridge, MA, Harvard University Press, 1996, pp. 1–22.
Hill, T., 'Kant on Imperfect Duty and Supererogation', *Kant-Studien*, 1971, vol. 62, pp. 55–76.

——, 'Kant's Argument for the Rationality of Moral Conduct', *Pacific Philosophical Quarterly*, 1985, vol. 66, pp. 3–23.

Hinman, L., 'On the Purity of Moral Motives: A Critique of Kant's Account of the Emotions and Acting for the Sake of Duty', *The Monist*, 1983, vol. 66, pp. 251–66.

Höffe, O., 'Kants kategorischer Imperativ als Kriterium des Sittlichen', in O. Höffe, (ed.) *Ethik und Politik*, Frankfurt, Suhrkamp, 1979, pp. 84–119.

Hooker, B., 'Ross-style Pluralism versus Rule-consequentialism', *Mind*, 1996, vol. 105, pp. 531–52.

Joseph, H. W. B., *Some Problems in Ethics*, Oxford, Clarendon Press, 1931.

Kagan, S., *The Limits of Morality*, Oxford, Clarendon Press, 1989.

Körner, S., *Kant*, Harmondsworth, Penguin, 1955.

Korsgaard, C., *Creating the Kingdom of Ends*, Cambridge, Cambridge University Press, 1996a.

——, *The Sources of Normativity*, Cambridge, Cambridge University Press, 1996b.

——, 'Kant's Analysis of Obligation: The Argument of *Groundwork I*', in *Creating the Kingdom of Ends*, Cambridge, Cambridge University Press, 1996c, pp. 43–76.

——, 'Skepticism about Practical Reason', in *Creating the Kingdom of Ends*, Cambridge, Cambridge University Press, 1996d, pp. 311–34.

——, 'Kant's Formula of Humanity', in *Creating the Kindom of Ends*, Cambridge, Cambridge University Press, 1996e, pp. 106–32.

——, 'The Right to Lie: Kant on Dealing with Evil', in *Creating the Kindom of Ends*, Cambridge, Cambridge University Press, 1996f, pp. 133–58.

——, 'Two Distinctions in Goodness', in *Creating the Kingdom of Ends*, Cambridge, Cambridge University Press, 1996g, Chapter 9.

Louden, R. B., 'Kant's Virtue Ethics', *Philosophy*, 1986, vol. 61, pp. 473–89.

McCarty, R., 'Motivation and Moral Choice in Kant's Theory of Rational Agency', *Kant-Studien*, 1994, vol. 85, pp. 15–31.

McDowell, J., 'Are Moral Requirements Hypothetical Imperatives?', *Proceedings of the Aristotelian Society*, vol. 52 (suppl.), 1978, pp. 13–29.

——, 'Values and Secondary Qualities', in T. Honderich (ed.) *Morality and Objectivity: A Tribute to J. L. Mackie*, London, Routledge and Kegan Paul, 1985, pp. 110–29.

MacIntyre, A., *After Virtue: A Study in Moral Theory*, London, Duckworth, 1981.

McNaughton, D., *Moral Vision*, Oxford, Blackwell, 1988.

Millgram, E., 'Williams' Argument Against External Reasons', *Nous*, 1996, vol. 30, pp. 354–88.

Moore, G. E., *Principia Ethica*, Cambridge, Cambridge University Press, 1994.

——, *Ethics*, London, Oxford University Press, 1966.

Nagel, T., *The Possibility of Altruism*, Princeton, NJ, Princeton University Press, 1979.

Nell (O'Neill), O., *Acting on Principle: An Essay on Kantian Ethics*, New York, Columbia University Press, 1975.

O'Connor, D., 'Good and Evil Disposition', *Kant-Studien*, 1985, vol. 76, pp. 288–302.

O'Neill, O., *Constructions of Reason: Explorations of Kant's Practical Philosophy*, Cambridge, Cambridge University Press, 1989a.

——, 'Consistency in Action', in *Constructions of Reason: Explorations of Kant's Practical Philosophy*, Cambridge, Cambridge University Press, 1989b, pp. 81–104.

——, 'The Public Use of Reason', in *Constructions of Reason: Explorations of Kant's Practical Philosophy*, Cambridge: Cambridge University Press, 1989c, pp. 28–50.

——, 'Between Consenting Adults', in *Constructions of Reason: Explorations of Kant's Practical Philosophy*, Cambridge: Cambridge University Press, 1989d, Chapter 6.

Parfit, D., 'Reasons and Motivation', in *Proceedings of the Aristotelian Society*, 1997, vol. 71 (suppl.), pp. 99–130.

Paton, H. J., *The Categorical Imperative: A Study in Kant's Moral Philosophy*, London, Hutchinson's University Library, 1947.

——, 'An Alleged Right to Lie: A Problem in Kantian Ethics', *Kant-Studien*, 1953–54, vol. 45, pp. 190–203.

——, 'The Aim and Structure of Kant's *Grundlegung*', *Philosophical Quarterly*, 1958, vol. VIII, pp. 121–5.

Pietroski, P., '*Prima Facie* Obligations, Ceteris Paribus Laws in Moral Theory', *Ethics*, 1993, vol. 103, pp. 489–515.

Quine, W. V. O., 'Quantifiers and Propositional Attitudes', in L. Linsky (ed.) *Reference and Modality*, Oxford, Oxford University Press, 1971, pp. 101–11.

Rawls, J., *A Theory of Justice*, Oxford, Oxford University Press, 1972.

——, 'Kantian Constructivism in Moral Theory', *Journal of Philosophy*, 1980, vol. 77, pp. 515–72.

Raz, J. (ed.) *Practical Reasoning*, Oxford, Oxford University Press, 1978.

Reath, A., 'Hedonism, Heteronomy and Kant's Principle of Happiness', *Pacific Philosophical Quarterly*, 1989a, Vol. 70, pp. 42–72.

——, 'Kant's Theory of Moral Sensibility: Respect for the Moral Law and the Influence of Inclination', *Kant-Studien*, 1989b, vol. 80, pp. 284–302.

——, 'The Categorical Imperative and Kant's Conception of Practical Rationality', *The Monist*, 1989c, vol. 72, pp. 384–410.

Ross, W. D., *The Foundations of Ethics*, Oxford, Clarendon Press, 1939.

——, *Kant's Ethical Theory*, Oxford, Clarendon Press, 1954.

——, *The Right and the Good*, Indianapolis, Hackett, 1988.

Scanlon, T., 'Contractualism and Utilitarianism', in A. Sen and B. Williams (eds) *Utilitarianism and Beyond*, Cambridge, Cambridge University Press, 1982, pp. 103–28.

——, *What We Owe to Each Other*, Cambridge, MA, Harvard University Press, 1998.

Scheffler, S., *Human Morality*, Oxford, Oxford University Press, 1992.

Searle, J., '*Prima Facie* Obligations', in J. Raz (ed.) *Practical Reasoning*, Oxford, Oxford University Press, pp. 81–90.

Sherman, N., *Making a Necessity of Virtue: Aristotle and Kant on Virtue*, Cambridge, Cambridge University Press, 1997.

Silber, J., 'The Copernican Revolution in Ethics: The Good Reexamined', in R. P. Wolff (ed.), *Kant: A Collection of Critical Essays*, Notre Dame, University of Notre Dame Press, 1968, pp. 266–90.

——, 'The Ethical Significance of Kant's Religion', Introduction to *Religion Within the Limits of Reason Alone*, trans. T. M. Grene and H. H. Hudson, New York, Harper & Row, 1960, pp. lxxix–cxxxvii.

——, 'The Highest Good in Kant's Ethics', *Ethics*, 1963, vol. 73, pp. 179–97.

Singer, M., *Generalization in Ethics*, New York, Alfred A. Knopf, 1961.

Smith, M., 'The Humean Theory of Motivation', *Mind*, 1987, vol. 96, pp. 36–61.

——, *The Moral Problem*, Oxford, Blackwell, 1994.

——, 'The Argument for Internalism: Reply to Miller', *Analysis*, 1996, vol. 56, no. 3, pp. 175–84.

Stocker, M., 'The Schizophrenia of Modern Ethical Theories', *Journal of Philosophy*, 1976, vol. 73, pp. 453–66.

Stratton-Lake, P., 'Formulating Categorical Imperatives', *Kant-Studien*, 1993, vol. 83, pp. 317–40.

——, 'In Defence of the Abstract', *Bulletin of the Hegel Society of Great Britain*, vol. 33, 1996, pp. 42–53.

Strawson, P., 'Ethical Intuitionism', in W. Sellars and J. Hospers (eds) *Readings in Ethical Theory*, New York, Appleton-Century-Crofts, 1952, pp. 250–9.

Walker, R., *Kant*, London, Routledge & Kegan Paul, 1978.

——, '*Achtung* in the *Grundlegung*', in O. Höffe (ed.) *Grundlegung zur Metaphysik der Sitten: Ein Kooperativer Kommentar*, Frankfurt am Main, Vittorio Klostermann, 1993, pp. 97–116.

Williams, B., 'Ethical Consistency', *Proceedings of the Aristotelian Society*, 1965, suppl. vol. 39, pp. 103–24.

——, 'Internal and External Reasons', in *Moral Luck: Philosophical Papers 1973–1980*, Cambridge, Cambridge University Press, 1981a, pp. 101–13.

——, 'Persons, Character and Morality', in *Moral Luck*, Cambridge, Cambridge University Press, 1981b, pp. 14–19.

Williams, T. C., *The Concept of the Categorical Imperative*, Oxford, Clarendon Press, 1968.

Wolf, S., 'Moral Saints', *Journal of Philosophy*, 1982, vol. 79, pp. 419–38.

——, 'Morality and Partiality', *Philosophical Perspectives*, 1992, vol. 6, pp. 243–59.

Wolff, R. P. (ed.) *Kant: A Collection of Critical Essays*, Notre Dame, University of Notre Dame Press, 1968.

Wood, A., 'Kant's Compatibilism', in A. Wood (ed.) *Self and Nature in Kant's Philosophy*, Ithaca, NY, Cornell University Press, 1984, pp. 73–101.

——, 'The Emptiness of the Moral Will', *The Monist*, 1989, vol. 73, pp. 454–83.

Yovel, Y., *Kant and the Philosophy of History*, Princeton, NJ, Princeton University Press, 1968.

INDEX